Wisdom is a living stream, not an icon preserved in a museum. Only when we find the spring of wisdom in our own life can it flow to future generations.
— THICH NHAT HANH

# AN INVITATION

This book is meant to be of use, to be a companion, a soul friend. It is a book of awakenings. To write this I've had to live it. It's given me a chance to gather and share the quiet teachers I've met throughout my life. The journey of unearthing and shaping these entries has helped me bring my inner and outer life more closely together. It has helped me know and use my heart. It has made me more whole. I hope it can be such a tool for you.

Gathering the insights for this book has been like finding bits of stone that glistened on the path. I paused to reflect on them, to learn from them, then tucked them away and continued. After two years, I'm astonished to dump my bag of broken stones to see what I've found. The bits that have glistened along the way are what make up this book.

Essentially, they all speak about spirit and friendship, about our ongoing need to stay vital and in love with this life, no matter the hardships we encounter. From many traditions, from many experiences, from many beautiful and honest voices, the songs herein all sing of pain and wonder and the mystery of love.

I was drawn to this form because as a poet, I was longing for a manner of expression that could be as useful as a spoon, and as a cancer survivor, daybooks have become inner food. In truth, over the last twenty-five years, the daybook has been answering a collective need and has become a spiritual sonnet of our age, a sturdy container for small doses of what matters.

All I can ask of this work is that it comes over you the way the ocean covers a stone stuck in the open, that it surprises and refreshes, that it makes you or me glisten, and leaves us scoured as we are, just softer for the moment and more clear.

It is my profound hope that something in these pages will surprise and refresh you, will make you glisten, will help you live, love, and find your way to joy.

— *Mark*

# FOREWORD

BY WAYNE MULLER, AUTHOR OF
*How Then Shall We Live*

One of the sweetest joys in my life is to hear Mark Nepo read his poetry. There is a tangible air of adventure. I am always surprised as Mark, unwrapping hidden treasure, carefully opening a simple moment, reveals the most extraordinary miracles. When he reads in public, you hear people catch their breath as they recognize something deep and true, something known but forgotten, or missed. Mark sees it, remembers it for us, and gives it back to us. In the end, there is a sense of gratitude for being awakened again to something truly precious.

Our life is made of days. It is only in the days of our lives that we find peace, joy, and healing. There are a thousand tiny miracles that punctuate our days, and Mark Nepo is a student of the miraculous. An alchemist of the ordinary, he invites us to see, taste, touch, dance, and feel our way into the heart of life.

Just as a life is made of days, so are days made of moments. A life well lived is firmly

9

planted in the sweet soil of moments. Mark Nepo is a gardener in this soil; he plants seeds of grace that grow only in the soil of loving attention and mindful time. We receive the deepest blessings of life when we fall in love with such moments — and Mark shows us how to fall in love deeply and with abandon.

Mark had cancer, and it shook him awake. His descent into illness gave birth to an astonishing mindfulness. Now, he invites us to use his eyes and heart to see and feel how awake our being alive can be. Having survived his cancer, Mark brings with him the eyes of a dying person who is grateful simply to breathe. But more than gratefulness he brings wisdom, clarity, kindness, and a passionate enthusiasm for sucking the marrow out of moments, out of the bones of time.

If you ache to live this way, Mark is your guide.

When Mark finished the final round of chemotherapy that helped cure his cancer, he rose early in the day, squeezed fresh orange juice, and placed the glass of juice on the table before him. Then he waited, reflecting on the promise of the day, until the sun rose over the trees outside his window. At that moment, he told me, the light from the sun pierced the juice and "diffused into orange, crystal light," at which point Mark lifted the juice to his lips.

Most sacraments are acts of breathtaking

simplicity: a simple prayer, a sip of wine and a piece of bread, a single breath in meditation, a sprinkling of water on the forehead, an exchange of rings, a kind word, a blessing. Any of these, performed in a moment of mindfulness, may open the doors of our spiritual perception and bring nourishment and delight.

This is a book of sacraments; it is Mark's generous gift to us, a banquet of miracles made from the stuff of days, the ordinary riches of a human life. Take your time, savor each page. Above all, be willing to be surprised. Life may already be more miraculous than you ever imagined.

# January 1
# Precious Human Birth

Of all the things that exist,
we breathe and wake and turn it into song.

There is a Buddhist precept that asks us to be mindful of how rare it is to find ourselves in human form on Earth. It is really a beautiful view of life that offers us the chance to feel enormous appreciation for the fact that we are here as individual spirits filled with consciousness, drinking water and chopping wood.

It asks us to look about at the ant and antelope, at the worm and the butterfly, at the dog and the castrated bull, at the hawk and the wild lonely tiger, at the hundred-year-old oak and the thousand-year-old patch of ocean. It asks us to understand that no other life form has the consciousness of being that we are privilege to. It asks us to recognize that of all the endless species of plants and animals and minerals that make up the Earth, a very small portion of life has

13

the wakefulness of spirit that we call "being human."

That I can rise from some depth of awareness to express this to you and that you can receive me in this instant is part of our precious human birth. You could have been an ant. I could have been an anteater. You could have been rain. I could have been a lick of salt. But we were blessed — in this time, in this place — to be human beings, alive in rare ways we often take for granted.

All of this to say, this precious human birth is unrepeatable. So what will you do today, knowing that you are one of the rarest forms of life to ever walk the Earth? How will you carry yourself? What will you do with your hands? What will you ask and of whom?

Tomorrow you could die and become an ant, and someone will be setting traps for you. But today you are precious and rare and awake. It ushers us into grateful living. It makes hesitation useless. Grateful and awake, ask what you need to know now. Say what you feel now. Love what you love now.

- Sit outside, if possible, or near a window, and note the other life forms around you.
- Breathe slowly and think of the ant and the blade of grass and the blue jay and what these life forms can do that you can't.

- Think of the pebble and the piece of bark and the stone bench, and center your breathing on the interior things that you can do that they can't.
- Rise slowly, feeling beautifully human, and enter your day with the conscious intent of doing one thing that only humans can do.
- When the time arises, do this one thing with great reverence and gratitude.

# JANUARY 2
# ALL FALL DOWN

Lead us from the unreal to the real.
— HINDU INVOCATION

It was a snowy night, and Robert was recalling the time two springs ago when he was determined to paint the family room. Up early, he was out the door, to the hardware store gathering the gallons of red, the wooden mixing sticks, the drop cloths, and the one-time brushes that always harden, no matter what you soak them in.

He mixed the paint outside and waddled to the door with a gallon in each hand, the drop cloth under his arm, and a wide brush in his mouth. He began to chuckle in telling what happened, "I teetered there for minutes, trying to open the door, not wanting to put anything down. I was so stubborn. I had the door almost open when I lost my grip, stumbled backward, and wound up on the ground, red gallons all over me."

At this point, he laughed at himself, as he has done many times, and we watched the snow fall in silence. I thought of his little story the whole way home. Amazingly, we all do this, whether with groceries or paint or with the stories we feel determined to share. We do this with our love, with our sense of truth, even with our pain. It's such a simple thing, but in a moment of ego we refuse to put down what we carry in order to open the door. Time and time again, we are offered the chance to truly learn this: We cannot hold on to things and enter. We must put down what we carry, open the door, and then take up only what we need to bring inside.

It is a basic human sequence: gather, prepare, put down, enter. But failing as we do, we always have that second chance: to learn how to fall, get up, and laugh.

- Meditate on some threshold you are having trouble crossing in your life. It might be at work, at home, in a relationship, or the doorway to greater peace.
- Breathe steadily and look to yourself to see if you are carrying too much to open the door.

- Breathe slowly and with each out-breath put the things you are carrying down.
- Breathe freely now and open the door.

# JANUARY 3
# UNLEARNING BACK TO GOD

The coming to consciousness is not a
   discovery
of some new thing; it is a long and painful
return to that which has always been.
                              — HELEN LUKE

Each person is born with an unencumbered spot — free of expectation and regret, free of ambition and embarrassment, free of fear and worry — an umbilical spot of grace where we were each first touched by God. It is this spot of grace that issues peace. Psychologists call this spot the Psyche, theologians call it the Soul, Jung calls it the Seat of the Unconscious, Hindu masters call it Atman, Buddhists call it Dharma, Rilke calls it Inwardness, Sufis call it Qalb, and Jesus calls it the Center of our Love.

To know this spot of Inwardness is to know who we are, not by surface markers of identity, not by where we work or what we wear or how we like to be addressed, but by feeling our place in relation to the Infinite and

17

by inhabiting it. This is a hard lifelong task, for the nature of becoming is a constant filming over of where we begin, while the nature of being is a constant erosion of what is not essential. Each of us lives in the midst of this ongoing tension, growing tarnished or covered over, only to be worn back to that incorruptible spot of grace at our core.

When the film is worn through, we have moments of enlightenment, moments of wholeness, moments of *satori,* as the Zen sages term it, moments of clear living when inner meets outer, moments of full integrity of being, moments of complete Oneness. And whether the film is a veil of culture, of memory, of mental or religious training, of trauma or sophistication, the removal of that film and the restoration of that timeless spot of grace is the goal of all therapy and education.

Regardless of subject matter, this is the only thing worth teaching: how to uncover that original center and how to live there once it is restored. We call the filming over a deadening of heart, and the process of return, whether brought about through suffering or love, is how we unlearn our way back to God.

- Close your eyes and breathe your way beneath your troubles, the way a diver slips to that depth of stillness that is always waiting beneath the churning of

18

the waves.

- Now, consider two things you love doing, such as running, drawing, singing, bird-watching, gardening, or reading. Meditate on what it is in each of these that makes you feel alive.
- Hold what they have in common before you, and breathing slowly, feel the spot of grace these dear things mirror within you.

# JANUARY 4
# BETWEEN PEACE AND JOY

We could never have guessed
We were already blessed
where we are. . . .

— JAMES TAYLOR

This reminds me of a woman who found a folded sponge all dried and compressed, and tucked inside the hardened fold was a message she'd been seeking. She carried the hardened sponge to the sea and, up to her waist in the deep, she watched it unfold and come to life in the water. Magically, the secret of life became visible in the bubbles being released from the sponge, and to her amazement, a small fish, trapped in sleep in the hardened sponge, came alive and swam out to sea. From that day on, no matter where she went, she felt the little fish swimming in the deep, and this — the swimming of the little fish that had for so long been asleep — gave her a satisfaction that was somewhere between peace and joy.

Whatever our path, whatever the color or grain of our days, whatever riddles we must solve to stay alive, the secret of life somehow always has to do with the awakening and freeing of what has been asleep. Like that sponge, our very heart begs to unfold in the waters of our experience, and like that little fish, the soul is a tiny thing that brings us peace and joy when we let it swim.

But everything remains hard and compressed and illegible until, like this woman, waist deep in the ocean, we take our sleeping heart in our hands and plunge it tenderly into the life we are living.

- With your eyes closed, meditate on the image of a hardened sponge unfolding like a flower underwater.
- As you breathe, practice seeing your heart as such a sponge.
- The next time you do the dishes, pause, hold the hardened sponge in the water, and feel your heart unfold.

# JANUARY 5
## SHOW YOUR HAIR

My grandmother told me,
"Never hide your green hair —
They can see it anyway."
— ANGELES ARRIEN

From the agonies of kindergarten, when we first were teased or made fun of in the midst of all our innocence, we have all struggled in one way or another with hiding what is obvious about us.

No one plans this. It is not a conspiracy, but rather an inevitable and hurtful passage from knowing only ourselves to knowing the world. The tragedy is that many of us never talk about it, or never get told that our "green hair" is beautiful, or that we don't need to hide, no matter what anyone says on the way to lunch. And so, we often conclude that to know the world we must hide ourselves.

Nothing could be farther from the truth. It is an ancient, unspoken fact of being that blackmail is only possible if we believe that we have something to hide. The inner corollary of this is that worthless feelings arise when we believe, however briefly, that who we are is not enough.

- Sit quietly, with your eyes closed, and with each in-breath feel the fact that who you are is enough.

# JANUARY 6
# THE SPOKED WHEEL

What we reach for may be different,
but what makes us reach is the same.

Imagine that each of us is a spoke in an Infinite Wheel, and, though each spoke is essential in keeping the Wheel whole, no two spokes are the same. The rim of that Wheel is our living sense of community, family, and relationship, but the common hub where all the spokes join is the one center where all souls meet. So, as I move out into the world, I live out my uniqueness, but when I dare to look into my core, I come upon the one common center where all lives begin. In that center, we are one and the same. In this way, we live out the paradox of being both unique and the same. For mysteriously and powerfully, when I look deep enough into you, I find me, and when you dare to hear my fear in the recess of your heart, you recognize it as your secret that you thought no one else knew. And that unexpected wholeness that is more than each of us, but common to all —

that moment of unity is the atom of God.

Not surprisingly, like most people, in the first half of my life, I worked very hard to understand and strengthen my uniqueness. I worked hard to secure my place at the rim of the Wheel and so defined and valued myself by how different I was from everyone else. But in the second half of my life, I have been humbly brought to the center of that Wheel, and now I marvel at the mysterious oneness of our spirit.

Through cancer and grief and disappointment and unexpected turns in career — through the very breakdown and rearrangement of the things I have loved — I have come to realize that, as water smoothes stone and enters sand, we become each other. How could I be so slow? What I've always thought set me apart binds me to others.

Never was this more clear to me than when I was sitting in a waiting room at Columbia Presbyterian Hospital in New York City, staring straight into this Hispanic woman's eyes, she into mine. In that moment, I began to accept that we all see the same wonder, all feel the same agony, though we all speak in a different voice. I know now that each being born, inconceivable as it seems, is another Adam or Eve.

- Sit with a trusted loved one and take turns:

23

- Name one defining trait of who you are that distinguishes you from others.
- Name one defining trait of who you are that you have in common with others.
- Discuss how you cope with the loneliness of what makes you unique from others, and how you cope with the experience of what makes you the same as others.

# JANUARY 7
# WE MUST TAKE TURNS

We must take turns:
diving into all there is
and counting the time.

The gift and responsibility of relationship is to take turns doing the dishes and putting up the storm windows, giving the other the chance to dive for God without worrying about dinner. While one explores the inner, the other must tend the outer.

A great model of this is how pearl divers search the deep in pairs. Without scuba tanks or regulators, one waits at the surface tending the lines tied to the other who soft-steps the sand for treasures he hopes he'll recognize.

He walks the bottom, watching the leaves

of vegetation sway and sways himself till she tugs the cord. He swallows the little air left as he ascends. Aboard, they talk for hours, placing what was seen, rubbing the rough and natural pearl. In the morning, she dives and fills their baskets and he counts the time, hands wrapped about her line.

Quite plainly, these pearl divers show us the work of being together and the miracle of trust. We must take turns: whoever is on the surface must count the air time left, so the one below can dive freely.

- Sit quietly and meditate on a significant relationship you are in with a friend or lover or family member.
- Breathe steadily and ask yourself if you take turns diving and counting the time.
- When moved to do so, discuss this with your loved one.

# JANUARY 8
## FEEDING YOUR HEART

---

No matter how dark,
the hand always knows
the way to the mouth.
— IDOMA PROVERB (NIGERIA)

Even when we can't see, we know how to feed

25

ourselves. Even when the way isn't clear, the heart still pumps. Even when afraid, the air of everything enters and leaves the lungs. Even when clouds grow thick, the sun still pours its light earthward.

This African proverb reminds us that things are never quite as bad as they seem inside the problem. We have inner reflexes that keep us alive, deep impulses of being and aliveness that work beneath the hardships we are struggling with.

We must remember: the hand cannot eliminate the darkness, only find its way to the mouth. Likewise, our belief in life cannot eliminate our suffering, only find its way to feed our heart.

- Sit quietly and, with your eyes closed, bring your open hands to your mouth.
- Inhale as you do this and notice how, without guidance, your hands know the way.
- Breathe slowly, and with your eyes closed, bring your open hands to your heart.
- Notice how, without your guidance, your heart knows the way.

# January 9
## Life in the Tank

Love, and do what thou wilt.
— SAINT AUGUSTINE

It was a curious thing. Robert had filled the bathtub and put the fish in the tub, so he could clean their tank. After he'd scrubbed the film from the small walls of their make-believe deep, he went to retrieve them.

He was astonished to find that, though they had the entire tub to swim in, they were huddled in a small area the size of their tank. There was nothing containing them, nothing holding them back. Why wouldn't they dart about freely? What had life in the tank done to their natural ability to swim?

This quiet yet stark moment stayed with us both for a long time. We couldn't help but see those little fish going nowhere but into themselves. We now had a life-in-the-tank lens on the world and wondered daily, In what ways are we like them? In what ways do we go nowhere but into ourselves? In what ways do we shrink our world so as not to feel the press of our own self-imposed captivity?

Life in the tank made me think of how we are raised at home and in school. It made me think of being told that certain jobs are not

27

acceptable and that certain jobs are out of reach, of being schooled to live a certain way, of being trained to think that only practical things are possible, of being warned over and over that life outside the tank of our values is risky and dangerous.

I began to see just how much we were taught as children to fear life outside the tank. As a father, Robert began to question if he was preparing his children for life in the tank or life in the uncontainable world.

It makes me wonder now, in middle age, if being spontaneous and kind and curious are all parts of our natural ability to swim. Each time I hesitate to do the unplanned or unexpected, or hesitate to reach and help another, or hesitate to inquire into something I know nothing about; each time I ignore the impulse to run in the rain or to call you up just to say I love you — I wonder, am I turning on myself, swimming safely in the middle of the tub?

- Sit quietly until you feel thoroughly in your center.
- Now rise and slowly walk about the room you are in.
- Now walk close to the walls of your room and meditate on life in your tank.
- Breathe clearly and move to the doorway and meditate on the nature of what is truly possible in life.

- Now step through the doorway and enter your day. Step through your day and enter the world.

# January 10
## Akiba

---

When Akiba was on his deathbed, he
bemoaned to his rabbi that he felt he was
a failure. His rabbi moved closer and asked
why, and Akiba confessed that he had not
lived a life like Moses. The poor man
  began
to cry, admitting that he feared God's
  judgment.
At this, his rabbi leaned into his ear and
whispered gently, "God will not judge Akiba
for not being Moses. God will judge Akiba
  for
not being Akiba."

— From the Talmud

We are born with only one obligation — to be completely who we are. Yet how much of our time is spent comparing ourselves to others, dead and alive? This is encouraged as necessary in the pursuit of excellence. Yet a flower in its excellence does not yearn to be a fish, and a fish in its unmanaged elegance does not long to be a tiger. But we humans find ourselves always falling into the dream

29

of another life. Or we secretly aspire to the fortune or fame of people we don't really know. When feeling badly about ourselves, we often try on other skins rather than understand and care for our own.

Yet when we compare ourselves to others, we see neither ourselves nor those we look up to. We only experience the tension of comparing, as if there is only one ounce of being to feed all our hungers. But the Universe reveals its abundance most clearly when we can be who we are. Mysteriously, every weed and ant and wounded rabbit, every living creature has its unique anatomy of being which, when given over to, is more than enough.

Being human, though, we are often troubled and blocked by insecurity, that windedness of heart that makes us feel unworthy. And when winded and troubled, we sometimes feel compelled to puff ourselves up. For in our pain, it seems to make sense that if we were larger, we would be further from our pain. If we were larger, we would be harder to miss. If we were larger, we'd have a better chance of being loved. Then, not surprisingly, others need to be made smaller so we can maintain our illusion of seeming bigger than our pain.

Of course, history is the humbling story of our misbegotten inflations, and truth is the corrective story of how we return to exactly who we are. And compassion, sweet compassion, is the never-ending story of how we embrace each other and forgive ourselves for not accepting our beautifully particular place in the fabric of all there is.

- Fill a wide bowl with water. Then clear your mind in meditation and look closely at your reflection.
- While looking at your reflection, allow yourself to feel the tension of one comparison you carry. Feel the pain of measuring yourself against another.
- Close your eyes and let this feeling through.
- Now, once again, look closely at your reflection in the bowl, and try to see yourself in comparison to no one.
- Look at your reflection and allow yourself to feel what makes you unique. Let this move through.

# January 11
## Ted Shawn

To know God
without being God-like
is like trying to swim
without entering water.

— Orest Bedrij

Underneath all we are taught, there is a voice

that calls to us beyond what is reasonable, and in listening to that flicker of spirit, we often find deep healing. This is the voice of embodiment calling us to live our lives like sheet music played, and it often speaks to us briefly in moments of deep crisis. Sometimes it is so faint we mistake its whisper for wind through leaves. But taking it into the heart of our pain, it can often open the paralysis of our lives.

This brings to mind the story of a young divinity student who was stricken with polio, and from somewhere deep within him came an unlikely voice calling him to, of all things, dance. So, with great difficulty, he quit divinity school and began to dance, and slowly and miraculously, he not only regained the use of his legs, but went on to become one of the fathers of modern dance.

This is the story of Ted Shawn, and it is compelling for us to realize that studying God did not heal him. Embodying God did. The fact of Ted Shawn's miracle shows us that Dance, in all its forms, is Theology lived. This leads us all to the inescapable act of living out what is kept in, of daring to breathe in muscle and bone what we know and feel and believe — again and again.

Whatever crisis we face, there is this voice of embodiment that speaks beneath our pain ever so quickly, and if we can hear it and believe it, it will show us a way to be reborn.

The courage to hear and embody opens us to a startling secret, that the best chance to be whole is to love whatever gets in the way, until it ceases to be an obstacle.

- Before work or during the day, sit quietly outside for a few moments.
- Close your eyes and be still. Feel the air on your closed lids.
- Let your love wash through your heart up your chest.
- Let your love breeze up your throat and behind your eyes.
- When you open your eyes, stretch and focus on the first thing you see.
- If it is a bench, say I believe in bench. If a tree, say I believe in tree. If a torn flower, say I believe in torn flower.
- Rise with a simple belief in what you feel and see, and touch what is before you, giving your love a way out.

# JANUARY 12
## SEEING INTO DARKNESS

Seeing into darkness is clarity . . .
This is called practicing eternity. . . .
— LAO-TZU

Fear gets its power from our not looking, at

33

either the fear or what we're afraid of. Remember that attic or closet door behind which something terrifying waited, and the longer we didn't look, the harder it was to open that door?

As a boy this obsessed me until I would avoid that part of the house. But, finally, when no one was home, I felt compelled to face the unknown. I stood before that attic door for the longest time, my heart pounding. It took all my small inner boy strength to open it.

I waited at the threshold, and nothing happened. I inched my way in and stood in the dark, even longer, until my breathing slowed, and to my surprise, my eyes grew accustomed to the dark. Pretty soon, I was able to explore the old musty boxes, and found pictures of my grandfather, my father's father, the only one in the family that I am like. Seeing those pictures opened me to aspects of my spirit.

It seems whatever the door, whatever our fear — be it love or truth or even the prospect of death — we all have this choice, again and again: avoiding that part of our house, or opening the door and finding out more about ourselves by waiting until what is dark becomes seeable.

- Sit quietly and bring to mind a door you fear going through.
- For now, simply breathe and, in your

34

mind's eye, grow accustomed to the threshold.
- For now, breathe deeply and simply feel safe around the closed door, vowing to return when you feel stronger.

# JANUARY 13
# WHY WE NEED EACH OTHER

A blind child
guided by his mother,
admires the cherry blossoms. . . .
— KIKAKOU

Who knows what a blind child sees of blossoms or songbirds? Who knows what any of us sees from the privacy of our own blindness — and, make no mistake, each of us is blind in a particular way, just as each of us is sighted uniquely.

Consider how each of us is blinded by what we fear. If we fear heights, we are blind to the humility vast perspectives bring. If we fear spiders, we are blind to the splendor and danger of webs. If we fear small spaces, we are blind to the secrets of sudden solitude. If we fear passion, we are blind to the comfort of Oneness. If we fear change, we are blind to the abundance of life. If we fear death, we are blind to the mystery of the unknown. And

35

since to fear something is thoroughly human, to be blind is unavoidable. It is what each of us must struggle to overcome.

With this in mind, Kikakou's little poem serves as an internal parable. For, in the course of our lives, we all stumble and struggle, repeatedly, in and out of relationship, and in and out of the grace of the hidden wholeness of life. It is, in part, why we need each other. For often our relationships help us experience the Oneness of things. We do this, in the course of our lives, by taking turns being the blind child, the loving guide, and the unsuspecting blossom — never knowing which we are called to be until we've learned what we are to learn.

- Close your eyes and repeat Kikakou's haiku three times, and each time, identify with a different position.
- The first time, breathe slowly and become the blind child admiring the blossoms he or she can't see.
- The second time, breathe deeply and become the loving other, guiding his or her blind child to a beauty they can share but never experience the same way.
- The third time, breathe without thinking and become the cherry blossom itself that stops both those who can see and those who cannot.

36

# JANUARY 14
# THE LIFE OF EXPERIENCE

Even if one glimpses God,
there are still cuts and splinters
and burns along the way.

So often we anticipate a reward for the uncovering of truth. For effort, we expect money and recognition. For sacrifice and kindness, we secretly expect acceptance and love. For honesty, we expect justice. Yet as we all know, the life of experience unfolds with a logic all its own. And very often, effort is seen, and kindness is embraced, and the risk of truth is held as the foundation of how humans relate. However, the reward for breathing is not applause but air, and the reward for climbing is not a promotion but new sight, and the reward for kindness is not being seen as kind, but the electricity of giving that keeps us alive.

It seems the closer we get to the core of all being, the more synonymous the effort and its reward. Who could have guessed? The reward for uncovering the truth is the experience of honest being. The reward for understanding is the peace of knowing. The reward for loving is being the carrier of love. It all becomes elusively simple. The river's sole purpose is to carry water, and as the force of the water deepens and widens the riverbed, the river fulfills its purpose more. Likewise, the riverbed of the heart is worn open over time to carry what is living.

All this tells us that no amount of thinking can eliminate the wonder and pain of living. No wall or avoidance or denial — no cause or excuse — can keep the rawness of life from running through us. While this may at times seem devastating, it is actually reassuring, because while the impermanence of life, if fixed on, can be terrifying, leaving us preoccupied with death, the very same impermanence, if allowed its infinite frame, can soothe us with the understanding that even the deepest pain will pass.

- Bring into view a recent moment of disappointment.
- Was there a particular outcome or response you were secretly hoping for?
- Rather than focusing on the fact that what you hoped for didn't happen, try to understand what is at the heart of what you were hoping for: was it being heard, being accepted, being loved, being seen as someone of value, or simply the need to be held?
- Accepting this disappointment, try to understand what you received from the life of experience.

38

# January 15
# How Does It Taste?

The more spacious and larger our
    fundamental
nature, the more bearable the pains in
    living.

— Wayne Muller

An aging Hindu master grew tired of his apprentice complaining, and so, one morning, sent him for some salt. When the apprentice returned, the master instructed the unhappy young man to put a handful of salt in a glass of water and then to drink it.

"How does it taste?" the master asked.

"Bitter," spit the apprentice.

The master chuckled and then asked the young man to take the same handful of salt and put it in the lake. The two walked in silence to the nearby lake, and once the apprentice swirled his handful of salt in the water, the old man said, "Now drink from the lake."

As the water dripped down the young man's chin, the master asked, "How does it taste?"

"Fresh," remarked the apprentice.

"Do you taste the salt?" asked the master.

"No," said the young man.

At this, the master sat beside this serious young man who so reminded him of himself and took his hands, offering, "The pain of life is pure salt; no more, no less. The amount of pain in life remains the same, exactly the same. But the amount of bitterness we taste depends on the container we put the pain in. So when you are in pain, the only thing you can do is to enlarge your sense of things. . . . Stop being a glass. Become a lake."

- Center yourself and focus on a pain that is with you.
- Rather than trying to eliminate the pain, try to breathe through it.
- With each in-breath, notice your efforts to wrap around the pain.
- With each out-breath, try to enlarge your sense of Self, and let the pain float within the depth of all we'll never know.

# JANUARY 16
# I SAY YES WHEN I MEAN NO

I say yes when I mean no
and the wrinkle grows.
— NAOMI SHIHAB NYE

There have been many times that I said yes when I meant no, afraid of displeasing others, and even more afraid of being viewed as selfish. I think the first time I decided to get married, I said yes when I meant no. Young and inexperienced in being myself, I agreed to be a fish out of water for as long as I could, so as not to hurt or disappoint or displease. Not surprisingly, it all ended badly.

And how many times, once trained in self-sacrifice, do we have the opposite conversation with ourselves; our passion for life saying yes, yes, yes, and our practical guardedness saying, don't be foolish, be realistic, don't leave yourself unprotected. But long enough on the journey, and we come to realize an even deeper aspect of all this: that those who truly love us will never knowingly ask us to be other than we are.

The unwavering truth is that when we agree to any demand, request, or condition that is contrary to our soul's nature, the cost is that precious life force is drained off our core. Despite the seeming rewards of compliance, our souls grow weary by engaging in activities that are inherently against their nature.

When we leave the crowded streets and watch any piece of nature doing what it does — tree, moose, snake, or lightning — it becomes clear that the very energy of life *is* the spirit released by things being what they are. And those of us committed to love must accept that care is the inner river flooding its banks. Yet if the soul's river can't be fed by its source, there will be no care.

- Sit quietly and meditate on the last time you said yes when you meant no.
- Breathe steadily and surface, if you can, why you didn't say no.
- Breathe deeply and identify the cost of not saying what you meant.
- Inhale slowly and invite your spirit to speak directly the next time you are asked to be other than you are.

# JANUARY 17
# THE FRICTION OF BEING VISIBLE

It is only by risking ourselves
from one hour to another
that we live at all.

— WILLIAM JAMES

Living through enough, we all come to this understanding, though it is difficult to accept: No matter what path we choose to honor, there will always be conflict to negotiate. If we choose to avoid all conflict with others, we will eventually breed a poisonous conflict within ourselves. Likewise, if we manage to attend our inner lives, who we are will

42

— sooner or later — create some discord with those who would rather have us be something else.

In effect, the cost of being who you are is that you can't possibly meet everyone's expectations, and so, there will, inevitably, be external conflict to deal with — the friction of being visible. Still, the cost of not being who you are is that while you are busy pleasing everyone around you, a precious part of you is dying inside; in this case, there will be internal conflict to deal with — the friction of being invisible.

As for me, it's taken me thirty of my forty-nine years to realize that not being who I am is more deadly, and it has taken the last nineteen years to try to make a practice of this. What this means, in a daily way, is that I have to be conscientious about being truthful and resist the urge to accommodate my truth away. It means that being who I really am is not forbidden or muted just because others are uncomfortable or don't want to hear it.

The great examples are legendary: Nelson Mandela, Gandhi, Sir Thomas More, Rosa Parks. But we don't have to be great to begin. We simply have to start by saying what we really want for dinner or which movie we really want to see.

- Center yourself and meditate on a decision before you that might generate

43

some conflict: either within you, if you withhold who you are, or between yourself and others, if you exert who you are.

- Breathe steadily and feel both the friction of being invisible and the friction of being visible.
- Breathe slowly and know that you are larger than any moment of conflict.
- Breathe deeply and know that who you are can withstand the experience of conflict that living requires.

# JANUARY 18
# THE SPIDER AND THE SAGE

I would rather be fooled
than not believe.

In India, there is a story about a kind, quiet man who would pray in the Ganges River every morning. One day after praying, he saw a poisonous spider struggling in the water and cupped his hands to carry it ashore. As he placed the spider on the ground, it stung him. Unknowingly, his prayers for the world diluted the poison.

The next day the same thing happened. On the third day, the kind man was knee deep in the river, and, sure enough, there was the spider, legs frantic in the water. As the man went to lift the creature yet again, the spider said, "Why do you keep lifting me? Can't you see I will sting you every time, because that is what I do." And the kind man cupped his hands about the spider, replying, "Because that is what I do."

There are many reasons to be kind, but perhaps none is as compelling as the spiritual fact that it is what we do. It is how the inner organ of being keeps pumping. Spiders sting. Wolves howl. Ants build small hills that no one sees. And human beings lift each other, no matter the consequence. Even when other beings sting.

Some say this makes us a sorry lot that never learns, but to me it holds the same beauty as berries breaking through ice and snow every spring. It is what quietly feeds the world. After all, the berries do not have any sense of purpose or charity. They are not altruistic or self-sacrificing. They simply grow to be delicious because that is what they do.

As for us, if things fall, we will reach for them. If things break, we will try to put them together. If loved ones cry, we will try to soothe them — because that is what we do. I have often reached out, and sometimes it feels like a mistake. Sometimes, like the quiet man lifting the spider, I have been stung. But it doesn't matter, because that is what I do. That is what we do. It is the reaching out that is more important than the sting. In

45

truth, I'd rather be fooled than not believe.

- Recall a time when you were kind for no reason. It could have been as simple as picking up what a stranger dropped. Or leaving an apple in the path of hungry birds.
- Meditate on what such acts have done for you. After being kind, have you felt lighter, more energized, younger, more open in your heart?
- Enter your day, not trying to consciously be kind, but rather with a kind outlook that allows you to naturally be who you are and do what you do.

# JANUARY 19
## REMEMBERING AND FORGETTING

What can I do to always remember who I really am?
— JUAN RAMON JIMINEZ

Most of our searching is looking for ways to discover who we already are. In this, we are a forgetful species, and perhaps what Adam and Eve lost when kicked out of Eden was their ability to remember what is sacred.

Thus, we continually run into mountains and rivers, run to the farthest sea, and into the arms of strangers, all to be shaken into remembering. And some of us lead simple lives, hoping to practice how not to forget. But part of our journey is this forgetting and this remembering. It is a special part of what makes us human.

So what can we do? Well, it is no secret that slowness remembers and hurry forgets; that softness remembers and hardness forgets; that surrender remembers and fear forgets.

It is beautifully difficult to remember who we really are. But we help each other every time we fill the cup of truth and hold each other up after drinking from it.

- Sit quietly, if you can, and allow a place where you don't feel to present itself.
- Breathe slowly into this place, for where we are numb, we have forgotten. So slow your way into remembering.
- Breathe softly over this place, imagining your breath is a cleansing water.
- After a time, try to recall the last time you felt something in this place.

# January 20
## Being Easily Pleased

One key to knowing joy
is being easily pleased.

So many of us have been trained to think that being particular about what we want is indicative of good taste, and that not being satisfied unless our preferences are met is a sign of worldliness and sophistication. I remember being at a party where a woman wouldn't accept her drink unless it was made with a certain brand of vermouth. She was, in fact, indignant about it. Or going to dinner with a colleague who had to have his steak prepared in a complex and special way, as if this particular need to be different was his special public signature. Or watching very intelligent men and women inscribe their circle of loneliness with criteria for companionship that no one could meet. I used to maintain such a standard of excellence around the sort of art I found acceptable.

Often, this kind of discernment is seen as having high standards, when in actuality it is only a means of isolating ourselves from being touched by life, while rationalizing that we are more special than those who can't meet our very demanding standards.

The devastating truth is that excellence can't hold you in the night, and, as I learned when ill, being demanding or sophisticated won't help you survive. A person dying of thirst doesn't ask if the water has chlorine or if it was gathered in the foothills of France.

Yet, to be accepting of the life that comes our way does not mean denying its difficulties and disappointments. Rather, it means that joy can be found even in hardship, not by demanding that we be treated as special at every turn, but through accepting the demand of the sacred that we treat everything that comes our way as special.

Still, we are taught to develop preferences as signs of importance and position. In fact, those who have no preferences, those who are accepting of whatever is placed before them, are often seen as simpletons or bumpkins. However, there is a profound innocence in the fact that sages and children alike are easily pleased with what each day gifts them.

The further I wake into this life, the more I realize that God is everywhere and the extraordinary is waiting quietly beneath the skin of all that is ordinary. Light is in both the broken bottle and the diamond, and music is in both the flowing violin and the water dripping from the drainage pipe. Yes, God is under the porch as well as on top of the mountain, and joy is in both the front

49

row and the bleachers, if we are willing to be where we are.

- Center yourself and bring to mind a time that you were demanding or particular beyond the need to take good care of yourself.
- Meditate on what it was you were truly asking for by being so demanding.
- If you needed attention, acknowledge that need now with your next breath, and give attention to whatever is near.
- If it was the need to be seen as special, exhale that need now, and see the things before you as special.
- If it was the need to be loved, release that need now, and love whatever is in your path.
- Enter your day and give what you need, and over time feel the specialness of the world return it to you.

# JANUARY 21
# TO SEE WITH LOVE

Enlightenment is intimacy with all things.
— JACK KORNFIELD

Each of us spins repeatedly from blindness to radiance, from dividedness to wholeness, and it is our impulse to stay in touch with all that

50

is alive that keeps us from staying lost. It is the impulse to be intimate.

It brings to mind the young, blind French boy, Jacques Lusseyran, who, in learning how to navigate his way among the other forms of life in his darkness, stumbled onto the secret of undivided living.

Young Lusseyran said, "It is more than seeing them, it is tuning in on them and allowing the current they hold to connect with one's own, like electricity. To put it differently, this means an end of living in front of things and a beginning of living with them. Never mind if the word sounds shocking, for this is love."

To live with things and not in front of them, to no longer watch, but to realize that we are part of everything we see — this is the love that keeps moving us back into wholeness when divided. To love by admitting our connection to everything is how we stay well. Allowing the current of another's inwardness to connect with our own is the beginning of both intimacy and enlightenment.

- Close your eyes and be still until you can sense the presence of the things about you.
- Breathe softly and feel the current of their silence.
- Breathe evenly and open your heart to all that you sense.

51

- Feel the electricity of being that informs the world.

# January 22
# Not Two

To reach Accord,
just say, "Not Two!"

— Seng-ts'an

Almost fourteen hundred years ago, one of the first Chinese sages we know of offered this brief retort to those who pestered him for advice — "Not Two!"

This reply is as pertinent as it is mysterious. To make sense of it, we need to understand what isn't said; that everything that divides and separates removes us from what is sacred, and so weakens our chances for joy.

How can this be? Well, to understand this, we must open ourselves to an even deeper truth: that everything — you and I and the people we mistrust and even the things we fear — everything at heart follows the same beat of life pulsing beneath all the distractions and preferences we can create.

Once divided from the common beat of life, we are cut off from the abundance and strength of life, the way an organ cut out of the body dies. So, to find peace, to live peace,

52

we need to keep restoring our original Oneness. We need to experience that ancient and central beat which we share with everything that exists. In feeling this common beat, we begin to swell again with the common strength of everything alive.

Yet we tend to lose our way when faced with choices. Tension builds around decisions because we quickly sort and name one way as good and another as bad. This quickly twists into an either/or sense that one way is right and another is wrong. In prizing what we prefer, we start to feel a thirst for something particular, which getting we call "success," and a fear of not getting it, which we then call "failure." From all this, we begin to feel the tightening pressure not to make a terrible mistake. Thus, we are often stymied and confused because we forget that — beneath our sorting of everything into good and bad, right and wrong, success and failure — all the choices still hold the truth and strength of life, no matter what we prefer.

To be certain, sharing a common beat does not mean that everything is the same, for things are infinite in how they differ. And faced with the richness of life, we can't value everything the same. But when we believe that only what we want holds the gold, then we find ourselves easily depressed by what we lack. Then we are pained by what we perceive as the difference between here and there, between what we have and what we need.

We still need to discern the ten thousand things we meet, but holding them to the light of our heart, we can say, "Not Two! Only One!" and realize there are no wrong turns, only unexpected paths.

- Meditate on a choice that is before you.
- Identify the distinct options you have.
- Try not to view these options with the urgency of what you prefer; rather focus on the experience each option might offer you.
- Try not to attach your sense of identity to any one option.
- If you don't get what you want, try not to see it as a failure but as an unexpected opening.

# January 23
## Getting at What Matters

If you want to be truly understood, you need to say everything three times, in three different ways. Once for each ear . . . and once for the heart.
— PAULA UNDERWOOD SPENCER

For years I felt so unheard that when asked a

54

question after speaking my heart, I'd take it as rejection or criticism. Often, though, it was just someone trying to understand. What was called for was for me to circle the unsayable and try again.

I've learned that true dialogue requires both speaker and listener to try several times to get at what matters. For sometimes, the truth is uttered just as I have to cough. Or your heart opens and closes while I am struggling to land.

So much depends on timing, and so, I've learned not to repeat myself, but to play what matters like a timeless melody, again and again, if the one before me is honest and sincere.

- This is a talking meditation. Sit with a loved one and take turns circling the unsayable:
- First, tell your loved one how you feel about them.
- Then, take some time in silence and say how you feel again.
- After some more time in silence, take each other's hands and say how you feel one last time.

# January 24
# Miracle Thinking

There are two ways to live your life.
One is as though nothing is a miracle.
The other is as though everything is a
  miracle.
— Albert Einstein

There is no end to worry, because there is no end to what exists out of view, beyond our very small eyes. So worry is a way to gamble with what might or might not happen.

It reminds me of a friend who had a flat tire on a country road. After finding he had no jack, he began walking, hoping to find a nearby farmer who would help him. It was getting dark and the crickets were getting louder. As he walked the overgrown road, he began to throw the dice of worry in his mind: What if the farmer's not home? What if he is and won't let me use his jack? What if he won't let me use his phone? What if he's frightened of me? I never did anything to him! Why won't he just let me use his phone?!

By the time he knocked on the farmer's door, my friend was so preoccupied with what could go wrong that when the friendly old man answered, my friend bellowed, "Well, you can keep your Goddam jack!"

56

Being human, we struggle constantly to stay with the miracle of what is and not to fall constantly into the black hole of what is not. This is an ancient challenge. As the Sufi poet Ghalib said centuries ago, "Every particle of creation sings its own song of what is and what is not. Hearing what is can make you wise; hearing what is not can drive you mad."

- Sit quietly and consider a situation that is causing you to worry.
- Breathe slowly and as you inhale, focus on accepting what is. Try to let in both the gifts and hardships of the reality you are in.
- Breathe evenly and as you exhale, focus on releasing what is not. Try to let go of all the imagined outcomes that are not yet real.
- Settle into the miracle of what is.

# JANUARY 25
# LOVING YOURSELF

I begin to realize that in inquiring about my own origin and goal, I am inquiring about something other than myself. . . . In this very realization I begin to recognize the origin and goal of the world.

— MARTIN BUBER

In loving ourselves, we love the world. For just as fire, rock, and water are all made up of molecules, everything, including you and me, is connected by a small piece of the beginning.

Yet, how do we love ourselves? It is as difficult at times as seeing the back of your head. It can be as elusive as it is necessary. I have tried and tripped many times. And I can only say that loving yourself is like feeding a clear bird that no one else can see. You must be still and offer your palmful of secrets like delicate seed. As she eats your secrets, no longer secret, she glows and you lighten, and her voice, which only you can hear, is your voice bereft of plans. And the light through her body will bathe you till you wonder why the gems in your palm were ever fisted. Others will think you crazed to wait on something no one sees. But the clear bird only wants to feed and fly and sing. She only wants light in her belly. And once in a great while, if someone loves you enough, they might see her rise from the nest beneath your fear.

In this way, I've learned that loving yourself requires a courage unlike any other. It requires us to believe in and stay loyal to something no one else can see that keeps us in the world — our own self-worth.

All the great moments of conception — the birth of mountains, of trees, of fish, of prophets, and the truth of relationships that last — all begin where no one can see, and it is our job not to extinguish what is so beautifully begun. For once full of light, everything is safely on its way — not pain-free, but unencumbered — and the air beneath your wings is the same air that trills in my throat, and the empty benches in snow are as much a part of us as the empty figures who slouch on them in spring.

When we believe in what no one else can see, we find we are each other. And all moments of living, no matter how difficult, come back into some central point where self and world are one, where light pours in and out at once. And once there, I realize — make real before me — that this moment, whatever it might be, is a fine moment to live and a fine moment to die.

- As you sit quietly, let each breath take you deeper into your center, and without sorting or selecting through what you find, become aware of an old and original part of who you are. It could be your laugh or your stubbornness or your love of flowers or your love of rain.
- Hold that old and original part of you in your breathing as you enter your day.
- Be open to finding this deep part of you in others, for the same wind touches many leaves.

59

# JANUARY 26
## BEING KIND – I

You often say, "I would give, but only to the deserving." The trees in your orchard say not so, nor the flocks in your pastures. They give that they may live, for to withhold is to perish.

— KAHLIL GIBRAN

The great and fierce mystic William Blake said, There is no greater act than putting another before you. This speaks to a selfless giving that seems to be at the base of meaningful love. Yet having struggled for a lifetime with letting the needs of others define me, I've come to understand that without the healthiest form of self-love — without honoring the essence of life that this thing called "self" carries, the way a pod carries a seed — putting another before you can result in damaging self-sacrifice and endless codependence.

I have in many ways over many years suppressed my own needs and insights in an effort not to disappoint others, even when no one asked me to. This is not unique to me. Somehow, in the course of learning to be good, we have all been asked to wrestle with a false dilemma: being kind to ourselves or being kind to others. In truth, though, being kind to ourselves is a prerequisite to being kind to others. Honoring ourselves is, in fact, the only lasting way to release a truly selfless kindness to others.

It is, I believe, as Mencius, the grandson of Confucius, says, that just as water unobstructed will flow downhill, we, given the chance to be what we are, will extend ourselves in kindness. So, the real and lasting practice for each of us is to remove what obstructs us so that we can be who we are, holding nothing back. If we can work toward this kind of authenticity, then the living kindness — the water of compassion — will naturally flow. We do not need discipline to be kind, just an open heart.

- Center yourself and meditate on the water of compassion that pools in your heart.
- As you breathe, simply let it flow, without intent, into the air about you.

# JANUARY 27
# BEING KIND – II

---

We love what we attend.

— MWALIMU IMARA

There were two brothers who never got along. One was forever ambushing everything in his path, looking for the next treasure while the first was still in his hand. He swaggered his shield and cursed everything he held. The other brother wandered in the open with very little protection, attending whatever he came upon. He would linger with every leaf and twig and broken stone. He blessed everything he held.

This little story suggests that when we dare to move past hiding, a deeper law arises. When we bare our inwardness fully, exposing our strengths and frailties alike, we discover a kinship in all living things, and from this kinship a kindness moves through us and between us. The mystery is that being authentic is the only thing that reveals to us our kinship with life.

In this way, we can unfold the opposite of Blake's truth and say, there is no greater act than putting yourself before another. Not before another as in coming first, but rather as in opening yourself before another, exposing your essence before another. Only in being this authentic can real kinship be known and real kindness released.

It is why we are moved, even if we won't admit it, when strangers let down and show themselves. It is why we stop to help the wounded and the real. When we put ourselves fully before another, it makes love possible, the way the stubborn land goes soft before the sea.

- Place a favorite object in front of you, and as you breathe, put yourself fully before it and feel what makes it special to you.
- As you breathe, meditate on the place in you where that specialness comes from.
- Keep breathing evenly, and know this specialness as a kinship between you and your favorite object.
- During your day, take the time to put yourself fully before something that is new to you, and as you breathe, try to feel your kinship to it.

# JANUARY 28
## MEETING THE WORLD

You must meet the outer world
with your inner world
or existence will crush you.

There is a wind that keeps blowing since the beginning of time, and in every language ever spoken, it continues to whisper, You must meet the outer world with your inner world or existence will crush you. If inner does not meet outer, our lives will collapse and vanish. Though we often think that hiding our inwardness will somehow protect or save us, it is quite the opposite. The heart is very much like a miraculous balloon. Its lightness comes from staying full. Meeting the days with our heart prevents collapse.

This is why ninety-year-old widows remain committed to tending small flowers in spring; why ten-year-olds with very little to eat care for stray kittens, holding them to their skinny chests; why painters going blind paint more; why composers going deaf write great symphonies. This is why when we think we can't possibly try again, we let out a sigh that goes back through the centuries, and then, despite all our experience, we inhale and try again.

- Center yourself and breathe slowly and deeply.
- As you breathe, feel your lungs fill and empty like a balloon.
- As you breathe, realize that your heart is filling and emptying itself of an inner air.
- During your day, let this inner air meet the world whenever you feel overwhelmed.

# January 29
## The Unspoiled Clearing

I am too alone in the world
and not alone enough
to make every moment holy.
— RAINER MARIA RILKE

It seems there are two basic ways to feel the fullness of life, and both arise from the authenticity of our relationships. One is from our love of life, and the other is from our love of each other.

Often, in our solitude, we can discover the miracles of life, if we take the time and risk to be alone until the glow of life presents itself. This is the reward of all meditation. It's like taking the path of our aloneness deep enough through the woods so we can reach that unspoiled clearing.

We can also reach that unspoiled clearing by taking the time and risk to be thoroughly with each other. This is the reward of love.

But our most frequent obstacle to experiencing the fullness of life, which I have suffered many times, is the hesitancy that keeps us from being either fully alone with life or fully alone with each other.

Being half anywhere is the true beginning of loneliness.

- Sit quietly and let a point of loneliness that you carry rise to your awareness.
- Breathe slowly and feel, if you can, which way you need to lean with it: more into yourself or more into the world.
- Breathe deeply and try to move your heart in that direction.

# JANUARY 30
## BEING A PILGRIM

To journey without being changed
is to be a nomad.
To change without journeying
is to be a chameleon.
To journey and to be transformed
by the journey
is to be a pilgrim.

We all start out as pilgrims, wanting to journey and hoping to be transformed by the journey. But, just as it is impossible when listening to an orchestra to hear the whole of the symphony for very long before we are drawn to hear only the piano or the violin, in just this way, our attention to life slips and we experience people and places without being affected by their wholeness. And sometimes, feeling isolated and unsure, we change or hide what lives within in order to please or avoid others.

The value of this insight is not to use it to judge or berate ourselves, but to help one another see that integrity is an unending process of letting our inner experience and our outer experience complete each other, in spite of our very human lapses.

I understand these things so well, because I violate them so often. Yet I, as you, consider myself a pilgrim of the deepest kind, journeying beyond any one creed or tradition, into the compelling, recurring space in which we know the moment and are changed by it. Mysteriously, as elusive as it is, this moment — where the eye is what it sees, where the heart is what it feels — this moment shows us that what is real is sacred.

- Center yourself and without judgment bring to mind a time that you refused to let your experience change you. Simply feel that time's presence.
- As you breathe, bring to mind a time that you changed yourself to please or avoid another. Again, simply feel that time's presence.
- As you soften, bring to mind a time that you journeyed forth and were changed by the journey. Feel this time's presence.
- Without judgment, give thanks by ac-

cepting all of this. Give thanks for being human.

# JANUARY 31
## PRACTICING

As a man in his last breath
drops all he is carrying
each breath is a little death
that can set us free.

Breathing is the fundamental unit of risk, the atom of inner courage that leads us into authentic living. With each breath, we practice opening, taking in, and releasing. Literally, the teacher is under our nose. When anxious, we simply have to remember to breathe.

So often we make a commitment to change our ways, but stall in the face of old reflexes as new situations arise. When gripped by fear or anxiety, the reflex is to hold on, speed up, or remove oneself. Yet when we feel the reflex to hold on, that is usually the moment we need to let go. When we feel the urgency to speed up, that is typically the instant we need to slow down. Often when we feel the impulse to flee, it is the opportunity to face ourselves. Taking a deep meditative breath, precisely at this moment, can often break the momentum of anxiety and put our psyche in neutral.

From here, we just might be able to step in another direction.

I'm not talking about external moments of anxiety here, but inner moments of truth. Certainly, when an accident is unfolding, we need to get out of the way; when a loved one falls, we need to try to hold them. Rather, I'm talking about fear of love and truth and God, fear of change and the unknown. I'm talking about how we all grip tightly to what we know, even if we hurt ourselves in the process.

Dropping all we carry — all our preconceptions, our interior lists of the ways we've failed and the ways we've been wronged, all the secret burdens we work at maintaining — dropping all regret and expectation lets our mentality die. Dropping all we have constructed as imperative allows us to be born again into the simplicity of spirit that arises from unencumbered being.

It is often overwhelming to imagine changing our entire way of life. Where do we begin? How do we take down a wall that took twenty-five or fifty years to erect? Breath by breath. Little death by little death. Dropping all we carry instant by instant. Trusting that what has done the carrying, if freed, will carry us.

- Sit by yourself, alone, in a safe place, and think of the last situation that made

69

you anxious.
- Ask yourself: What specifically made you uncomfortable? In tensing, what did you cling to in your mind?
- Place both your discomfort and your clinging before you now.
- In this safe place, touch what scared you. It can't hurt you now.
- In this safe place, drop what your mind clung to. It can't help you now.
- Repeat this several times while breathing slowly and deeply.
- Breathe. Feel in detail what rises in you without the discomfort or the clinging.
- Breathe. This is the God in you. Bow to it.

# FEBRUARY 1
## LIVE SLOW ENOUGH

Live slow enough
and there is only the beginning of time.

Follow anything in its act of being — a snowflake falling, ice melting, a loved one waking — and we are ushered into the ongoing moment of the beginning, the quiet instant from which each breath starts. What makes this moment so crucial is that it continually releases the freshness of living.

The key to finding this moment and all its freshness, again and again, is in slowing down.

Often, when we are inconvenienced, we are being asked to slow down. When we are delayed in our travel or waiting for a check in a restaurant, we are being asked to open up and look around. When we find ourselves stalled in our very serious and ambitious plans, we are often being asked to refind the beginning of time. Unfortunately, we are all so high-paced, running so fast to where we want to be, that many of us are forced to slow down through illness or breakage. In this, we are such funny creatures. If we could see ourselves from far enough away, we would seem like a colony of insects running into things repeatedly: thousands of little determined beings butting into obstacles, shaking our little heads and bodies, and running into things again.

Like the Earth that carries us, the ground of our being moves so slowly we take it for granted. But if you should feel stalled, numb, or exhausted from the trials of your life, simply slow your thoughts to the pace of cracks widening, slow your heart to the pace of the earth soaking up rain, and wait for the freshness of the beginning to greet you.

- Place a dry sponge and a glass of water

71

before you. Set them aside for the moment.
- Center yourself by letting the energy of all that feels urgent rush through you. Exhale and try to let it go.
- Now drip a small amount of water on the sponge and, as you breathe slowly, watch how the sponge opens.
- Keep dripping water on the sponge as you breathe slowly, and feel your heart open.

# FEBRUARY 2
# TWO HEART CELLS BEATING

If you place two living heart cells from different people in a Petrie dish, they will in time find and maintain a third and common beat.

— MOLLY VASS

This biological fact holds the secret of all relationship. It is cellular proof that beneath any resistance we might pose and beyond all our attempts that fall short, there is in the very nature of life itself some essential joining force. This inborn ability to find and enliven a common beat is the miracle of love.

This force is what makes compassion possible, even probable. For if two cells can find

72

the common pulse beneath everything, how much more can full hearts feel when all excuses fall away?

This drive toward a common beat is the force beneath curiosity and passion. It is what makes strangers talk to strangers, despite the discomfort. It is how we risk new knowledge. For being still enough, long enough, next to anything living, we find a way to sing the one voiceless song.

Yet we often tire ourselves by fighting how our hearts want to join, seldom realizing that both strength and peace come from our hearts beating in unison with all that is alive. It feels incredibly uplifting that without even knowing each other, there exists a common beat between all hearts, just waiting to be felt.

It brings to mind the time that the great poet Pablo Neruda, near the end of his life, stopped while traveling at the Lota coal mine in rural Chile. He stood there stunned, as a miner, rough and blackened by his work inside the earth, strode straight for Neruda, embraced him, and said, "I have known you a long time, my brother."

Perhaps this is the secret — that every time we dare to voice what beats within, we invite some other cell of heart to find what lives between us and sing.

- Breathe deeply in silence and feel the

beat of your heart.
- Meditate on the common beat the cells of your heart carry.
- Let this beat sound like a beacon from you.
- As you enter your day, keep sending the beat of your heart to everything around you. Do this with your regular breathing.
- Be aware of the moments you feel energized or filled with emotion. It is in the life of these moments that you are in full relationship with the world.

# FEBRUARY 3
## YEARNING

Before we blink,
we know each other.

We speak before we speak, with eyes and lips, in how we tip our heads, in how we lean like trees tired of waiting for the sun. We tell our whole story before we even open our mouths. Yet we frequently pretend that nothing is conveyed. We pretend we are strangers and deny what we learn before words.

We are all made up of yearning and light, searching for a way out, afraid we will be shut in or cut off or repelled back into the ground from which we are reaching.

This is enough to begin: To know, before all the names and histories drape who we are, that we want to be held and left alone, again and again; held and left alone until the dance of it is how we survive and grow, like spring into winter into spring again.

- As you move through your day, let in what you learn of others by how their being passes you.
- Without a word, bestow a blessing on each as they walk away.

# February 4
# A Set of Inner Doors

The stuff of our lives doesn't change.
It is we who change in relation to it.
— Molly Vass

Whatever our gifts or wounds or life situation — whether we have been married several times or have never been in love, whether we have plenty of money or are sorely in need of more — the core issues of our lives will not go away.

There exists for each life on Earth a set of inner doors that no one can go through for us. We can change jobs or lovers, travel around the world, become a doctor or lawyer or expert mountain climber, or nobly put our life on hold to care for an ailing mother or father, and when we are done, though the worthy distraction could take years, the last threshold we didn't cross within will be there waiting. There is no substitute for genuine risk.

Stranger still is how the very core issues we avoid return, sometimes with different faces, but still, we are brought full circle to them, again and again. Regardless of how we may try to skip over or sidestep what we need to face, we humbly discover that no other threshold is possible until we use our courage to open the door before us. Perhaps the oldest working truth of self-discovery is that the only way out is through. That we are returned repeatedly to the same circumstance is not always a sign of avoidance, but can mean our work around a certain issue is not done.

In my own life, it is not by chance that struggling to adulthood with a domineering and critical mother, I have been thrust again and again into situations with dominant men and women, struggling painfully for their approval and fearing their rejection. For years, I tried to manage the circumstance better, which was like sanding and varnishing the door without ever opening it. I was destined to repeat the pain of rejection, no matter how skillfully I handled it, until I opened the door of self-worth.

Even my calling to be a poet became a distraction that lasted many years. Feeling rejected and insecure at heart, I quietly made a mission of becoming a famous writer, only to find myself one day replaying the issues of approval and rejection a hundredfold at the mailbox, as I awaited word from countless critical strangers known as editors. I was stunned and relieved to finally discover myself at the same threshold of loving myself that I had run from years before.

The thresholds go nowhere. It is we who, in our readiness and experience, keep coming back, because the soul knows only one way to fulfill itself, and that is to take in what is true.

- Meditate on an issue that keeps returning to you.
- Relate to it as a messenger and ask the messenger what door it is trying to open for you.
- How will your life change if you move through this threshold?
- How will your life be affected if you do not?

# BENEATH PROBLEM SOLVING

---

Beneath most headaches
is a heartache.

---

Often we find it easier to think our way around things rather than to feel our way through them: What can we do to pull ourselves out of a bad mood? What can we buy, remove, or repair that will reduce or solve a loved one's anger or sadness?

In retrospect, I realize I have spent many hours problem solving emotional facts I just needed to feel. I know now that my frequent labors to understand what went wrong, while somewhat useful, often were distractions from feeling the sadness and disappointment necessary to heal and move on.

It's all very human. No one wants to feel pain, especially when you can't quite point to a specific cut or wound. So it is with the heart. There's nothing to show or stitch up, yet everything is affected.

The truth is that while analyzing and strategizing and preparing ourselves can occupy our minds, and may even help prevent us from being hurt the same way twice, there is no substitute for giving the wound air, which in the case of the heart means saying deeply, without aversion or self-pity, "Ouch."

- Sit quietly and allow a recent discomfort of heart to rise within the safety of your breathing.
- Breathe slowly and allow yourself to move through the discomfort by feeling it.
- Breathe deeply and trust that your heart has the wisdom to filter and process this discomfort, if you will only give it the chance.

# FEBRUARY 6
## ALONG THE WAY

I learn, by going, where I have to go.
— THEODORE ROETHKE

We drove to a lake that one of us had heard of. Around it was a path. We brought a few simple things: bread, water, bananas. We circled the lake, stopping at certain patches of light. Huge acorns were dropping from the canopy and small ravens were preening on branches sagging over the water.

Along the way, Christine stopped, drawn to a clearing she couldn't walk by. We followed, stepping slower, breathing deeper, and off the path, the ancient trees were growing and we lost the urge to go at all. With nothing but each other and our breathing, we heard a thread of stream unravel in a song that birds imitate.

We didn't talk about it, but it is the path off the path that brings us to God. For our hearts are just small birds waiting.

- Center yourself and imagine your life as a path about a beautiful lake.
- Breathe slowly and trace your path to where you are today.
- Breathe deeply and imagine tomorrow's part of the path coming into view. Smell the unmarked trails.
- As you enter your day, stay open to the unexpected clearings that call to you.

# FEBRUARY 7
# A LEGACY OF SADNESS

Atlas wasn't forced to hold up the world.
He was convinced that if he didn't,
the world would fall.

Many of us are raised by well-intending parents to be the carriers of their sadness. Often the one child who is softer than the rest, who is more sensitive than the family is used to, is the one selected to deal with what

80

no one else will deal with. It is an odd fate.

I was one of those children. I was often called too sensitive, too emotional, too day-dreamy. But as I grew older, as life visited us with the hardships that life inevitably brings to all families, it was I who was needed to carry the burden of my family's inability to feel. Without having my capacity to feel ever valued or acknowledged, I was the one to shoulder the family sadness with the brunt of my heart.

I have come to understand that there is a huge difference between sharing someone's pain and bearing it. Too many times, those in pain use the concern of loved ones as a way to ground what they don't want to feel themselves. The way electricity runs off into the ground during a storm, they mistakenly use others to run their sadness and pain into the ground of those who care. Too often, we want others to hold our sadness or pain because we won't take the risk to ask them to hold us while we are hurting.

As an adult trying to be my own person, understanding which feelings are genuinely mine and which are those I have inherited is often confusing. People like me, and maybe you identify, so let me say people like us, frequently feel responsible for the emotional condition of others.

It is delicate and never-ending work, this sorting of what is truly ours and what is not.

When unable to stay within ourselves, we become codependent, never feeling at peace until the emotions of everyone around us are managed and tended — not so much out of compassion, but as the only way to quiet our anxious burden as carriers of sadness. Or when rebounding the other way, we can isolate, becoming not only dispassionate to others, but also numb to ourselves.

The work becomes that of making an accurate inlet of the heart without closing off to the feelings of others or to the depth of things that are ours to feel. Though some of us were trained to carry the sadness and pain of others, the fiber of the one heart we were given is strong and light enough by itself to bring us to the wind that is whispering, Let down, let go, the world will carry you.

- If you are a parent, think of how you share your feelings with your child. If you have a lover, think of how you share your feelings in that love. If you have a close friend, think of how you share your feelings in that friendship.
- Meditate on the last time you shared a sadness or a pain with this special person.
- Through this example, look honestly at how you share such things and see if you try to transfer or unload your sadness or pain or if you simply give voice

to what troubles you.

- If you can, recall your mood as you shared. Did you want the relief of surfacing what was building inside? Or did you want your loved one to make you feel better? Did you feel closer to yourself after sharing or more distant?
- If you think you have given them what's yours to carry, go to them and thank them for holding your sadness. Lift it off their hearts and take it back. Ask them to hold you instead.

# FEBRUARY 8
## GREED

The greedy one gathered all the cherries,
while the simple one tasted
all the cherries in one.

We suffer, often unknowingly, from wanting to be in two places at once, from wanting to experience more than one person can. This is a form of greed, of wanting everything. Feeling like we're missing something or that we're being left out, we want it all. But being human, we can't have it all. The tension of all this can lead to an insatiable search, where our passion for life is stirred, but never satisfied. When caught in this mindset, no amount of travel is enough, no amount of love is enough, no amount of success is enough.

I am not saying that we shouldn't explore our curiosity and venture into the unknown. I very much want to experience the world and love to encounter new people in my life. What I'm referring to here is that seed of lack that makes us feel insufficient, and then, somehow, to compensate, we start to race through life with one eye on what we have and one eye on what we don't.

Greed is not restricted to money. It can work its appetite on anything. When we believe we are behind or less than, we somehow start to want more than we need, as if what we don't have will fill in our pain and make us feel whole, as if the thing we haven't tasted will be the thing to bring us alive. The truth is that one experience taken to heart will satisfy our hunger to be loved by everyone.

- Bring to mind something you want to experience.
- Meditate on what this experience might give you.
- Breathe openly and meditate on what part of this gift is already at work in you.

84

# FEBRUARY 9
# THE THING IN THE WAY

We tend to make the thing in the way
the way.

We were up early, eager to walk the Botanical
Gardens of Montreal, where they have the
largest bonsai collection in the world outside
of Asia. We strolled toward the Chinese
Temple Garden, a lush yet simple retreat
from the streets that covers acres, a place of
renewal originally constructed in the 1600s
in China and moved stone by stone to Montreal in 1990.

As we approached the massive gate, it was
locked. I panicked, ready to demand entry
after driving 400 miles from another country
to see this. Robert calmly, like an Oriental
sage himself, treated the situation as if it were
a koan, a riddle to be entered until its very
assumptions shifted.

He began to walk the outer wall of the
Garden. It seemed insurmountable. I was
frustrated. He kept walking slowly along the
high wall. Since the Garden stretched for
acres, I wondered if we would have to walk
its entire perimeter. The thought made me
cranky. He kept strolling.

Suddenly, when we had walked farther than

was originally in our view, the walls disappeared. It turned out that the Garden had no walls, save for the facade at its entrance. So we simply walked through the open grass to a path that welcomed us.

How many thresholds that seem blocked or barred or locked only seem so from their initial viewing? How many opportunities for true living are barrier-free, if we can only remove ourselves and our minds from their traditional points of entry?

- Center yourself and consider a barrier or threshold you are facing.
- Breathe slowly and relax your insistence. Stop beating the door down.
- Breathe evenly and circle the barrier or threshold with your spirit.
- Breathe patiently and see if there is another way in.

# FEBRUARY 10
# WHAT YOUR LIFE ASKS OF YOU

How are you tending
to the emerging story of your life?
— CAROL HEGEDUS AND
FRANCES VAUGHAN

Like many of us, I seem to be continually

challenged not to hide who I am. Over and over, I keep finding myself in situations that require me to be all of who I am in order to make my way through.

Whether breaking a pattern of imbalance with a lifelong friend, or admitting my impatience to listen to my lover, or owning my envy of a colleague, or even confronting the self-centeredness of strangers stealing parking spaces, I find I must be present — even if I say nothing. I find I must not suppress my full nature, or my life doesn't emerge.

Aside from the feeling of integrity or satisfaction that comes over me when I can fully be myself, I am finding that being who I am — not hiding any of myself — is a necessary threshold that I must meet or my life will not evolve. It is a doorway I must make my way to or nothing happens. My life just stalls.

Tending our stories means that our lies must open if we are to live in the mystery; our ways of hiding, no matter how subtle, must relax open if we are to be.

- Center yourself and meditate on the emerging story of your life.
- Breathe slowly and consider what your life asks of you so that it can emerge.
- Breathe fully and consider how you can better meet this inner requirement.

87

# FEBRUARY 11
## SIMPLICITY

I have just three things to teach:
simplicity, patience, compassion.
These are your greatest treasures.
Simple in actions and in thoughts,
you return to the Source of Being.

— LAO-TZU

In the sixth century B.C.E., the legendary Chinese sage Lao-tzu gave us this threefold instruction. I will talk about simplicity here and devote separate entries later to both patience and compassion.

But regarding the three as a whole, let me confess that while stumbling about my own path, I have found that I must continually learn and relearn these things — not just once, but again and again, in deeper and deeper ways. They appear now like a spiral staircase and with each stepping, I find myself deeper in the life of my soul.

So, what does it mean to be simple? In a world that is complicated, we are often misled to believe that being simple is being stupid, when in truth, it holds the reward for living directly, which is that things appear, at last, as they really are.

How many times have I seen the gestures of a loved one or colleague and then struggled privately to uncover what it all really meant? How many times have I done everything possible but ask directly? How often do I refuse to be direct: not saying what I mean, not showing what I feel, not letting the life around me really touch me?

Amazingly, nothing else in nature is indirect. The leopard trying to scale the mountain strains and shows its effort. The frightened squirrel in the tree hovers and trembles, showing its fright. The wave mounting toward shore saves nothing as it bows and spreads itself over and over against a shore that openly crumbles to be so loved. Only humans say one thing and mean another. Only we go one way and wish we were somewhere else.

Like so many other tasks that await us, the reward is hardly what we imagine. It seems that Lao-tzu reveals to us a secret tool of living, kept secret by our unwillingness to accept its truth. This ancient sage tells us quite openly that the act of simplicity — of living directly — is the doorway to the Source of all Being.

Imagine if this is true. I implore you, when feeling lost or far away, try it — try being direct — and the Universe without a word will come alive.

- Breathe slowly and recall a time when

89

things were direct and uncomplicated.
- Keep breathing slowly and recall a time when things were indirect and a burden.
- As you inhale, feel the burden.
- As you exhale, feel the simplicity.
- What did the burden take from you?
- What did the simplicity awaken in you?

# FEBRUARY 12
# MAKING TEA

Given sincerity, there will be enlightenment.
— THE DOCTRINE OF THE MEAN, 200 B.C.E.

If we stop to truly consider it, making tea is a miraculous process. First, small leaves are gathered from plants that grow from unseen roots. Then boiling water is drained through the dried leaves. Finally, allowing the mixture to steep creates an elixir that, when digested, can be healing.

The whole process is a model for how to make inner use of our daily experience. For isn't making tea the way we cipher through the events of our lives? Isn't the work of sincerity to pour our deepest attention over the dried bits of our days? Isn't patience the need to let the mixture of inner and outer brew until the lessons are fragrant and soothing on the throat? Isn't it the heat of our sincerity that steams the lessons out of living? Isn't it the heat of those lessons that makes us sip them slowly?

Yet perhaps the most revealing thing about all this is that none of these elements alone can produce tea. Likewise, only by using them together, can we make tea of our days and our sincerity and our patience. And none of it is healing without a willingness to drink from the tea of life.

- Slowly, and with symbolic care, make a cup of tea.
- As the tea is steeping, be mindful of your life and how you bring your sincerity and patience to bear on your days.
- Sip slowly and feel gratitude coat your throat.

# FEBRUARY 13
# WHAT IS NOT EXPRESSED

What is not *ex*-pressed is *de*-pressed.

It seems the more we express, that is, bring out what is in, the more alive we are. The more we give voice to our pain in living, the less build-up we have between our soul and our way in the world. However, the more we depress, the more we push down and keep in, the smaller we become. The more we stuff between our heart and our daily experience, the more we have to work through to feel life directly. Our unexpressed life can become a callus we carry around and manicure, but never remove. Experience can in effect lose its essential tenderness and poignancy, as we mistakenly conclude that life is losing its meaning. To a man unaware of the cataracts filming his eyes, the world seems dimmer, not his seeing. How often do we find the world less stimulating, unaware that our heart is diminished because of its encasement in all that remains unexpressed?

Let me give a personal example. I have, for many reasons, including issues of my own making, forever felt invisible in family or group settings. Initially, this stemmed from fearfully pleasing a self-centered mother at all cost. It led to years of unexpressed hurts and rejections that accrued into a callus that guarded the heart within my heart. I am and have always been a very open and emotionally accessible person, but at a certain depth, my core could not be touched. Though this started with Mother, it effected the level at which I could relate with anyone.

Eventually, this was not enough. I realized the world was not losing color, but that I was screening the deepest emotional colors out. That I state this so calmly and clearly in one sentence hardly reflects the difficult and slow, elusive way this awareness pained itself into my daily consciousness. Rather, it emerged in me gradually as I began to acknowledge and voice the feelings of invisibility I have carried all my life.

Whatever your own example, it seems our authenticity is tied to what is de-pressed and what is ex-pressed. Just as flowers need healthy root systems in order to blossom, feelings can only express their beauty when they are rooted cleanly within us, breaking ground in some manner, sprouting outside us. It is that delicate paradoxical inch of ground between surface and deep, between flower and root, between what is allowed out and what is allowed in, that continually determines whether we are living our lives or not.

- Recall the last time you felt depressed.
- Sit quietly and look inside and see if there is anything lodged or pressing there against your mind or heart.
- It might be a disappointment or injury that you don't want to accept about yourself or others.
- Treat whatever you find like a splinter, and soften yourself with the slowness of your breathing, so it can be removed.
- As you breathe, remember that you are larger than this hurt pressing in on you.

# FEBRUARY 14
# LOVE AT FIRST SIGHT

Where two deliberate, the love is slight.
Whoever loved, not having loved at first
 sight.
— CHRISTOPHER MARLOWE

The true power of love at first sight is often
missed because we insist on limiting its
meaning to the sweep of falling into another
person upon first meeting. To appreciate the
deeper sense of this, we must uncover and
reclaim the importance of first sight itself,
which has more to do with seeing things essentially, rather than physically, for the first
time.

We all walk around within the numbness of
our habits and routines so often that we take
the marvels of ordinary life for granted. It is
first sight that opens the freshness of each
moment, unencumbered by any of our habits
and routines. First sight is the moment of
God-sight, heart-sight, soul-sight. It is the
seeing of revelation, the feeling of oneness
that briefly overcomes us when nothing
remains in the way.

At its deepest and most real level, the notion of love at first sight is spoken of in every
spiritual tradition as the reward for being

94

fully awake. Such seeing anew restores our sense of being alive. Paradoxically, first sight is recurring. In the same way that we wake every day, we regularly return to first sight in the rhythm of our wakefulness of spirit. Whenever we can see with that original vision — with nothing between us and the life around us — we can't help but love what we see. To see so fundamentally opens us to love. To love so fundamentally is to see the world we're a part of as the vibrant, ongoing creation that it is. So, it really manifests this way: at first sight, we find love; at our first true seeing, the love that is already there touches us.

In this regard, first seeing is an ever-present threshold to the majesty of what is. Certainly and beautifully, this happens with other people when we, upon first truly seeing another, fall sweetly into the miracle of their presence. But this is also possible, on a daily basis, upon first truly seeing ourselves, our world, our sense of God — again and again.

I can work across from the same person for years, and one day, because my own suffering has opened me more fully than I can remember and because the light floods that person's face, I can for the first time truly see who they are and feel love for them. I can walk by the same willow, season after season, and one day, because of the sheen of after-rain and the lowness of the wind, I can truly see the willow like never before, and feel love for the willow in all of us. I can, in the mirror late at night, after seeing myself hundreds of times, see the willow and the light and the other in my tired face, and know that sameness as the stuff of God.

In truth, it has never been about first meeting, though this can happen, but more about first coming into view. As a breeze all spun out lets the water go clear, we finally stop talking, stop performing, stop pretending, and all tired out, we go clear, and the heart that rests in everything beats before us.

- Close your eyes and breathe away your mind-sight, your past-sight, your future-sight, your wounded-sight.
- With each slow breath, feel the cool air of your birth-sight, your first-sight.
- Breathe slowly and imagine that the beat of your heart carries up the beginning-of-time-sight.
- At the moment that you feel original, however briefly, open your eyes and bow with love to the first thing you see.

# FEBRUARY 15
# BEING A SPIRITUAL WARRIOR

Until the heart becomes an inlet,
it cannot be free.

It is true; there is such sadness in the world. But there is a difference between feeling the pain of things breaking, ending, or drifting apart, and the sharper pain that comes from measuring the inevitable events of life against some ideal of how we imagine things are supposed to be. In receiving hardships this way, life is always a falling off. Life is hard enough without viewing all our pain as evidence of some basic insufficiency we must endure.

There is a beautiful Tibetan myth that helps us to accept our sadness as a threshold to all that is life-changing and lasting. This myth affirms that all spiritual warriors have a broken heart — alas, must have a broken heart — because it is only through the break that the wonder and mysteries of life can enter us.

So what does it mean to be a spiritual warrior? It is far from being a soldier, but more the sincerity with which a soul faces itself in a daily way. It is this courage to be authentic that keeps us strong enough to withstand the heartbreak through which enlightenment can occur. And it is by honoring how life comes through us that we get the most out of living, not by keeping ourselves out of the way. The goal is to mix our hands in the earth, not to stay clean.

I remember, in getting to know a new friend, how we shared our stories in an increasingly personal way. As I kept taking my turn, I heard myself tell of loved ones who have died, of my struggle through cancer, of a marriage that, despite the deepest commitment, didn't last, of years of being rejected as an artist, of losing a teaching job that was dear to me, of suffering a brutal estrangement from my parents — and just as I was feeling a strength come over me for facing life and being authentic, he wiped his mouth and said, "What a sad life you've had."

It took me some time to withstand his judgment and his pity, but I looked at him across the night and kept breathing deeply through the break in my heart. In daily ways, we are judged, discounted, and even pitied for glories that only we can affirm. In the end, life is too magnificent and difficult for us to give away our elemental place in the journey.

- Stand quietly by the sink and let the water run.
- Close your eyes and meditate on how life — like the water you hear — runs through our broken hearts, cleansing

our hurt.
- Breathe deeply and feel the mystery wash through the break in your heart.
- Open your eyes and enter your day.

# FEBRUARY 16
# MISERY

If peace comes from seeing the whole,
then misery stems from a loss of
 perspective.

We begin so aware and grateful. The sun somehow hangs there in the sky. The little bird sings. The miracle of life just happens. Then we stub our toe, and in that moment of pain, the whole world is reduced to our poor little toe. Now, for a day or two, it is difficult to walk. With every step, we are reminded of our poor little toe.

Our vigilance becomes: Which defines our day — the pinch we feel in walking on a bruised toe, or the miracle still happening?

It is the giving over to smallness that opens us to misery. In truth, we begin taking nothing for granted, grateful that we have enough to eat, that we are well enough to eat. But somehow, through the living of our days, our focus narrows like a camera that shutters down, cropping out the horizon, and one day we're miffed at a diner because the eggs are runny or the hash isn't seasoned just the way we like.

When we narrow our focus, the problem seems everything. We forget when we were lonely, dreaming of a partner. We forget first beholding the beauty of another. We forget the comfort of first being seen and held and heard. When our view shuts down, we're up in the night annoyed by the way our lover pulls the covers or leaves the dishes in the sink without soaking them.

In actuality, misery is a moment of suffering allowed to become everything. So, when feeling miserable, we must look wider than what hurts. When feeling a splinter, we must, while trying to remove it, remember there is a body that is not splinter, and a spirit that is not splinter, and a world that is not splinter.

- Breathe steadily and focus on one thing that is annoying or paining you. It might be how your car is running, or how your relationship is running, or how your sleep was disturbed by the noise of strangers.
- Breathe deeply and, keeping what is bothersome in view, widen your focus.
- Breathe thoroughly and accept the energy of all that exists outside your bother.

## ENDGAME

Now there's nothing left
but to keep dancing.

I don't know if it is human nature or the way of life on Earth, but we seldom become all of who we are until forced to it. Some say that something in us rises to the occasion, that there is, as Hemingway called it, "a grace under pressure" that comes forth in most of us when challenged. Others say this talk of grace is merely a way to rationalize hard times and painful experience, a way to put a good face on tragedy.

Yet beneath all the talk of tragedy and grace, I have come to believe that we are destined to be opened by the living of our days, and whether we like it or not, whether we choose to participate or not, we will, in time, every one of us, wear the deeper part of who we are as a new skin.

Either by erosion from without or by shedding from within — and often by both — we are forced to live more authentically. And once the crisis that opened us passes, the real choice then becomes: Will we continue such authentic living?

It is no secret that cancer in its acuteness

pierced me into open living, and I've been working ever since to sanctify that open living without crisis as its trigger. But can this be done without crisis pushing us off the ledge? That's the question now, years from the leap — how to keep leaping from a desire to be real, so as not to be shoved by an ever-lurking crisis.

Perhaps the greatest moment of shedding and breaking for me came as I was being wheeled to rib surgery. I found myself numbly afraid, spinning from the Demerol shot, watching the hospital ceiling roll on by, and I found myself repeating over and over the following words as I waited on my stretcher:

"Death pushed me to the edge. Nowhere to back off. And to the shame of my fears, I danced with abandon in his face. I never danced as free. And Death backed off, the way dark backs off a sudden burst of flame. Now there's nothing left, but to keep dancing. It is the way I would have chosen had I been born three times as brave."

We are often called further into experience than we'd like to go, but it is this extra leap that lands us in the vibrant center of what it means to be alive.

- Sit quietly with a trusted loved one and discuss a time of adversity you have endured and what it opened in you.
- Now that the adversity is behind you,

how has your inner view of life changed?
- Discuss what it is like for you to sustain these new inner ways.

# FEBRUARY 18
# WHEN FEELING STUCK

The same stream of life
that runs through the world
runs through my veins.
— RABINDRANATH TAGORE

We are so achievement-oriented that we often surge right by the true value of relating to what's before us, because we think that accomplishing things will complete us, when it is experiencing life that will.

Yet, if we can outlast the urge to judge everything we encounter, a miracle starts to surround us in which painting, music, poetry, running water, flowers, wind through trees, open vistas — all touch and draw out their counterpart that lives quietly within us.

The nineteenth-century poet Gerard Manley Hopkins called this inner terrain "inscape." And just as no landscape can flourish without sun and water, our inscape must be irrigated and drenched with many forms of life if we are to thrive.

So, when feeling stuck or disconnected

103

from the miracle of life, as will happen to us all, try to listen, see, feel, and just take in. Try to let the energies of life stir their counterparts within you.

In order to be whole, suspend your criticism. For life is not a matter of taste, but of awakening, not a matter of finding things pleasing or disturbing, but of finding things completing, not a matter of liking or disliking, but of opening the geography of one's soul.

- This is a meditation done to music. Close your eyes and listen to a piece of music that is new to you.
- As you breathe evenly, allow yourself to feel your like or dislike for it, and try to let that go.
- As you breathe, allow yourself to meet the sheer energy of the music with the sheer energy of what is new in you.

# FEBRUARY 19
## INSTEAD OF BREAKING

The glassblower knows:
while in the heat of beginning,
any shape is possible.

Once hardened, the only way
to change is to break.

With the precise tools of modern medicine,
unborn children who are malforming or
experiencing obstructions can now be oper-
ated on in utero. Profoundly, these state-of-
the-art techniques reveal a deep timeless
truth about growth and healing. For just as
amazing as the fact of these operations, is the
fact that these surgeries leave no scars once
the infant is born.

What this tells us is that if we tend to things
at the deepest level, our repair will be so
much a part of who we are that there will be
no scar. It is easier to bend underneath the
surface, in the deep timeless fluid of the
beginning, than to break once fully grown.

But it is too late for me, you might say, I
am already full-grown. Not so, for in the
world of our inwardness, we are always growing and are blessed to carry that fluid beginning within us. It is never really out of reach.

We can return and begin again by facing
ourselves. In this way, we can go below our
hardened ways to the soft impulses that birth
them. Instead of breaking the bone of our
stubbornness, we can nourish the marrow of
our feeling unheard. Instead of breaking the
bone of our fear, we can cleanse the blood of
our feeling unsafe. Instead of counting the
scars from being hurt in the world, we can

find and re-kiss the very spot in our soul where we began to withhold our trust.

- Sit quietly and bring to mind an aspect of your personality that tends to get in the way. It might be your own brand of stubbornness or distrust or envy.
- As you breathe steadily, allow yourself to trace this trait to its soft beginning.
- Without trying to name it or change it, simply surround this soft inner spot with your love.

# FEBRUARY 20
## NICODEMUS AND THE TRUTH

How can one be born again?
— NICODEMUS TO JESUS

I often think of Nicodemus, the one Pharisee who secretly believed in Jesus and who would meet with him anonymously at night to have deep spiritual conversations, but who would never acknowledge his questions of spirit or his association with Jesus in the light of day. Of course, this did nothing to the essence of Jesus, but traumatically thwarted and plagued Nicodemus for the rest of his days.

This story shows us the quiet pain that comes from not honoring what we know to be true, even if all we know to be true are the questions we are asking. It is even more useful to realize that we each carry a Jesus and a Nicodemus within us; that is, we each have a divine inner voice that opens us to truth and a mediating social voice that is reluctant to show its truth to others.

The famous British child psychologist D. W. Winnicott called these aspects of personality our True and False Self. It is the True Self that lets us know what is authentic and what has become artificial, while the False Self is a diplomat of distrust, enforcing a lifestyle of guardedness, secrecy, and complaint.

In everyday terms, this means that each time we experience a change in reality as we know it, we must choose whether to declare or hide what we know to be true. At such moments, we either need to bring the way we have been living into accord with that shift of reality, or we need to resist the change. Thus, in daily ways, whether we live in our True or False Self depends on our willingness to stay real. And so, over time, staying real becomes the work of keeping our actions in the world connected to the truth of our inner being, allowing our True Self to see the light of day.

Very often, we continue, out of habit or fear, to behave in old ways, even though we know that the way of things has changed. Time and again, I have found myself at this crucial juncture: having to admit that what

107

was essential is no longer essential and then needing to summon the courage to make the act of living essential again.

I know that every time I hear or see the truth but hold to the old way — of being or thinking or relating — I am giving my life over to the Nicodemus in me. And in so doing, I embark on a divided life, in which I listen to the divine inner voice secretly at night, but deny it day after day.

But this moment of inner embarrassment, when we catch ourselves in the act of split living, is also the recurring chance for us to honor once again what we know to be true. For anyone, no matter how wounded or distressed, can in a moment of truth let the God within show itself out here in the world. However small or fleeting, this one repeatable act can restore our common and vital sense of being alive.

- Sit quietly and recall the last time you felt a moment of inner embarrassment — that is, the last time you realized what you were doing was no longer authentic, but you kept doing it anyway.
- If you can, meditate on what made you keep doing what you knew to be untrue. What were you afraid would happen if you honored the truth as you felt it?
- If a similar situation were to happen

108

tomorrow, how might you act differently?

- If you can, don't blame yourself for struggling like Nicodemus. Rather, comfort the Nicodemus in you that it is safe to honor what it knows in the light of day.

# FEBRUARY 21
## CLEANING OUT THE WOUND

If I had experienced different things,
I would have different things to say.

So often, I have felt troubled and guilty bearing witness to my pain, and yet, not to makes things worse. Somehow, in saying just what Mother had done in her cruel need to be the center, or just what Father couldn't do out of his fear of facing my mother; somehow, telling the truth as I know it makes me feel like a bad person — as if I'm making my pain up, as if I'm hurting others by saying bad things about them.

But the unshakable bottom of all this is that I'm not making things up. If I have unkind things to say, it's because I've experienced unkind things. And so, my only guide in this witnessing is to be accurate and honest. While I am not a victim, I didn't ask for certain shaping experiences to happen to me. I didn't ask to be slapped or ridiculed as a boy or to be mistreated by lifelong friends later in life. In truth, If I had experienced different things, I would have different things to say.

What is most healing about bearing witness to things exactly as they are, including my own part in my pain, is that when the voice of the pain fits the pain, there is no room for distortion or illusion. In this way, truth becomes a clean bandage that heals, keeping dirt out of the wound.

To voice things as they are is the nearest medicine.

- Center yourself and, in the safety of your heart that has carried you this far, give voice to a wound you carry.
- Breathe deeply and try to be accurate, naming all those responsible for the wound, including yourself, if that is the case.
- Soothe the wound with your deepest breathing.
- Soothe yourself with the cleanness of the truth.

# FEBRUARY 22
## OPPOSING VOICES

Let the opposing voices in your head
   speak.
They are only finding their part
in a larger, yet-to-be-heard song.

Being alive is a paradox, an ongoing mix of things that on the surface don't always seem to make sense. But voicing what doesn't seem to make sense helps. It's like an orchestra tuning up to play together. We have no chance of discovering the fullness of our inner music, if we don't let the players in our hearts and minds and spirits tune.

Often, confusion is the tension of trying to make sense of things too soon, before enough of the inner players have learned their parts. Often, experience is the way that the heart and mind and spirit practice what they need to play.

Isn't the trail of our relationships the time it takes for the heart to practice its part in the movement we call Love? Isn't the trail of our honest questions the time it takes for the mind to practice its part in the movement we call Wisdom? Isn't the trail of our changing beliefs the time it takes for the spirit to practice its part in the movement we call God?

And isn't our trail of Oneness, those brief moments when everything comes together, isn't this the time it takes for Love and Wisdom and God to bring the common place in us alive?

- This is a guided thought meditation. Center yourself and bring into view an issue that carries indecision or confusion for you right now.
- Though it will feel initially chaotic, breathe slowly and let the opposing views of this issue bubble up uncensored.
- Take your time, breathe deeply, and let the opposing energies play themselves out.
- Rather than struggle to understand how these things go together, breathe steadily and, as if each energy is an instrument, feel the duet they are trying to play in you.
- Enter your day humming that tune.

# FEBRUARY 23
## TO HOLD NOTHING BACK

To hold nothing back
in every breath
is a spiritual practice.

For forty-nine years I have found that hesitation, more than anything, has been the invisible hitch that has kept me from joy. I've found that the moment with all its meaning often moves on by the time I've reconsidered whether or not to enter it. I am not saying we should always be impulsive. More to the point, I have discovered, again and again, that I usually know what I need to do but just deny it, and it is this small hesitation, this small resistance to enter what is real, that makes life feel neutral or out of reach.

To hold nothing back in every breath means staying committed to letting whatever we experience make its way in and letting whatever is in make its way out. Holding nothing back means holding the intention to be an open vessel, in a daily way.

Simply and profoundly, our very breath can serve as a reminder that life is only possible if the exchange of inner and outer is undisturbed. Letting things in, feeling their impact, and, in turn, letting things out, expressing

cleanly what we feel, is a spiritual practice
that rinses the mind and heart.

- Meditate on a glass of water.
- When feeling centered, drink the water
  slowly without hesitation.
- Exhale deeply and say softly to yourself:
  I will hold nothing back in my effort to
  live. I will not hesitate to be.

# FEBRUARY 24
## BEHIND THE URGENCY

---

When feeling urgent,
you must slow down.

I learned this, over and over, during the many
crises of cancer. Unless someone is bleeding
or can't breathe, unless there is some true
physical requirement to act swiftly, a sense of
urgency is a terrible illusion, a trick that happens, again and again, because life inside our
skin and outside our skin are forever different.

It is as hard as it is humbling. When feeling
like I can't sit still, I need, more than ever, to
sit still. When feeling like I will die if I don't
have your approval, I need, more than ever,
to die to my need for your approval. What we
need is always harshly and beautifully right

before us, disguised in the wrapping of our nearest urgency. We just refuse to accept this, because it feels so difficult to face.

The doorway to our next step of growth is always behind the urgency of now. Now more than ever, when all feels urgent, you must cut the strings to all events. Now more than ever, when the weights you carry seem tied to your wrists, you must not run or flail. Now more than ever, when each decision feels like the end, you must believe that each question is a beginning. Now more than ever, when you fear that being who you are is a knife to those you love, you must be strong inside where no one has seen you, for loving from there can only make those you love grow. Now more than ever, when feeling that you are the source and recipient of all pain, you must bow your head till the ancient channel from sky to heart can reopen, till you remember that you are a blessed piece of spirit-dust in spirit-wind. Now more than ever, you must breathe till your ounce of breath becomes the sky, again and again.

In this way, pray to know your place in the human family like you've never known it. In this way, pray to have your True Self inch through your turmoil. In this way, love yourself the way you love the emptiness of time. Love yourself the way you love your children or your dog or your dearest friend, without reservation. In this way, today with all its hardships will spill into tomorrow, and decisions will become as clear as streams thawing.

- Center yourself and feel the urgencies that pull at you.
- Feel the tension of each like a string stretched taut.
- With each breath, untie yourself, one urgency at a time.
- However briefly, breathe freely, even for a moment, untied to any urgency at all.

# February 25
## Cutting a Path

No matter where we dig or climb,
we come upon the fire we left untended.

Carl Jung had a dream that he was cutting a path in the woods, unsure where it was leading, but working hard at it nonetheless. Tired and sweating, he came upon a cabin in a clearing. He dropped his tools and approached the cabin. Through the window he saw a being in prayer at a simple altar. The door was open and Jung went in. As he drew closer, he realized that the being in prayer was himself and that his life of cutting a path was this being's dream.

What Jung brings to us is the never-ending task of deciding to whom we entrust our life: our True or False Self. For all the seriousness with which we run about in the world — fixing, denying, projecting, and sacrificing — for all the schemes and strategies and alliances and positioning for reward, it is all an unreal dream to the center of our being that waits for us far inside while we hack our way through.

Without knowing it, we, like Jung, work hard at cutting a path to our deeper self that waits patiently for us to arrive, all tired, aching, and out of breath. Once that path is cleared and once the being at our center is discovered, we can return to the world in relationship with our soul. We can discover a deeper, more peaceful sense of home.

- Be still and close your eyes, and as you meditate, journey inwardly to the cabin where your soul awaits.
- Drop all you are carrying at the door. Drop all that waits to be done. Or redone.
- As you breathe, enter the cabin and wait with open arms for the center of your being to realize you are there.
- As you breathe, feel your soul embrace you. Embrace back. Savor that moment.

# February 26
## At the Pace of What Is Real

---

Stop talking, stop thinking,
and there is nothing you will not
   understand.

— SENG-TS'AN

Like most people I know, I struggle with taking too much on, with doing too many things, with moving too fast, with overcommitting, with overplanning. I've learned that I must move, quite simply, at the pace of what is real. While this pace may vary, life always seems vacant and diminished when I accelerate beyond my capacity to feel what is before me.

It seems we run our lives like trains, speeding along a track laid down by others, going so fast that what we pass blurs on by. Then we say we've been there, done that. The truth is that blurring by something is not the same as experiencing it.

So, no matter how many wonderful opportunities come my way, no matter the importance placed on these things by others who have my best interests at heart, I must somehow find a way to slow down the train that is me until what I pass by is again see-able, touchable, feel-able. Otherwise, I will pass by everything — can put it all on my résumé — but will have experienced and lived through nothing.

- Consider three things you must do today.
- Carefully put two down.
- Immerse yourself in the one thing that is left.

# FEBRUARY 27
# THE ROPES AND WHEELS
# THAT CARRY US

---

Beauty is Truth, Truth Beauty —
that is all you know on earth,
and all you need to know.

— JOHN KEATS

These are the famous last lines of "Ode on a Grecian Urn" uttered by the young English poet dying of tuberculosis at the age of twenty-four. The poem is an understandable complaint by a tender being against the harshness of life. But suddenly, by voicing his pain of living, the young poet comes upon a profound realization.

When Keats says, "Beauty is Truth, Truth Beauty," we are forced to ask: Are they the same? Deeply, I think not. Rather, like X and Y chromosomes, they make up the fundamental elements of life that no one can do without. They are the yin and yang of existence — one cleanses the wound, while the other heals the wound.

This is "all you need to know." Beauty, wherever we find it, is the salve that keeps us vital and fresh. But Truth, in its uncompromised and naked story, no matter how harsh, has a Beauty all its own that is cleansing.

This is why we must remember the Holocaust and other atrocities exactly as they were. This is why it is essential to bear honest witness to our own naked stories.

Still, as wise as the message he came upon is, there is an equal lesson in how young Keats came upon it. For only by voicing our tender pains can we find our way to the deeper Beauties and Truths that like ropes and wheels can carry us.

- Sit quietly and feel your own tenderness in being alive.
- Breathe slowly, and as you inhale, allow the naked truth of one tenderness to cleanse you.
- Breathe fully and, in the next breath, allow the beauty around you to revitalize the place in you that is raw.

# FEBRUARY 28
## THE STONES AT CHIMAYO

I'd rather learn from one bird how to sing
than teach ten thousand stars how not to
dance.

— E. E. CUMMINGS

On the way to Chimayo, a woman saw two
Spanish farmers repositioning stones in a
riverbed to redirect the flow; she felt compelled to help. She had the feeling that this
had been done for centuries — their mothers
and fathers, their grandmothers and grand-
fathers, each in their own time and way, picking up the same stones pushed about by
storm or drought and putting them back so
the water can continue.

It seems this is the never-ending work of
relationship, each of us in our own time and
way moving the stones between us, repositioning the heavy things that get in the way,
so the life of feeling can continue.

The weather of simply living jams things
up, and we, like every generation before us,
must roll up our pants and sleeves, step into
the river, and unclog the flow. Of course, we
need to ask, What are the stones pushed
about between us? What are the heavy things
that keep getting in the way?

No doubt, they are infinite and particular, but often, they are made of habits of not: not seeing, not hearing, not feeling, not being present, not risking the truth, not risking the heart's need to live out in the open.

That we close off, jam up, spill over, and dry up are all part of being human in the gravity of time. That we feel compelled to stop and help even strangers move the heavy thing out of the way is an impulse known as love.

- Identify something heavy within you that seems to be in the way.
- Does it have to do with a habit of not? If so, try to name what it is you are not allowing to flow freely within you?
- If you are not seeing, breathe slowly and begin the vow to see. If you are not listening, breathe slowly and begin the vow to listen.
- Be honest in assessing how heavy this stone in you is.
- If you need help in moving it, whom will you ask and when?

# FEBRUARY 29
# WHO'S TO SAY

Who's to say
the effort to be real
isn't the beginning of wings?

Who's to say that the budding of wings from the ribs of small birds doesn't begin with the impulse within them to live? Who's to say that the butterfly breaking through its cocoon isn't the result of its being tired of living in a tight weave of its own making?

Who's to say that the migration of flamingoes from South America to Africa doesn't begin with a yearning to eat the yellow ribbon that keeps lining the horizon?

And who's to say the color of passion doesn't line our faces the instant we grow tired of living in a tight cocoon of our own making? Who's to say the journey to love doesn't begin the instant we give voice to that loneliness that no one wants to hear? Who's to say the journey to peace doesn't sprout like a small wing the instant we let our feelings find their place in the world?

In truth, every effort that is allowed its full beat within will ripple as a birth of some kind in the world.

- Center yourself and breathe deeply.
- At the high point of inhalation, imagine the still center as the inner sun of spirit.
- Let it flood you with its light each time you exhale.
- Enter your day, inviting one deep feeling to sprout from you.

# March 1
# The One Direction

Live deep enough
and there is only one direction.

No matter whom the apprentice talked to, if she listened close enough and long enough, the words all went back to the same source, as if there were only one large thing speaking. No matter how many eyes she looked deeply into, they all eventually revealed the same shimmer, as if there were only one large thing seeing. No matter how many pains she soothed, the cries all sounded from the same human hurt, as if there were only one large thing feeling.

When she brought all this to her master, her master walked her in silence through the woods to a clearing, where they sat on a fallen tree. The light was flooding through, covering everything. The master placed a stone in her one hand and a small flower in her other hand, and said, "Feel the warmth from both stone and flower. See how both are covered differently with the same light. Now trace the light of each back to the sun."

The apprentice heard the one large thing speaking in the master's voice, saw the one large thing shimmer in the master's eyes, and even felt the same human hurt in the master's soft silence. The light grew even stronger and the master said, "We are all just small stones and little flowers searching for our sun. What you have seen under words, behind many eyes, and beneath all cries is the one direction."

- Meditate on one recent moment of lightheartedness you have felt. Breathe deeply and smile.
- Now meditate on one recent moment of lightheartedness you witnessed in a loved one or friend. Breathe deeply and smile.
- Continue your deep breathing, and let these two moments find their sameness.
- Focus on this lightness of heart as you would a sun out of view, and feel the one direction.

# MARCH 2
## MORE POWER TO YOU

Originally, the word *power* meant able to
  be.
In time, it was contracted to mean to be
  able.
We suffer the difference.

I was waiting for a plane when I overheard
two businessmen. One was sharing the good
news that he had been promoted, and the
other, in congratulation, said, "More power
to you."

I've heard this expression before, but for
some reason, I heard it differently this time
and thought, what a curious sentiment. As a
good wish, the assumption is that power is
the goal. Of course, it makes a huge difference if we are wishing others worldly power
or inner power. By *worldly power,* I mean
power over things, people, and situations —
controlling power. By *inner power,* I mean
power that comes from being a part of
something larger — connective power.

I can't be certain, but I'm fairly sure the
wish here was for worldly power, for more
control. This is commonplace and disturbing,
as the wish for more always issues from a
sense of lack. So the wish for more power

really issues from a sense of powerlessness.

It is painfully ironic that in the land of the free, we so often walk about with an unspoken and enervating lack of personal freedom. Yet the wish for more controlling power will not set us free, anymore than another drink will quench the emptiness of an alcoholic in the grip of his disease.

It makes me think of a game we played when I was nine called King of the Hill, in which seven or eight of us found a mound of dirt, the higher the better, and the goal was to stand alone on top of the hill. Once there, everyone else tried to throw you off, installing themselves as King of the Hill. It strikes me now as a training ground for worldly power.

Clearly, the worst position of all is being King of the Hill. You are completely alone and paranoid, never able to trust anyone, constantly forced to spin and guard every direction. The hills may change from a job to a woman to a prized piece of real estate, but those on top can be so enslaved by guarding their position that they rarely enjoy the view.

I always hated King of the Hill — always felt tense in my gut when king, sad when not, and ostracized if I didn't want to play. That pattern has followed me through life. But now, as a tired adult, when I feel alone and powerless atop whatever small hill I've managed to climb, I secretly long for anyone to join me. Now, I'm ready to believe there's more power here together.

- Sit quietly and recall a recent situation in which you exerted control.
- What did having a sense of control do for you?
- What did having a sense of control require of you?
- How much of your need to control was necessary?
- What would have happened if you let others join you on the hill of your control?

# MARCH 3
## IN THE LIVING

Every person's condition is a solution in hieroglyphic to those inquiries they would put. We act it as life, before we apprehend it as truth.

— RALPH WALDO EMERSON

Each life is a language no one knows. With every heartbreak, discovery, and unexpected moment of joy, with every lift of music that touches us where we didn't think we could be touched, with every experience, another letter in our alphabet is decoded. Take a step;

learn a word. Feel a feeling; decode a sign. Accept a truth; translate a piece of the mystery written in your heart.

Before we live what's next, it always seems like there is some answer we need to arrive at. But daring to enter, we are humbled to discover, again and again, that the act of living itself unravels both the answer and the question. When we watch, we remain riddles to be solved. When we enter, we become songs to be sung.

When life feels far off, remember that a flute is just something hard with holes until it's played. So, too, the heart. As matches are just sticks until lit, as ice is not quenching until thawed, questions and problems remain obstacles until lived. In this way, the life of every soul waits like sheet music to be played. What good are we if never played?

- Simply close your eyes and breathe, feeling your mouth as a hole in your being.
- Breathe simply and evenly, knowing that only when life moves through do holes become openings.
- Open your eyes and breathe with your heart.
- Feel the music of life moving through you as silence.

If the love I have isn't working,
what good is money?

So often we put externals first. Out of worry, out of fear, out of obligation, we think we're being good Puritans by saying no to what stirs us.

In the '60s, the well-known psychologist Abraham Maslow conceived of a hierarchy of needs, in which he established that human beings must provide for basic physical needs, such as food and shelter, before they can attend to inner needs, such as self-esteem and right relationship.

While this is in part true, I believe there is a dimension of the inner life that is as imperative and equivalent as food and shelter. Without the fulfillment of these basic inner needs, we are just fed and sheltered bodies void of life. Without love, truth, and compassion, all the comforts of modern life don't matter, because we are simply reduced to biological machines, not even as present as animals.

Without this understanding, we often defer the risk to love: I need to establish myself before I can get involved. I need nice clothes first. I'll become physically desirable first. I'll eliminate all my problems first. We also defer love once it is before us, under the guise of safeguarding our future: I won't call long distance now, because I'll need the money when I retire. I won't meet them at this concert now, because I'll need money for a new car in six years. I can't afford to enter counseling with my partner because we need storm windows. Certainly, we have to balance and make choices, but with no love in the house, there is no need for storm windows.

When I was ill, I faced the very real possibility of dying, and suddenly the little money I'd saved, however prudent I was, didn't matter. It was all worthless. It became immediately clear that the only true purpose of money was to help make love work. When ill, I didn't hesitate to make all those long-distance calls I always put off. I met friends at concerts and bought albums and sent flowers instead of waiting for the perfect occasion. I bought plane tickets to the Caribbean for my wife and my dearest friends — and we went!

Once well, I couldn't go back to deferring my life under the guise of saving. I still save some, but now I feel compelled to use whatever money I can afford to make love work, to bring truth into being, to allow generosity and compassion to flourish. This is more than altruistic. It is necessary to be fully alive. It's part of the wood that keeps the inner fire burning.

I am now forced to ask, Beyond rent and health insurance, for what are we saving? If the love we have is not brought to life out here in the world, we risk saving for a future that may never come or that, in fact, may find us just ghosts of spirit, unable to live it because we've squandered our chances to love along the way.

- Sit quietly and meditate on the love you carry for someone dear.
- Breathe deeply and allow yourself to feel that love and how it wants to express itself now.
- Without hurting yourself — without borrowing on your rent or spending money you don't have — act on the love you feel now.
- Do not defer its expression. Call. Send flowers. Gas up the car and go.
- If you truly don't have the money, call out with your love anyway. Entrust it to the Universe.
- Be the love you feel now.

---

So hard to feel the stone
and not the ripple.

The moment we stray from where we are, we create a tension between two places — where we are and where we are thinking of being. It is this tension that blocks us from the sensation of being fully alive, because being split in our attention prevents us from being authentic — even though managing many tasks at once (being skillful in splitting our attention) is considered intelligent.

For each of us, straying from where we are and coming back is a never-ending task, very much like blinking or breathing. When we incorporate this fullness of attention into our daily lives, we seldom notice it. But if we should interrupt our flow of being, we will stumble just as surely as if we were to stop seeing or breathing.

That we stray from the moment is not surprising. The more crucial thing is that we return.

- Center yourself and enter the moment at hand.
- Breathe steadily and feel yourself stray:

to somewhere else, to tomorrow, to the future or the past.
- Breathe through your straying, without judgment, and re-enter the moment at hand.

# MARCH 6
## RETURNING

We carry a center
that is always returning.

We all stray from the moment in particular ways. If we meet someone and begin a new relationship, it isn't long before we're walking hand in hand, while wondering if we will sleep together; and if and when we do, we are wondering if we will live together; and if and when we do, we are wondering if we will have children — and on and on.

This happens with fear and pain as well. In diagnosis, I feared surgery. In surgery, I feared treatment. In treatment, I feared stronger treatment. In recovery, I fear recurrence.

No one can avoid this straying, but our health depends on the breath that stops us from straying further. No matter how far we've gone, it is the practice of returning to whatever moment we are living now that restores us, because only when fully in each moment can we draw strength from the Oneness of things.

- Center yourself and feel the moment at hand.
- Note the vitality of energy that appears when you stop focusing on yourself.
- Breathe steadily and feel yourself stray. Note how that vitality lessens while straying.
- Breathe through your straying and re-enter the moment at hand.
- Note the resurgence of vitality.

# MARCH 7
## LET GO OF THE RICE

In a world that lives like a fist
mercy is no more than waking
with your hands open.

So much more can happen with our hands open. In fact, closing and stubbornly maintaining our grip is often what keeps us stuck, though we want to blame everything and everyone else, especially what we're holding on to.

There is an ancient story from China that makes all this very clear. It stems from the way traps were set for monkeys. A coconut was hollowed out through an opening that was cut to the size of a monkey's open hand. Rice was then placed in the carved-out fruit which was left in the path of the monkeys. Sooner or later, a hungry monkey would smell the rice and reach its hand in. But once fisting the rice, its hand could no longer fit back out through the opening. The monkeys that were caught were those who would not let go of the rice.

As long as the monkey maintained its grip on the rice, it was a prisoner of its own making. The trap worked because the monkey's hunger was the master of its reach. The lesson for us is profound. We need to always ask ourselves, What is our rice and what is keeping us from opening our grip and letting it go?

It was upon hearing this story that I finally understood the tense ritual of rejection that exists between my mother and me. Like any child, I've always wanted her love and approval, but suddenly I realized that this has been my rice — the more it has not come, the tighter my grip. My hunger for her love has been master of my reach, even in other relationships. I have been a caught monkey, unwilling to let go.

I have since unfolded the grip in my heart, and humbly, I can see now that the real challenge of surrender, for all of us, is not just letting go — but letting go of something we yearn for.

The truth is that food is everywhere. Though the stubborn monkey believes in its moment of hunger that there is no other food, it only has to let go for its life to unfold. Our journey to love is no different. For though we stubbornly cling, believing in our moment of hunger that there is no other possibility of love, we only have to let go of what we want so badly and our life will unfold. For love is everywhere.

- Sit quietly and meditate on what is the rice in your fist.
- Breathe deeply and try to see what is keeping you from letting it go.
- Practice opening the fist of your heart by actually making a fist while inhaling, and then opening it as you exhale.

# MARCH 8
## RESPONSIBILITY

I felt angry toward my friend.
I told my wrath. My wrath did end.
I felt angry toward my foe.
I told him not. My wrath did grow.
— WILLIAM BLAKE

137

True inner responsibility centers on our willingness to give voice to whatever is happening to us in the midst of a relationship. This is important both for you and the person you are relating to. If you are not present, there is nothing to respond to. And love only becomes real in the world through our ability to respond. Bringing who you are to a relationship — being your True Self — gives others the opportunity to transcend their limitations by acting on their love. It gives the other person a chance to show up.

If you remain voiceless, then I can unconsciously keep living out whatever inequity or imbalance I am involved in with you. But once you show your hurt or frustration or confusion or question, then I have the chance to stop my unconscious participation in the pattern of our relationship. The key to whether I will respond to you or not often has to do with love, the one thing that can break the inertia of old behavior.

We can be driving along the endless summer highway locked in some pattern that has become suffocating to you. But until you are moved by some sudden wind that shows the willow's trunk as we speed by, until you are moved to say, "I can't go on like this," I can't have the chance to say, "I don't want it to be like this either." Until you break your silence, I can't have the chance to say, "What can we do to change all this?"

Often, we spend so much time waiting for the other to catch on and see our pain, getting more and more frustrated and wounded the longer they don't. But this is the definition of a limitation: not being able to see what is obvious.

So, while we dread voicing our fears and hurts to one another, love has no way of being acted on without something truthful to respond to.

- Center yourself and bring to mind a fear or hurt that you are bearing quietly in a relationship that matters to you.
- Breathe fully, and in the safety of your private space, voice what you are feeling without words. Just let it surface freely in your mind and heart.
- Keep breathing deeply and just get comfortable with the truth of this feeling.
- This is enough for today. Trust that you will know if and when and how to voice this truth to the person in your life who needs the chance to hear it.

# MARCH 9
## OPENING OUR DEEPEST EYES

> The inner life of any great thing will be incomprehensible to me until I develop and deepen an inner life of my own.
> — PARKER J. PALMER

Everyone has an inner life; it's just a matter of opening it. What Parker Palmer wisely suggests is that we can only feel something to the degree that we are willing to meet its depth. Just as we must open our eyes — must raise our lids — to see, we must raise our barriers and open our hearts and minds, if we are to see and feel the essence of the life around us.

To develop our own inner life is tantamount to opening our deepest eyes. It has much to do with raising our walls, with living from our own depths so we can experience the depths around us.

Too often, while cut off from our inwardness, we complain that the things about us are shallow and boring, not worth our attention, when, more often than not, it is we who are out of touch.

To see deeply, we must open deeply.

- Bring to mind something or someone

you've dismissed, and bring it or this person before your heart's opened eye.
- Surround the image with your deepest breathing.
- After a time, ask yourself, Does this thing or person seem any different?

# MARCH 10
# THE CREATOR'S CYCLE

We survive . . . and then we die.
— OJIBWAY ELDER

Nothing escapes the Creator's cycle. Not plants, horses, trees, birds, or human beings. Not the life of the mind. Not the life of the heart. Not the life of the spirit. All living things emerge, gather, spark new life, fall apart, die, and emerge in new ways. Each soul is a gust of God's breath unfolding in the great energy that surrounds us like an ever-moving stream. The goal is not to cheat death, but to live in the stream with a humility and aliveness that only an acceptance of death can release.

When we try to deny death, we can grow sick from frantically chasing any challenge that will occupy our minds. In living the other extreme, we can grow sick from thinking only of death, from letting death be all that we see. This makes a sad career of fear.

Beyond all design and desire, we survive, and like stones that are eroded by forces that can never be seen or stopped, our reward is the pain and wonder of baring our inner beauty to the sky. What we carry deep within, if we live honestly, will inevitably be worn outwardly. The experience of living this fully has nothing to do with removing ourselves from the Creator's cycle. Too often, we struggle stubbornly in an attempt to protect ourselves from the friction of being alive, when it is precisely that friction that works our spirit into a seeable gem. We are more malleable than we think, more durable and changeable than all hope.

Thin and fragrant petals do not hide from the wind. They survive to die and break ground again. Even within one life, we shred and re-root. We break, bleed, and rearrange into yet another beautiful thing that learns how to reach. Resisting this process doubles our pain. Singing our way through it is the source of wisdom and beauty.

- What is your greatest fear about dying?
- What is your greatest fear about living?
- Do these fears have anything in common?
- How would you shape your life if you didn't have these fears?

- What if you shaped your life in this way anyway?

# MARCH 11
## BENEFIT OF THE POSE

As long as you do not live totally in the
    body,
you do not live totally in the Self.
                        — B. K. S. IYENGAR

In studying Yoga, teachers of all traditions will advise students to be still after certain positions in order to feel the benefit of the pose. This is a great practice for all of life. In countless ways, we work so hard to get there, only to bypass feeling the deep rewards of inhabiting the space we arrive in.

This is especially true in how we touch each other. We are often so preoccupied with the next move — or if there will be a next move — that we seldom feel the deep rewards of simply holding each other.

By treating each moment of touch as a consummation in itself, we can practice feeling eternity.

With your partner:

- Sit quietly and breathe deeply while touching each other's arms.

- Feel each other's being in the bodies that carry you.
- After several minutes, kiss each other slowly with your eyes open.
- Now keep touching each other's arms lightly while searching each other's eyes.

With yourself:

- Sit quietly in front of a mirror and focus on the body you are in.
- Breathe deeply and enter the field of your eyes.
- Breathe slowly and feel your soul like a pool of clear water just beneath your eyes.
- Breathe fully and feel the water of your spirit wash against the shore of your body.

# MARCH 12
# IN THE LIKENESS OF EVERYTHING

Everything in the Universe is
   interconnected.
Within each it is reflected.
                    — LOURDES PITA

I think this insight explains why we are so

drawn to certain things: why, of all the fallen branches, I will go to the one that most resembles the way I've had to bend all my life; why, of all the places you could return to, you choose the lip of a cliff worn featureless by wind, because it lets you feel the worn lip of your heart that you show no one.

It seems that we humans have always been drawn to find ourselves in the life about us. But too often, in doing so we break everything down until everything resembles us. Too often, though we seldom mean to, we take in life the way we do food, chewing it into unrecognizable bits that need to be swallowed. But the kind of food that living offers must be taken in whole, as it is, or it loses its wisdom and power and grace.

So, this is our ongoing challenge: not to turn everything into us. In truth, the deepest function of humility is that it helps us take experience in on its own terms, not violating its own nature — all in an effort to be nourished by life that is different from us. Through this effort, we find the corresponding seeds of such life in us. They are the common seeds of grace that can sustain us.

In truth, we each carry within our own innate makeup, like chromosomes, the minute aspects of everything that forms the Universe. And so, the art of freedom becomes the necessary adventure of grasping the secrets that are everywhere in the open and stirring

145

their aspects within us, in such a way that we come alive: learning from the fish how to surface and dive, from the flower how to open and accept, from the stone how to crack and let light in, and from the birds that wings are more useful at times than brains.

Rather than finding ourselves in everything, we are challenged daily to find everything in ourselves, till being human is evolving inwardly in the likeness of everything, shaping ourselves to the wonders we find, until like birds, who have known this forever, we too make song at the mere appearance of light.

- Sit quietly and bring to mind a favorite place in nature where you like to go. It might be an open field, or a waterfall, or a stream, or a path in the woods.
- Go there in your mind and feel the one aspect that keeps bringing you back there. It might be the wind through the grass, or the sound of the water, or the light through colored leaves.
- In your mind, enlarge the one compelling aspect and enter it more fully. Become the grass or the water or the leaf.
- Breathe slowly and let what you love about this place teach you how you are grasslike or waterlike or leaflike.

# MARCH 13
## OPENING TO FAITH

Once a man was about to cross the sea. A wise man tied a leaf in a corner of his robe and said to him: "Don't be afraid. Have faith and walk on the water. But look here — the moment you lose faith you will drown."
— SRI RAMAKRISHNA

We often move away from pain, which is helpful only before being hurt. Once in pain, it seems the only way out is through. Like someone falling off a boat, struggling to stay above the water only makes things worse. We must accept we are there and settle enough so we can be carried by the deep. The willingness to do this is the genesis of faith, the giving over to currents larger than us. Even fallen leaves float in lakes, demonstrating how surrender can hold us up.

We can learn from the leaves that ducks swim around. In life as in water, when we curl up or flail we sink. When we spread and go still, we are carried by the largest sea of all: the sea of grace that flows steadily beneath the turmoil of events. And just as fish can't see the ocean they live in, we can't quite see the spirit that sustains us.

Again and again, the onset of pain makes

us clutch and sink. But life has taught me that how we first open after doubling over is crucial to whether we will heal at all.

- When you can, walk or sit by a lake or pond and watch the leaves float on the surface.
- Breathe like a fallen leaf and think of nothing.
- Just breathe and let your heart and mind be carried, however briefly, by the spirit you can't quite see.

# March 14
## Ancient Friends

One climbs, one sees. One descends, one sees no longer, but one has seen. There is an art in conducting oneself in lower regions by memory of what one has seen higher up. When one can no longer see, one can at least still know.

— Rene Daumal

In the 700s in the Tang Dynasty in China, the poet Li Po wrote what is now a famous poem, "Letter in Exile." It is for his "ancient friend," So-Kin of Rakuyo. In the poem, we learn that the two have been deep, lifelong friends, though they have only been together a handful of times. By the end, Li Po is awash with his old friend's presence: "What is the use of talking, and there is no end of talking. There is no end of things in the heart."

We are moved to ask how is it possible: they have spent more time apart than together. Yet the presence of a friend like this can shape one's entire life. If blessed, we have one, or maybe, if wealthy in blessings, two friends like this during our time on Earth. It's as if Li Po and So-Kin are stars in each other's constellation, brief but enduring points of light. The difficulty then has always been how to make it across the dark from point of light to point of light. This is the province of faith, the preservation of presence when we are not lighted.

This friendship itself is a metaphor for another kind of friendship, our lifetime kinship with Truth, with Love, with Unity, with God. Like Li Po without So-Kin, we may spend much of our time unaware and unenlightened, yet the presence of Truth and God, like a deep and ancient friend, can shape our entire lives. So the inner task becomes how do we make a lasting friendship with the Unities that are larger than us? How do we keep their light in our heart when no stars appear in sight?

- Breathe deeply and recall one special moment of truth in your life that has

149

guided you over the years.

- Breathe lovingly and bring this truth into view.
- Smile and bow to this truth like an old friend you haven't seen in years.
- Pray to it with gratitude.

# March 15
# The Power of Symbols

If you truly hold a stone,
you can feel the mountain it came from.

A caveman picking berries was cornered by a wild and now extinct creature, and when he was spared by the sudden snap of a tree limb that scared the beast off, he took a piece of the fallen bough as a good luck charm. And so the story of symbols began.

People have always saved scraps of their experience to help remind them of the forces of life that can't always be seen. Filled with the timeless rhythm of the ocean, we pocket a shell and carry it thousands of miles to know that presence of ocean when we are hours from the sea. It is why we treasure certain songs, why we save ticket stubs and dried out flowers.

Symbols are living mirrors of the deepest understandings that have no words. I know of two friends who made it through Vietnam. They were rehabilitated in Italy, and before coming home, they split a copper lire, each holding dear the other's half, as if it were the break of heart forever left in that godforsaken jungle.

We ask the smallest items of everyday life to carry unbearable meaning for us, and the dearest ones work like Aladdin's lamp. All we have to do is rub them slowly, and feelings and times long gone come and live again, or basic truths hard to keep in view return.

As a boy, I remember visiting my grand-father's house. He had a milk-white bowl filled with M&M's. It was a simple magical treasure to me. No matter how often I reached on tiptoe, it never emptied. It has been thirty years since he died, and now when depressed, I hold that milk-white bowl in my lap and eat a few M&M's.

And I feel better. This isn't illusion or escapism, but rather using the milk-white bowl filled with M&M's as a living symbol that can call into my moment of sadness a deeper sense of plenitude and generosity that is always there, but not always accessible.

This is the proper use of symbols, not to coldly represent ideas, but to call into being all that lives in us and about us. They help us bear witness to the painful mystery of living, and whether a crucifix, a small weeping Bud-dha, or a broken shell from a long-forgotten sea, they help us bear the days.

- Recall a special moment in growing up.
- Meditate on the feeling of that moment until the scene comes into view.
- Slowly feel your way about this special moment and focus on a detail — a certain chair or smell of lilac or a rainy piece of glass.
- With reverence, lift up this detail as a living symbol of all this special moment means to you.
- The next time you feel less than, bring yourself in contact with this very personal symbol.
- Let it open you to gifts you don't always remember.

# MARCH 16
## NATURE'S SWAY

When the wind stops,
the trees still move,
the way my heart creaks
long after it bends.

I am always surprised at the aftereffect of being moved deeply by something. I can be hurt or disappointed or feel the warmth of being loved or the gentle sway of being temporarily left, and then I'm ready to chew on something else, seldom allowing for the feelings to digest completely. In fact, I've come to see that much of my confusion in life comes from giving my attention to the next thing too soon, and then wrapping new experience in the remnants of feeling that are not finished with me.

For example, the other day I felt sad because an old friend is ill. I addressed my sadness directly and thought I'd been with this mood enough, so I continued on my way. The next day I found myself in the usual frustration of traffic and shopping, and the indifferent reactions of waitresses and clerks were suddenly making me sad. Or so I thought. Though it seems obvious here in the telling, it wasn't in the happening, and I spent a good deal of misguided energy wondering if it was time to change my lifestyle. But really I was feeling ripples of sadness about my friend's illness.

The deeper lesson involves nature's sway: its approach, its impact, and, especially, its echo. Everything living encounters it, especially us in the unseeable ripples of what we think and feel. Being alive takes time.

- Sit quietly and focus on one feeling that recently came upon you strongly.
- As you breathe, attend whatever traces of its impact are still effecting you.

153

- Breathe slowly like a flag and let these traces of feeling ripple through.

# MARCH 17
## A GREAT BATTLE RAGING

There is a great battle raging: for my mouth not to harden and my jaws not to become like heavy doors of an iron safe, so my life may not be called pre-death.
— ISRAELI POET YEHUDA AMICHAI

There is an ancient Greek myth that carries within it, like a message in a bottle, one of the most crucial struggles we face as living beings. It is the story of a gifted musician, Orpheus, whose love, Eurydice, is taken by Hades, the god of the underworld. Orpheus is so grief-stricken that he travels to the land of the dead to plead with Hades to give Eurydice back. After a cold and deliberate consideration, Hades says, "You can have her. It will take you three days to bring her back to the land of the living. There is one condition. You must carry her and you must not look upon her face until you reach the light. If you do, she will return to me forever."

Unfortunately, unknown to Orpheus, Hades tells Eurydice the opposite, "He will carry you to the land of the living, and you must

154

look upon him before you reach the light. If you do not, you will return to me forever." Their colossal struggle fails, and Eurydice is lost forever.

The struggle for us, though, is ongoing. For there is an Orpheus in each of us that believes, if I look, I will die. There is also a Eurydice in each of us that believes, if I don't look, I will die. And so, the great spiritual question, after "To be or not to be?" is to look or not to look. The personal balance we arrive at determines whether we make it out of hell or not.

Though it shifts throughout our lives, according to our devotions, I believe each of us is born with a natural leaning toward looking or not looking. Not surprisingly, I am one of those feminine seers: I believe that if I don't look, I will die. This probably has a lot to do with my calling to be a poet. So, I admit my bias. For though, like staring into the sun too long, there are times we mustn't look to preserve our sight, more often we need to look to stay alive.

Like each of us, I struggle with both: to be the keeper of secrets or the discoverer of truths. Though no one can tell us how, we have to work this great battle again and again: to leave the underworld — not to harden — and to make our way back into the land of the living.

- Center yourself and breathe steadily. Bring to mind the stream of life decisions that have brought you this far.
- As you slow your breathing, try to understand which has defined your time on Earth: the need to look or the need not to look.
- As you breathe evenly, try to feel which you need right now — to look or not to look. Which will bring you more fully into the land of the living?

# MARCH 18
## THE LIFE OF A CARETAKER

Accept this gift,
so I can see myself as giving.

I have been learning that the life of a caretaker is as addictive as the life of an alcoholic. Here the intoxication is the emotional relief that temporarily comes when answering a loved one's need. Though it never lasts, in the moment of answering someone's need, we feel loved. While much good can come from this, especially for those the caretaker attends, the care itself becomes a drink by which we briefly numb a worthlessness that won't go away unless constantly doused by another shot of self-sacrifice.

It all tightens until what others need is anticipated beyond what is real, and then, without any true need being voiced, an anxiety to respond builds that can only be relieved if something is offered or done. At the heart of this is the ever-present worry that unless doing something for another there is no possibility of being loved. So the needs of others stand within reach like bottles behind a bar that, try as he or she will, the caretaker cannot resist.

I have experienced this even in the simple issue of calling a loved one while away from home. Even when no one expects to hear from me, I can agonize over whether to call. Often, unable to withstand the discomfort of not registering some evidence of my love, I will end up going to great lengths to call.

In truth, caretaking, though seeming quite generous, is very self-serving, and its urgent self-centeredness prevents a life of genuine compassion. In all honesty, to heal from this requires as rigorous a program of recovery as alcoholics enlist, including sponsors who will love us for who we are.

Within one's self, the remedy of spirit that allows for true giving resides somewhere in the faith to believe that each of us is worthy of love, just as we are.

- Center yourself and bring to mind a loved one you seem to meet more than

157

halfway.
- Meditate on what makes you take the extra step.
- Imagine them loving you if you did nothing.
- Imagine loving yourself if you did nothing.
- Breathe and do nothing until you feel a sense of love rising for yourself.

# MARCH 19
## WEAKNESS

Our strength will continue if we allow ourselves the courage to feel scared, weak, and vulnerable.

— MELODY BEATTIE

This is a prayer for the ages. In fact, it helps to define weakness, in spiritual terms, as any habit of mind or heart that prevents us from seeing things exactly as they are, or in their entirety, or with our entire capacity to feel. These are the blindnesses that continually keep us from Truth, Oneness, and Compassion.

We are all frail. We all make mistakes. We all fall prey to a thousand emotions and exaggerations. But these things make us rich, not weak — if we are willing to face them squarely. In truth, it is not the tissue of our humanity that defeats us, but rather our refusal to accept who we are and to live accordingly, limitations included.

Underneath it all, this blindness, in its many recurring forms, is the cause of most cruelty. For it is during those moments when we think we see so clearly that we break things that are irreplaceable, not even realizing they were precious.

After breaking many things in my life — hearts, heirlooms, robins' eggs — I am humbled to admit that the only difference I see on Earth between being strong or weak is the honesty with which we face ourselves, accept ourselves, and share ourselves, blemishes and all.

- For this meditation, hold a picture of someone you care about. It might be a picture of yourself.
- Close your eyes and center yourself. When opening your eyes, focus on the picture and allow yourself to see your relationship with this person exactly as it is.
- Close your eyes again. When opening your eyes this time, focus on the picture and allow yourself to accept this being entirely, blemishes and all.

# MARCH 20
## STIRRING THE WATER

> To let knowledge produce troubles, and then use knowledge to prepare against them, is like stirring water in hopes of making it clear.
> — LAO-TZU

This cycle of producing troubles and then preparing against them is very much like pulling a thread that really should have been left alone. The more we pull it, the more the fabric unravels, and now we must re-sew it all. Or very much like planning too many things, or committing to too many people in too short a time, and then exhausting yourself and those around you trying to make it all happen.

We have all done this. A more subtle form of this revolves around the struggle to accept ourselves. Feeling unworthy or insecure, we create a goal, in hopes that achieving this will make us feel good about ourselves. Then we're off scheming for success, preparing against failure, stirring the water, hoping it will go clear.

All the while, the very deep resources of heart and spirit are being misapplied. Isn't this how we launch into careers that really don't call us? Isn't this how we enter relationships that really don't embrace us? Isn't this how we sometimes bring children into the world, hoping they will help us go clear?

The mind is a spider that, if allowed, will tangle everything and then blame the things it clings to for the web it wants to be free of. I have done this with dreams of greatness and hopes of love, wanting so badly to see myself clearly in the water, while I kept stirring and stirring. Perhaps the hardest thing I've learned, and still struggle with, is that I don't have to be finished in order to be whole.

- Sit quietly and bring to mind one thread in your heart that you have recently unraveled.
- Breathe deeply and consider how you have been involved in re-sewing this.
- Breathe evenly and try to stop, try to put everything aside, as is, and let the pulled thread be.

# MARCH 21
# TO HARBOR OR RELEASE

How can you follow the course of your life
if you do not let it flow?

— LAO-TZU

The pollen collects until the rain washes away

161

whatever has not been taken as seed. The moss forms on stumps and rocks until the feet of animals wear it off. The leaves that cover the path disintegrate in time to show the lost their way.

It is the same with us. Our dreams collect like pollen until the sweat and tears of our living them washes away whatever has not become possible. Our soft gnarly clumps of attachment grow out of our stone — joy and sorrow alike — until what is food is eaten and what is not is worn away. Like fallen leaves, our memories cover our path until they are remembered out of existence, setting us free.

Often the pain of resisting makes us rust like iron, and in order to re-enter the flow of life, we need to be scraped back to our original surface. Our feelings, if not released, bread the heart with their grit. Like windows filmed by weather, we wait on loving hands to be rubbed clear. It is inevitable. Experience covers us over, and the expressive journey lets us come clean to the table of light. Again.

All things in existence participate in this involuntary cycle. For human beings, the process of living stains us repeatedly with the grit of being here, with heartache and disappointment and the pointedness of being human, which can sicken us if harbored or make us whole if released. Again and again, we, more than any other life form, have this majestic and burdensome power to harbor or release the impact of our experience.

Humbly, we are asked to keep the flow real between what is taken in and what is let out. We have only to breathe to remember our place as a living inlet. Experience in, feelings out. Surprise and challenge in, heartache and joy out. In a constant tide, life rushes in, and in constant release, we must let it all run back off. For this is how the earth was made magnificent by the sea and how humankind is carved upright, again and again, by the ocean of spirit that sets us free.

- As you cross the doorway of your home into the world today, breathe deeply and ask yourself, What is it about being human that you are most grateful for?
- Be with this question as you move through your day.
- Tonight as you re-enter your nest, breathe deeply again and ask yourself, What is it about being human that continues to surprise you?
- Be with this question as you rest and sleep through the night.

# MARCH 22
## SABBATH TIME

Work when there is work to do. Rest when you are tired. One thing done in peace will most likely be better than ten things done in panic. . . . I am not a hero if I deny rest; I am only tired.

— SUSAN MCHENRY

When I need to be refreshed or renewed, I return to doorways of heart that have opened me before. I walk and stand beside the big willow and wait for its familiar sway to speak to me. I replay that special piece of piano music that made its way into the sore crease of my heart and let things unfold. I make some tea and sit in my favorite chair and carefully pull out my old and tattered e. e. cummings book and read "i thank you god for most this amazing day. . . ."

I try to open the hours with softness and silence — the two threads that unravel into gratitude — and wait for the miracle to return. This is the renewing atom of Sabbath for me. I try to start each day with such a small endearing moment, before the bumps and nicks and noise rush in, before the confusions and conflicts tighten my sense of things.

For me, the heart constricts and dilates like

the eye. When it's constricted, there is no rest; the world seems smaller and meaner and full of danger. So Sabbath time becomes essential as a practice that dilates everything tight. These private moments of rest restore — make ore out of rest — and loosen the knots of the world by slowing down the heart.

In rest, I always remember that what ties me to the earth is unseen. Just the other day, I was constricted. My heart was beating like a heron awakened in the weeds, no room to move. Tangled and surprised by the noise of my mind, I fluttered without grace to the center of the lake which humans call silence. I guess, if you should ask, peace is no more than the underside of tired wings resting on the lake, while the heart in its feathers pounds softer and softer.

- Practice loosening the knot in your heart by placing your hands, palm up, in your lap.
- With each inbreath, tighten your hands briefly.
- With each outbreath, relax your hands till they rest like the tired wings they are.

# March 23
# Never Knowing Where
# We Fly

Birds learn how to fly, never knowing
where flight will take them.

There is a deep and humbling lesson in the way of birds. Their wings grow and stretch and span patches of air. First tentatively and then with confidence, they lift, they pump, they glide, they land. It seems, for birds, it is the act of flying that is the goal. True, they migrate and seek out food, but when flying, there is the sense that being aloft is their true destination.

Unlike birds, we confuse our time on Earth, again and again, with obsessions of where we are going — often to the point that we frustrate and stall our human ability to fly. We frequently tame and hush our need to love, to learn, to know the truth of spirit, until we can be assured that our efforts will take us somewhere. All these conditions and hesitations and yes-buts and what ifs turn the human journey upside down, never letting the heart, wing that it is, truly unfold.

Yet, without consideration or reservation, it is simply the presence of light that stirs birds to sing and lift. They do not understand concepts such as holding back or only investing if the return seems certain. In this, we are the only creatures that seek out guarantees, and in so doing, we snuff the spark that is discovery.

Just how often do we cripple ourselves by not letting love with all its risks teach us how to fly? How many times do our hearts stall because we won't let the wingspan of our passion open us fully into our gifts? How frequently do we search for a song of guidance that can only come from inside us?

I know that over the years, through fear and expectation, my mind has gathered and hoarded places I needed to go, things I needed to have, selves I needed to be. But here I am, without most of them — the goals and wants all used up in learning how to love.

So, try as I do to imagine and construct where I am headed, try as I will to plan and know what this life of feeling means, it is the pulse of what I feel itself that lifts me into spirit. In truth, wings don't grow any differently to fit south or east or west, and our lives, no matter how we train ourselves, are more fundamental than any direction of worldly ambition. We, like the birds, are meant to fly and sing — that's all — and all our plans and schemes are twigs of nest that, once outgrown, we leave.

167

- Meditate on some desire you have hesitated to give life to. It might be your want to dance or play the piano. Or an impulse to travel somewhere that is calling you. Or the urge to get to know someone, even yourself.
- Breathe, letting the feeling rise unencumbered.
- Breathe and focus on your hesitation. It might stem from a fear of failure or rejection or a fear of the unknown.
- Breathe through your hesitation, knowing that, just as wings can only fly if they flap, your ability to live deep things — to be in relation to other life — will grow only if you try.

# MARCH 24
## EVEN IN THE DARK

To be broken is no reason
to see all things as broken.

Seldom seen, growing along the ocean floor, the white-plumed anemone is a watery blossom. It is white lace opening under tons of black, opening as if bathed in the sun, while so far from the sun.

This is the trick to staying well, isn't it: to feel the sun even in the dark. To not lose the truth of things when they go out of view. To grow just the same. To know there is still water, even when we are thirsty. To know there is still love, even when we are lonely. To know there is still peace, even when we are suffering.

None of this invalidates our pain, but only strengthens our way back into the light.

- Close your eyes and feel the fact of the sun. It will be there when you can see again.
- Inhale deeply through the part of your heart that is closed and feel the fact of love. It will be there when you can feel again.
- Breathe slowly through the part of you that doubts and feel the fact of life. It will be there when you can open your spirit, as you did when you were born.

# MARCH 25
# THE EAR AS PETAL

The ear is only a petal
that grows from the heart.
When we hear each other,
it all becomes a garden.

Just what does it mean to listen? We have all

exhibited the remarkable mental dividedness whereby we choose not to pay attention, and yet when asked, we can recite word for word what has been said.

Listening arises from a deeper place, and it seems we can only hear the living to the extent that we have truly lived, only understand pain and joy to the extent that we have allowed ourselves to be touched by life. If the ear grows from the heart like a petal, then as roots absorb rain and sun until a simple flower opens, the heart must absorb both tears and joy in order to sprout an ear that can truly hear.

I remember, years before cutting my feet in search of a path, sitting on my immigrant grandmother's hospital bed, watching her wince as they put gauze on her bedsore heels. I remember, years before I saved my golden retriever from drowning, watching a coworker cry for his dead dog, trying to understand how he could love an animal more than a person. I remember, years before having to start my life over, racing down a farmhouse road in the middle of the night to see my father-in-law's proud eyes jut as the barn he built thirty years before was burning to the ground.

It was only later that I felt their pain, and even more, their true joy in caring for things. To be sure, we do not have to experience the same things to receive each other, but we do have to experience what is ours to live through before life will show its roots.

What does it take to truly listen? The breakdown of everything that parades between our hearts. If I dare to hear you, I will feel you like the sun and grow in your direction, and you in mine. For when we hear each other, it all becomes a garden. It all becomes edible.

- Sit with a trusted loved one and meditate on a story of joy or pain that you have heard more fully over time.
- Share with each other why this story has stayed with you.
- How has your understanding of this story deepened over time?
- Breathe slowly and open your heart more fully to one human moment you chose not to pay attention to during the last week.

# MARCH 26
## FEELING YOUR FEELINGS

The fastest way to freedom is to feel your feelings.
— GITA BELLIN

This sounds pretty simple, but though it's

easy to know you have feelings, easy to know their weight and agitation and suddenness of mood, it is another, more subtle matter to feel them — that is, to let them penetrate your being the way wind snaps through a flag.

This is necessary because if we don't feel our feelings all the way through, they never leave us, and then we do all kinds of unusual things to get out from under them. This is the cause of many an addiction.

I've diverted myself many times by becoming involved in what surrounds my pain or sadness, while never feeling the thing itself. So when someone asks me how I feel, I wind up retelling the circumstance of the pain, but not feeling it. Or strategizing what to do next, but not feeling it. Or anticipating reactions, but not feeling what is mine to feel. Or swimming in the anger of injustice, but not diving through the wound.

Though we fear it, feeling our feelings is the only clear and direct way to free our hearts of pain.

- Meditate on the ways you might avoid your feelings.
- In your silence, stop holding them off with words or reasons or busyness.
- Simply be a shore and let your feelings wash against you like waves.

# MARCH 27
## WE ARE BORN SINGING

Song is not a luxury,
but a necessary way of being in the world.

Somehow we have been fooled into thinking that song is entertainment, something we can do without, like dessert. But to give voice to what lives inside is what keeps all things possible. In truth, the minute we arrive we are born singing, though this is often mistaken for crying. Yet without this deep reflex, the lungs won't work and the lifelong exchange between inner and outer can't begin.

I remember my first day alone at home after my rib surgery. For the first time in months, everything was still, the morning light now filling the space where my rib used to be. Suddenly, finally, I began to weep, loudly, as pockets of fear and pain and exhaustion escaped. This release was a song, and what I hadn't realized was that, once released, once the buildup of my journey was given a way out, life with its thousand energies and softnesses could come in.

Such a simple secret: by letting things out, we also let things in. So if you're cut off, in pain, estranged, numb — sing, give voice to anything. It needn't sound pretty. Simply,

173

bravely, open despite the difficulty, and let what is in out, and what is out in. Sing, and your life will continue.

- Center yourself and locate one pocket of pain or fear or exhaustion that is building inside you.
- Breathe your way into that pocket. Inhale into the buildup. Exhale, letting what's in there make its way into the world.
- Realize that your breath is the passageway that connects your inner buildup with the air of the world.
- Realize that the sound of your breath is the quietest of songs.

# MARCH 28
## THE GIFT OF SHEDDING

From the beginning,
the key to renewal has been
the casting off of old skin.

It is interesting that the earliest peoples believed in something that we, in our modern hive of manufacturing, have forgotten — that immortality is attainable by shedding. The Dusuns of North Borneo have believed for centuries that when God finished creating the world, He announced that "Whoever is able to cast off his skin shall not die."

But what does this mean? Not that we can live forever, but that the way to stay closest to the pulse of life, the way to stay in the presence of that divine reality which informs everything is to be willing to change. Still, change what? To change whatever has ceased to function within us. To shed whatever we are carrying that is no longer alive. To cast off our dead skin because dead skin can't feel. Dead eyes can't see. Dead ears can't hear. And without feeling, there is no chance of wholeness, and wholeness remains our best chance to survive the pain of breaking.

Of course, for human beings, dead skin takes many forms, the most significant of which remain intangible but suffocating, such as a dead way of thinking, a dead way of seeing, a dead way of relating, a dead way of believing, or a dead way of experiencing.

In essence, shedding opens us to self-transformation. Paradoxically, those of us who refuse such renewal will, sooner or later, be forced to undergo transformation anyway as a result of being broken or eroded by the world. Very often both occur at the same time: that is, we shed from within while being eroded from without.

• Center yourself and meditate on what

175

you are carrying that is dead skin for you.

- Breathe cleanly and deeply and ask yourself, What are you being called to shed, to put to rest, in order to gain greater access to the hidden wholeness of life.

# MARCH 29
# WHAT KEEPS US FROM SHEDDING

Often we give up our right to renewal to accommodate the anxiety of those around us.

For sure, living is not easy, and living openly is both wondrous and dangerous. The fact is that shedding, no matter how useful or inevitable, always has a pain of its own. Unfortunately, there is no escaping this underside of growth. So it is not surprising that there are many feelings peculiar to human beings that prevent us from shedding what has ceased to work, including fear, pride, nostalgia, a comfort in the familiar, and a want to please those we love. Often we give up our right to renewal to accommodate the anxiety of those around us.

The Melanesians of the New Hebrides

176

contend that this is how we lost our immortality. Sir James Frazer has preserved their story. It seems, at first, human beings never died, but cast their skins like snakes and crabs and came out with youth renewed. But after a time, a woman, growing old, went to a stream to change her skin; according to some, she was Ul-ta-marama, Change-skin of the world. She threw her old skin in the water and observed that as it floated it caught on a stick. Then she went home, where she had left her child. But the child refused to recognize her, crying that its mother was an old woman, not this young stranger. So to pacify the child she went after her old skin and put it on. From that time, human beings ceased to cast their skins and died.

And so, when we cease to shed what's dead in us in order to soothe the fear of others, we remain partial. When we cease to surface our most sensitive skin simply to avoid conflict with others, we remove ourselves from all that is true. When we maintain ways we've already discarded just to placate the ignorance of those we love, we lose our access to what is eternal.

- Sit quietly and ask yourself, What voices are asking you to keep your old skin and not to change?
- Center yourself and ask, What is the

cost to you for not renewing your connection with all that is eternal?

# MARCH 30
# THE ENERGY OF BEING REAL

Do not seek any rules or method of
   worship.
Say whatever your pained heart chooses.
— RUMI

"Mana" is a term originally used in Polynesian and Melanesian cultures to describe an extraordinary power or force residing in a person or an object, a sort of spiritual electricity that charges anyone who touches it. Carl Jung later defined the term as "the unconscious influence of one being on another." What Jung speaks to is the fact that the energy of being real has more power than outright persuasion, debate, or force of will. He suggests that being who we are always releases an extraordinary power that, without intent or design, affects the people who come in contact with such realness.

The beautiful and simple truth of this can be seen in looking at the sun. The sun, without intent or will or plan or sense of principle, just shines, thoroughly and constantly. By being itself, the sun warms with its light, never withholding or warming only certain things of the Earth. Rather, the sun emanates in all directions all the time, and things grow. In the same way, when we are authentic, expressing our warmth and light in all directions, we cause things around us to grow. When our souls like little suns express the light of who we are, we emanate what Jesus called love and what Buddha called compassion, and the roots of community lengthen.

In this way, without any intent to shape others, we simply have to be authentic, and a sense of mana, of spiritual light and warmth, will emanate from our very souls, causing others to grow — not toward us, but toward the light that moves through us. In this way, by being who we are, we not only experience life in all its vitality, but, quite innocently and without design, we help others be more thoroughly themselves. In being real, in staying devoted to this energy of realness, we help each other grow toward the one vital light.

- Center yourself and let the stream of your feelings move through.
- After a time, give direct voice to the particular feelings as they rise, saying simply on each outbreath whatever moves through you: sadness, fear, confusion, peace, boredom, joy.
- After a time, let the stream of feelings

179

continue to rise as you return to breathing in silence.

- Now feel the very things about you — rug, chair, window, wall — feel them lean in your direction.

# MARCH 31
## THE PRACTICE OF BEING REAL

As the sun cannot withhold its light,
we cannot withhold what feels real.

As the Earth keeps going by turning itself toward the light day after day, we have no choice, despite all forms of etiquette and training, but to keep turning toward what we feel is real. Otherwise, we become cold little planets spinning in the dark.

Very often, when I am confused or depressed for a long period of time, it is because I have stopped turning toward the light of what feels real. At times like this, I have to break the darkness of my spinning with a very small and simple step that often seems huge and difficult because I have been spinning in on myself — I have to practice being real by saying what I feel, not just once, but continually.

I have struggled my whole life with this. Like most of us, I learned to survive by withholding what feels real. When events happen — when someone says or does something that hurts me — I have learned to absorb the hit and pretend that nothing has changed, that everything is the same. But when I do this, my energy is used up in maintaining the pretense that nothing has happened, and I begin to spin coldly in the dark.

It is so simple and yet so brave to say that we are hurt when we are hurt, that we are sad when we are sad, that we are scared when we are scared. In very direct and daily ways, this energy of realness — this mana — changes situations because the immediate expression of our truth releases light and warmth that influences the life we are a part of. This is the way our spirit shines.

- Center yourself and, once again, let the stream of your feelings move through.
- After a time, give direct voice to the particular feelings as they rise. Be careful this time to voice your feelings as yours: I feel sad, I feel cold, I feel light, I feel weary.
- During your day, try to be mindful of how the pulse of what feels real shifts.
- Try to keep turning toward it.

181

# APRIL 1
## WORK OF THE WORM

---

What the worm eats
feeds the root.

The story is told by a member of the Ojib-way tribe that the Creator was having trouble keeping the world together, when a little worm said he could help. The Creator paused, and the little worm spun its imperceptible silk, connecting all of creation with an unsee-able web. The Creator's gift to the worm was to let it live forever, allowing that when the little worm enclosed itself in the unseeable web, it would after a time emerge with the thinnest wings full of color — as a butterfly.

The story tells us that everything in Cre-ation is connected and that what holds it all together comes from the humble work of liv-ing on Earth. It tells us that the experience of eternity is possible if we immerse ourselves firsthand in the unseeable web of life. It tells us that if we still ourselves long enough within the web of all there is, we will eventu-ally come to know the lightness of transfor-mation.

Humbly, like a little worm, it is in us to work our experience — our pain and frustra-tion and confusion and wonder — into

182

threads of silk. And freely, it is in our realm of choice to first connect everything with our experience and then to make a cocoon of those connections. Finally, we can enter that cocoon of experiential connection — the way a Native American sweats in his lodge, the way a yogi holds his third eye, the way a monk maintains his vow of silence — until we emerge wearing our deepest colors for everyone to see.

Amazingly, the Universe is held together by the unseeable threads of our own experience, and our reward for keeping the web of connection alive is that our spirit emerges through what is personal into the center of All Being. And so, by being who we are, we are suddenly enlivened, however briefly, into the web of All Creation.

No matter how important we imagine others to be, it is each of us who holds things together, in our small humble way of working through the days with all that we have. This is the quiet miracle of spinning connection from our very humanness. This humble practice, that no one can stop, is the work of the worm.

- When the chance presents itself, watch a loved one breathe in their sleep.
- Look upon them as you would a flower, with gratitude and wonder that they even exist.

- Watch quietly and, if you can, breathe in rhythm with their unconscious breath.
- Feel the air move between you both as you breathe, and know this human moment as a common silk that connects everything.

# APRIL 2
# WE SHARE THE SAME RIVER

The river's now in me.

I was traveling in South Africa and felt very tender one morning, when my friend Kim came upon me as I was weeping. She asked if I was okay. I told her it was only the waters of life splashing up my shore. Later that day, I found her near tears and checked in with her. She said, "The river's now in me."

We looked into each other and realized that we all share the same river. It flows beneath us and through us, from one dry heart to the next. We share the same river. It makes the Earth one living thing.

The whole of life has a power to soften and open us against our will, to irrigate our spirits, and in those moments, we discover that tears, the water from within, are a common blood, mysterious and clear. We may speak different languages and live very different lives, but when that deep water swells to the surface, it pulls us to each other.

We share the same river, and where it enters, we lose our stubbornness the way fists wear open when held under in the stream of love.

- If you can, sit and watch a stream or brook as you meditate on the life of feeling that joins us all.
- If you can't get to a stream or brook, meditate just the same while watching rain trickle down the street.
- Note how the same river touches everything and moves on.
- As you breathe, feel the life of everything swell through you.

# APRIL 3
## TALKING FAST

---

Live loud enough in your heart
and there is no need to speak.

There was a time in my life during my years in college when I was so talkative that the waterfall of words kept others at a safe distance. Of course, in time, this cascade pushed others away. But what I didn't realize till much later was that I kept talking faster and louder to the world around me because I couldn't hear the world within me. Of course, the more noise I made, the less chance I had of having what was real enter me or rise from me. It became a damning cycle.

So often, we mistake the need to hear with the need to be heard. All that talk was a way of reaching out to others with my heart. Ultimately, it was all based on the fear that if I didn't throw my heart out there — through endless words and gestures and questions — I would be left alone. It's taken me many years to learn that the world comes flooding in if I can only keep myself open.

It remains important to reach out and to express oneself, but underneath that is the need to be porous and real. Through the opened heart, the world comes rushing in, the way oceans fill the smallest hole along the shore. It is the quietest sort of miracle: by simply being who we are, the world will come to fill us, to cleanse us, to baptize us, again and again.

- Center yourself by breathing steadily.
- Bring into view one thing you are reaching for. As you exhale, reach without moving and let it open up your body.
- Bring into view one thing you are needing to express. As you inhale, feel with-

186

out speaking and let it open up your
heart.

# APRIL 4
# MAKING AMENDS

There is hurt and there is love.
They roll us through the days
like a turtle down a hill.
All we can do when on our back
is roll one more time
and head for the sea.

Stones loosened by storms cover paths, and
uprooted trees break newly formed nests, and
crisis after crisis throws us into each other. It
is inevitable. Stay alive and you will be hurt,
and you will also hurt others.

Unintended hurt is as common as branches
snapped in wind. But it is the unacknowl-
edged hurt that becomes a wound. Just as
our only recourse to falling down is getting
up, our only recourse to hurting others is to
acknowledge what we've done and clean up
the mess. This is known as making amends, a
simple yet enormous act of integrity that
restores trust, and trust, after all, is the soil
that holds the roots of humankind. Without
it, life on Earth begins to eat itself dry.

What causes us to hurt each other? It's hard

187

to say. But it seems that, being human, we are subject to many ancient and powerful opposites found in life. Among those that impact us constantly are light and dark, yes and no, and especially fear and peace. For it is out of fear that we feel the need to isolate ourselves or to control others, and it is often in the act of elevating ourselves that we hurt one another, not to mention ourselves. When not afraid, when in a moment of peace, we feel quite a different need. We feel a sudden requirement to connect and belong to other living things, and it is then in the act of true embrace that we love one another.

Still, as no one in daily life is exempt from both sleeping and waking, no one can escape feeling both fear and peace, and so, no one can escape being both hurtful and loving. But the world is kept whole by those who can overcome their fear, however briefly. The blood of life itself is kept vital by those who can simply and bravely repair their separations, time and time again.

Even if our awareness of being hurtful comes years after delivering the hurt, the smallest word or gesture — owning what we've done — can reopen the heart.

- Sit quietly and bring to mind and heart an act of isolation or control that you invoked which hurt another.
- Breathe deeply and try to see the fear

that prompted your need to isolate or control.

- Breathe slowly and in your heart make amends; that is, own the fear that prompted you, the act of isolation or control that arose from it, and the hurt that resulted.
- Just for yourself, express your amends in a letter or card addressed to the person you hurt.
- Enter your day and let your heart tell you whether to mail the amends or not.

# APRIL 5
# THE COURAGE OF THE SEED

All the buried seeds
crack open in the dark
the instant they surrender
to a process they can't see.

What a powerful lesson is the beginning of spring. All around us, everything small and buried surrenders to a process that none of the buried parts can see. And this innate surrender allows everything edible and fragrant to break ground into a life of light that we call spring.

In nature, we are quietly given countless models of how to give ourselves over to what appears dark and hopeless, but which ultimately is an awakening that is beyond all imagining. This moving through the dark into blossom is the threshold to God.

As a seed buried in the earth cannot imagine itself as an orchid or hyacinth, neither can a heart packed with hurt imagine itself loved or at peace. The courage of the seed is that once cracking, it cracks all the way.

- This is a walking meditation. Find and watch some buds barely breaking ground.
- Meditate on their unseen beginnings underground.
- Breathe slowly and let your breath draw whatever is budding in you to the surface of your life.

# APRIL 6
# QUESTIONS PUT
# TO THE SICK – I

When was the last time you sang?
— QUESTION PUT TO THE SICK BY A
NATIVE AMERICAN MEDICINE MAN

I was lying flat on a stretcher in a large hospital room after one of my surgeries. I had just been wheeled in, rejoining four others all mending in the one open room. There was a deep silence as we looked at each other; there was only the slight breathing of machines and the clear drip of fluids and the hum of old radiators. Suddenly, an older man began to laugh, and without a word, our eyes bounced back and forth to each other, and one by one, we joined in what became a cascade of coughing laughter interspersed with short moans; for with each laugh, our incisions and bedsores poked us sharply. But we laughed and hurt and laughed and hurt, like a flock of broken birds dreaming of their next flight.

That laughter was a raw and primal sort of song, an elemental way of giving voice to our suffering. It was remarkably healing. I learned a great truth from that unexpected chorus. I learned that even when we feel powerless, we can always give voice to our pain and hope, to the slim, ongoing fact of our being alive.

We often underestimate the power of giving voice, but it is real and sustaining. It is the basis of all song. It is why prisoners break into song. It is why the blues are sung, even when no one is listening. It is at the heart of all hymns and mantras.

And it works its healing, not so much by being heard as by the fact that in giving voice to what lives within, even through the softest whisper, we allow the world of spirit to soften our pain. In this way, the smallest moan is in itself a lullaby. In giving voice to what we feel, the darkest cry uttered with honesty can arrive as the holiest of songs.

- Sit quietly and breathe slowly until you feel a catch in your breathing.
- Focus on the catch, for something is pressing there on your heart.
- Place your hand on your heart and inhale deeply.
- On the exhale, give voice to what is pressing, even if you don't know what it is.
- Even if all you express is the slightest sigh, it is the beginning of a song.

# APRIL 7
## BEING SHAPED BY OTHERS

The whole world could praise Sung
    Jung-Tzu
and it wouldn't make him exert himself.
The whole world could condemn him and it
wouldn't make him mope. He drew a clear
line between the internal and the external.
— CHUANG TZU

These words were spoken by Chuang Tzu in the fourth century B.C.E. I read them fifteen years ago and taped them to my closet, so I could be reminded not to let the opinion of others shape me.

I have changed a great deal since then: what I do, where I live, who I am. Many things have come and gone. The closet to which Chuang Tzu's words were taped is holding someone else's clothes. But the words are in my heart, though I still struggle not to be shaped by what others think.

This is at once the clearest of spiritual intents and yet the hardest to stay true to: how to stay open to what others feel and not to what they think. We cannot live without being affected by others, but we are only real when we let truth and love shape us from within. Our want to be liked, our want to avoid conflict, our want to be understood — all these traits tease us away from taking the voice within seriously.

Though the Earth is touched by everything alive, it never stops turning around the fire at its center, and though we are touched by the stories of strangers and the far-off songs of birds lost in wind, we find our way by following the spirit's voice at our center. Too much is lost in waiting for someone else to tell us that what moves us is real.

- As you breathe, feel the Earth beneath you holding you up as it slowly turns about its center.

- Breathe deeply and feel how you are like the Earth.
- Inhale cleanly and feel the many things that you hold up.
- Exhale cleanly and keep turning about your own center.

# APRIL 8
## CENTER OF THE EYE

In keeping the center of the I empty,
the miracle of life can enter and heal.

It's not by chance that the dark center of the human eye, the pupil, is actually an empty hole through which the world becomes known to us. Likewise, in a spiritual sense, the *I* is the empty center through which we see everything. It's revealing that such a threshold is called the pupil, for it is only when we are emptied of all noise and dreams of ego that we become truly teachable.

Like the center of the eye, both the Buddhist and Zen traditions speak of an unbreakable emptiness at the heart of all seeing from which all living things emerge. The Hindu *Upanishads* tell us that in the center of the seed of the great nyagrodha tree there is nothing, and out of that nothing the great tree grows. We are then reminded that in our time on Earth we grow like this tree — out of that nothing. As the essence of the tree is the empty center of its seed, so the essence of our life is the intangible presence at the center of our soul.

Therefore, our chief work as human beings rests in the sincere effort to allow that central presence to in-form us. Thus, all forms of prayer and meditation are aimed at keeping the center of the I empty, so the miracle of life in its grace and immensity can enter and heal us.

- Close your eyes and erase the many thoughts and images that arise, one after another, as if your mind is a blackboard and your breath is a sponge wiping each appearance clean.
- Do this until you experience a slowing down of messages. Then open your eyes as if waking for the very first time.
- Keep breathing slowly and take in the first thing you see. Feel what is before you. See and feel the wood that makes up the chair next to you and resist preempting its presence by pronouncing it a chair.

How many ways can a statue dream of
   living?
Every time I reach for you, we begin.
We begin.

The line between living and watching is very
thin. A moment's rest or pause for reflection
can spread into a thickness of hesitation, and
the next thing we know, reaching out or saying something or picking up the phone or
stopping in unannounced is difficult, as if
there is suddenly some huge wall to climb
just to be heard.

This is how we isolate ourselves, digging
moments of healthy solitude into holes in the
yard, and, of course, the dirt we dig and pile
up becomes a small mountain that separates
us from everyone we love. We all know how
not phoning that friend because we were
busy, if allowed to go too far, turns into a
vastness that seems impossible to cross. The
truth is that the phone is the same six inches
from our hands as it has always been. The
challenge is to remember this when everything seems so far away.

To feel isolated is part of the human journey. But when we obey the feelings of hesita-

tion and separation more powerfully than those of love, we start to experience numbness and depression. This is when we start to live like statues, believing that all we can do is watch.

Hard as it feels, it is just at this moment that we must break back into living by reaching for anything, no matter how small or close. If it is fall, rub a leaf across your face. If winter, break a piece of ice. If spring, touch a small flower.

- Surround yourself with small precious things: a stone, a feather, a shell.
- Center yourself and meditate on the space that exists between you and these small precious things.
- As you inhale, practice being a statue that comes alive with each breath.
- As you exhale, reach for the small precious things before you.

# APRIL 10
# AT HOME IN OUR SKIN

The spiritual life is about becoming more at home in your own skin.
— PARKER J. PALMER

Anything that removes what grows between

our hearts and the day is spiritual. It might be the look of a loved one stirring their coffee as morning light surprises their groggy eyes. It might be the realization while watching a robin build its nest that you are only a temporary being in this world. It might be a fall on ice that reminds you of the humility of your limitations.

As Parker Palmer suggests, the aim of all spiritual paths, no matter their origin or the rigors of their practice, is to help us live more fully in the lives we are given. In this way, whatever comes from a moment's grace that joins us to our lives and to each other — this is spiritual. For example, I was having coffee the other day in a café and suddenly, from the rain of noise around me, there arose a word of truth in the exposed voice of a stranger whose face I couldn't even see.

I don't know her context or her story or whom she was revealing herself to. I didn't even turn around to see her face, because in that moment, there was a perfect beauty in our staying anonymous. I only felt, simply and deeply, that without her ever knowing, her moment of pointed and unexpected truth made me more at home in my own skin.

The life of spirit is everywhere: in dust waiting for light, in music waiting to be heard, in the sensations of the day waiting to be felt. Being spiritual is much more useful and immediate than the books about books would have us think.

- Center yourself, and as you breathe, realize that your spirit fills your life the way your bones and blood fill your hand.
- As you breathe, realize that your life fits the world the way your warm and living hand fits a glove.
- As you breathe, feel your spirit fill your skin and feel your skin fit the world.

# APRIL 11
## TURNING LIGHT INTO FOOD

We still might feed the dark thing in us
that grows away from the light
until against all sense
we mysteriously flower
in the other direction.

Quietly, each spring, things in the plant world start growing slowly toward the light, while their roots finger their way underground. But once breaking surface, the most amazing thing happens again and again without a sound: the exposed thing growing toward the light stays alive by turning light into food. We've all learned about this. It's called "photosynthesis," the process by which leaves turn sunlight into sugar, which feeds their roots; then the roots, once nourished, make the stems and leaves grow further.

The smallest plant life in spring reveals to us both the challenge of being a spirit in human form and the quiet courage necessary to grow inwardly. For this is our deepest calling: how to turn light into food.

How often we are told, "You can't live on air." Yet if we dare to make our way into the open, we are drawn into the air and the light, and the rest somehow happens. For like the nubs of shoots yet to break ground, we can't help it. Something in our very fiber knows where the light is, even when we can't see it.

My most profound experience of this was in the midst of my worst despair after being diagnosed with a tumor pressing on my brain. Inexplicably, despite the fear and terror and sadness, despite doctors and technicians telling me the worst of what they imagined for me — though they really didn't know — somehow, though I was digging deeper in the dark like a stubborn root, some essential vein of being was, for all that, growing toward the light.

And I am here to tell you, you *can* live on air. The light is our home.

- In early spring, choose one twig or stem and watch it grow. Follow its progress

every other day.
- As you notice its changes, be aware of its complex relationship to both the light above and the dark below.
- As you watch this piece of life grow, imagine it as a mirror of something in you about to break ground.
- What is this small piece of greenery teaching you about yourself?

# APRIL 12
## THE NEED TO SPEAK

Just by speaking I can break out of my
  self-made prison.
— JUNE SINGER

So many times we suppose ourselves out of existence, imagining that if we speak our heart we will be rejected or ignored.

I once watched a man reach to call a friend, excited to share a deep idea that had overcome him. But as the phone was ringing, I saw him imagine a cool reception, saw him try on the pain of not being heard, and quickly, with a sigh of deflation, he hung up before the fourth ring.

Still, the expression — whether misunderstood, well received, or rejected — matters. For the cost of not making the call is that a piece of us dies. Consider how fish swim and birds fly. They do so because it is in their nature. For it is the swimming and the flying that makes them fish and birds.

Likewise, it is the speaking of one's heart that makes a human being human. For even if no one hears us, it is the act of speaking that frees us by letting the spirit swim and fly through the world.

- Sit quietly and allow yourself to be as still as lake water when there is no wind.
- Breathe slowly and look into yourself. Look to your bottom.
- Inhale deeply and feel whatever rises from your bottom.
- Exhale cleanly and, though you are alone, speak what you are feeling, aloud to yourself.

# APRIL 13
# A PROFOUND BOW

All streams flow to the sea
because it is lower than they are.
Humility gives it its power.

— LAO-TZU

There is a Yoga mudra, a kneeling posture of exercise, where by bringing your head to your

202

chest while extending your arms up and out behind you, you can practice placing your head beneath your heart. And from this humbling position, you can't help but tire, and so, you must put your arms down. With your head beneath your heart, you must stop doing.

Soon after learning this, I came upon a woman who had been a nun, and she told me that she would practice for days upon days similar postures of Gregorian Chant: incline, bow, and profound bow — each bringing the head lower and lower to the earth.

This holds a powerful lesson: Time and time again, the head must be brought beneath the heart or the ego swells. If you do not bend, life will bend you. In this way, humility is accepting that your head belongs beneath your heart, with your thinking subordinate to your feeling, with your will subordinate to the higher order. This acceptance is key to receiving grace.

Lay your head down and the world of being will open its joys.

- Sit quietly on your knees, and as you breathe, incline forward.
- After a time, breathe deeply, and as you exhale evenly, bring your head below your heart while extending your arms behind you.

- After a time, bring your head, if you can, to touch the floor and offer thanks for being humbled.

# APRIL 14
## SELF-CONFIDENCE

*It may have nothing to do with me, but if a friend or loved one is sad or angry, I can secretly wonder, What did I do? What can I do? Why didn't I do it all better to begin with?*

I am often surprised and humbled by how quickly in my insecurity I can begin to assume responsibility for all the wrongs and sufferings I see around me. When thrown off-center, when old patterns return, when feeling exhausted or depressed, I so quickly become the exaggerated cause of all that is not right with the world.

I know I am not alone in this. Perhaps it is one of the laws of emotional weather: sudden lows result in isolated storms. It has happened to me enough over the years that I have to acknowledge the power of negative self-centeredness. We typically think of the ego-centered as being conceited and self-inflated and quite selfish. But this recurring struggle with exaggerated responsibility has made me realize that more often we are ego-centered when feeling deflated, when feeling shaken from our sense of oneness with things. In that place of separation, we become darkly self-centered, blaming ourselves for not fixing things or making things right or for letting bad things happen. Underneath these self-recriminations is the grandiose assumption that we have the power, in the first place, to control events that are really beyond any human being's influence.

Certainly, we affect each other, and often, but to assume that other people's inner moods hinge on my presence is an egocentric way to keep myself in a cycle of sacrifice and guilt. Further, to assume that another's condition or way of being in the world hinges on my presence is the beginning of self-oppression and codependence. In extreme moments of negative self-centeredness, we can even assume magical proportions of burden, in which we feel acutely responsible for a loved one's illness or misfortune because we weren't good enough or there enough or perfect enough.

It is helpful to note here psychologist Michael Mahoney's definition of *self-confidence.* He traces confidence to the Latin *confidere,* "fidelity," and understands self-confidence as a fidelity to the self. Indeed, it is only a devotion to that sacred bottom beneath our moods of insecurity that brings us back in accord with the center of the heart which shares the same living center with all beings. This is what the Hindu tradition calls Atman, the shared immortal self.

So now, when I trip into moments of low-esteem and feel certain that I am the cause of all this bad weather, I try to feel the pace of the Earth turning beneath my feet and the pace of the clouds drifting over my head and the pace of my heart opening after a lifetime of pain. When these align, I am weakened of my ordinary will and awakened into a power greater than any one heart, greater than the weather of any one day or the mood of any one life.

- Sit quietly and become centered. Now bring to mind the last time you felt a loved one's mood sink in your presence. Try not to deflect the discomfort you felt.
- Try to let go of all your self-questioning. Try to breathe through to the calm you felt before bringing this to mind.
- Breathe deeply and bring to mind the depth of heart you see in this person that makes you love them. Try to feel the love that lives beneath all moods.

# APRIL 15
# THE NEXT STEP TO HEALTH

The deeper the cry,
the more clear the choice.

I have a friend who has called into question whom he should love. This opened a field of complexities, and life quickly became an endless consideration of possibilities and allegiances.

But beneath the endless inventories, his soul was calling out from way inside, and through his pain, my friend kept hearing this far-off cry surface at the oddest times. Soon, he realized this cry was, indeed, much deeper than "Who?" His very soul was begging to feel. This seemed more serious, more urgent, more filled with terror than a choice between one woman and another.

As he began to struggle with facing himself, my friend began to realize that all the decisions to be made about who and where and when were really heartfelt distractions from a deeper cry. Underneath all the painful ambiguities and assessments, his very soul was drowning, sinking out of reach of the feel of life. Once hearing the deeper cry within himself, his choice became extremely basic and very straightforward: How do I regain my wonder at being alive? What must I do to keep my heart from sinking?

Time and again, we are shown by the quiet courage of others that if we can let the deeper cry through, the next step to health will come plainly into view.

- Center yourself and bring to mind a complex decision that needs to be made.
- Breathe slowly and try to relax your spirit beneath the decision to be made.
- Breathe cleanly and try to let the deeper cry through.
- Feel your basic life position way inside and admit — that is, accept and let in — what you need to be well.

# APRIL 16
## ONE DROP OF TRUTH AT A TIME

It is the fullness of our attention
to whatever is near
that has birds fly out of God's mouth.

The months relax and the ice enclosing a bent-over branch thaws, and the snow drops and the branch springs back up after its deathlike sleep. The tree coming into spring teaches us how to let go into renewal. For this is how the freeze around a broken heart thaws. In another part of the world, small brilliant fish mouth pebbles along the ocean sand, sucking off bits of food and spitting back the rest. This is how they comb the bottom, and these small limbless creatures teach us how to suffer and move on, how to sift through what is nourishing and how to give back the rest. And high in the mountains, away from the eyes of others, a small cave with its singular drip collects clear water that is the heartbeat of the mountain. So the center of the Earth itself shows us how to be: one drop of clearness at a time, collecting in the moist center that keeps the soul alive.

These are just a few examples of an essential relatedness that exists between all things. In practice, if we look closely with our whole being at anything — plants, trees, the human heart, emptiness, fish, even the worn gears of a watch — the same core of deep instruction will rise before us in a language that waits beneath words. The world, it seems, both natural and constructed, is an endless net of particular lessons, each made of the same compelling thread that is always hiding in the open, simply waiting for our complete attention to reveal itself. By pulling at these threads, I have discovered, again and again, the deep and common way of things that is embedded in everything.

So when confusion or pain seems to tighten what is possible, when sadness or frustration shrinks your sense of well-being, when worry or fear agitates the peace right out of you, try lending your attention to the nearest thing. Try watching how the dust lifts and resettles when you blow on it. Watch how the paw-prints of your neighbor's retriever, if stared at long enough, turn into unexpected symbols. Watch how the one shell you brought back three years ago from the sea reveals itself, at last, as a face that is telling you how to continue. Give your full attention over to the nearest patch of life — to how an apple peels and juices — and after a while each thing attended will reveal yet another way back to the center.

- This is a walking meditation. Center yourself and breathe deeply as you slowly step into the world nearby.
- Once centered, look around and focus on one thing that seems to have the rhythm of what you are feeling. It might be the slight sway of a bush or the tumble of a cup blowing down the street.
- Breathe slowly and give your full attention to the small outer rhythm that is matching your mood.
- Breathe and watch until the rhythm you

210

are seeing and the rhythm you are feeling reveal their common truth.

# APRIL 17
# A WISDOM MOMENT OF TRUST

If you can't cross over alive,
how can you cross when you're dead?
— KABIR

The need to step into what we fear and, in so
doing, disperse its hold on us is powerfully
brought to life by a moment in the film
*Indiana Jones and the Last Crusade.* After
searching everywhere within reason and
memory for the Holy Grail, Jones stands on
an enormous precipice, a deep chasm before
him, the Grail waiting on the other side. His
father, wounded and depending on the Grail
to heal, cries out possible interpretations of
the clues Jones has been given to reach the
Grail.

After what seems a lifetime of inner debate
and escalating fear, he dares, against everything he knows, to step into the void above
the chasm, and as he does, an enormous
stone foundation appears beneath his feet, a
bridge that was there all along.

This is a moment of risk and trust, a
wisdom moment that repeats itself in our

lives in both small and large ways. Over and over, the cup we need to drink from, the ancient ever-healing cup of wholeness waits beyond some deep chasm we are afraid to cross.

Often we are driven to the edge by the cries and clues of elders and loved ones, only to find that nothing makes sense, that there seems nowhere to go. And then the atom of risk begins to replay itself in those brought to the edge.

Then, when all known ways of seeing have failed, we sometimes dare to step into the void. Whether that void is a chasm of purpose or self-esteem or a ravine in relationship or a canyon of addiction, this crazy-wisdom step — that begins with risk and lands in trust — reveals a foundation that was there all along, but which is only made visible by our risk to think and see in new ways and our trust to step into what we fear.

- Breathe deeply and know that even the smallest moment of risk and trust is difficult.
- Center yourself and meditate on a chasm of your own making. It might be a trench of stubbornness or pride that no one can cross, or the echo of your own pain that isolates you, or the vastness that builds when you are afraid to tell someone the truth of your heart, or

the absence of belief that you deserve
what waits on the other side.

- Lean into your chasm gently until the
  fear subsides.
- Lean into your chasm and offer, through
  your breathing, a wordless compassion
  for yourself and all others in our very
  human struggle to step with risk and
  land with trust.

# APRIL 18
# THE PURPOSE OF FULL
# ATTENTION

This is the ongoing purpose of full
    attention:
to find a thousand ways to be pierced into
    wholeness.

A most profound and helpful learning came
to me when struggling with the pain of having a rib removed. For weeks I felt a corset of
pain girdling each breath. But watching the
winter water of a stream begin to thaw and
flow, over and over, I finally saw that to make
it through the pain, I had to be more like
water and less like ice.

For when trees fell into the ice, the river
shattered. But when large limbs fell into the

flowing water, the river embraced the weight and flowed around it. The trees and winter water were teaching me that the pain was more pointed and hurtful when I was tense and solid as ice. Then, each breath was shattering. But when I could thaw the fear and tenseness I carried, the pain was more absorbed, and I could, like the thawing stream, move on — not pain-free, but no longer shattered.

It is this way with much of nature. By opening fully to our own experience, we can feel and see the resilience of life around us. Feeling our woundedness, we can learn from the hollowed stump how to root smaller greens. Feeling our sadness, we can learn from the leaves too tired to be blown along how to surrender. Feeling our tenderness, we can learn from the caterpillar how to endure the tremble that precedes the appearance of wings. But it is only by showing up, by denying nothing, that other living things reveal to us the secrets of how they manage to live. In deep counterpoint to the old saying, "An eye for an eye," there is a deeper law that guides us to wholeness: a truth of being for a truth of being. So the purpose of full attention is to invite through personal surrender the particular example of life force in whatever is around us to show itself: a truth of being for a truth of being.

Yes, when in pain, be like flowing water.

When suffering near the bottom, feed off what you can, like the brilliant ocean fish, and spit back the rest. When feeling burdened, watch small birds to see how they begin to fly. When feeling finished, watch newborn animals open their wet little eyes and imitate their innocence. Once giving full attention, you will come back — one drop at a time — into the tide of the living.

- This is also a walking meditation. Meditate on a particular pain that is troubling you.
- As you walk about, breathe steadily and see through the lens of this pain, not to turn everything into your pain, but to locate something that might teach you about pain.
- Look for something that resembles your pain. It might be a bottle abandoned once broken, or a slim branch splitting, or a fence sagging. It could be a shrub aching to bloom.
- Breathe steadily, and by feeling your pain while watching, invite this piece of life to open its secret to you.

# APRIL 19
## OUTWAITING CLOUDS

The bud in half-bloom
outwaits the cloud.

Some days I wake with a cloud around my heart, and it dulls everything except the weight I carry deep inside. Yet, just because I can't make it to the light today doesn't mean that the light has vanished. In truth, the heart, like the Earth, is continually blanketed by ever-changing atmospheres that come and go between who we are and how we live our days.

So faith, it seems, can be defined as the effort to believe in light when we're covered by clouds, and though it feels like the sun will never come again, the truth is it has never stopped burning its light. In fact, its heat and warmth is burning steadily, right now, on the far side of whatever cloud we are under.

If we could only suspend our judgment when clouded in the heart. For many skepticisms are born from conclusions drawn while unable to see, as if any kind of understanding will prevent the clouds from coming or going, again and again.

But no cloud lasts forever. The Earth and all that grows from it knows this well. So does

216

the heart and everything that grows from it, in spite of all our very understandable pains.

- Sit outside, when you can, and watch the clouds come and go.
- Breathe slowly and evenly, and feel the sky open and close above you.
- Note how the trees and flowers do not collapse when the clouds roll in.
- Draw strength from this.

# APRIL 20
## BIRDS AND ORNITHOLOGISTS

Birds don't need ornithologists to fly.

We spend so much time wanting to be seen and named: as intelligent or good or handsome or pretty or successful or popular or as nobody's fool. Yet the spirit doesn't know it's being spiritual anymore than water rushing knows it's a stream, and the heart doesn't know it's expanding with compassion anymore than a hawk spreading its wings knows it's being a hawk. Nor does someone acting out of love often realize they are being kind.

From an early age, we are taught that to live fully is to be accepted, and to be accepted, we need to be seen. So we base success and even love on the effort to be seen, on how much we stand out.

However, the often painful truth we discover along the way is that to survive in an inner way that matters — that keeps us connected to all that has ever lived and is living — we sorely need to know how to be accepting.

By this I don't mean being passive. By this I mean inhabiting our capacity to see and affirm the common pulse of life we find in others, no matter how different they may seem from us.

When we do this, we no longer need to be different to be valued and no longer need to be accepted to know love. In short, we no longer need an audience to fly. We simply have to extend our sincerity to each abiding day and we will be in accord with all that is valuable.

Like flowers waiting on rain, our hearts wait on love. As much as we want to be seen and known, it is the giving of attention that keeps us awake. For giving attention opens us to love. And accepting that deep things wait like seed between us is believing in the world. So wake me by accepting me, and the world will sprout us up like grass.

- Be still, close your eyes, and quiet your mind until you feel the air as you breathe.
- On the inbreath, open yourself to what

it feels like to get attention.
- On the outbreath, open yourself to what it feels like to give attention.
- As you breathe, allow yourself to feel how the two merge — in and out — get and give.
- As they merge, consider what it means to you to be awake.

# APRIL 21
# THE GIFT OF SURPRISE

Another name for God
is surprise.
— BROTHER DAVID STEINDL-RAST

While rushing to complete your dearest plans that you tell no one, you can bump into another and groceries will fly, and while picking up the ketchup, you might fall in love. Or in your second year of college, while studying what Mommy and Daddy want you to be, you can accidentally open a book on Albert Schweitzer and discover that you feel compelled to go to Africa. Or, understanding geometry, you might decide to become a gardener, finding endless joy in creating landscapes. Or the death of your grandmother might open a side of you that is starving for history. In my case, losing a rib to cancer made me discover the Adam in me.

It seems that any moment of interest or pain or adversity can surprise us into the larger totality of life, breaking our current limits and allowing us the chance to redefine ourselves in regard to the larger sense that is upon us. That we are opened — so suddenly, so often — is the way the soul unfolds on Earth.

We can never be prepared for everything. No one person can anticipate all of life. In fact, overpreparation is yet another way to wall ourselves in from life. Rather, we can only prepare for how we might respond to the gift of surprise that often moves in on us faster than our reflex to resist.

Life is surprising, thank God, and God, the chance to know Oneness, lives in surprise. For God is seldom in our plans, but always in the unexpected.

- Center yourself and pray for the strength of spirit to be open to surprise.
- As you exhale, try to relax your resistance to the unexpected.
- As you inhale, try to make a passageway for everything larger than you.
- Enter your day.

# April 22
# It Is Enough

If you can't see what you're looking for,
see what's there.

One of the most difficult things for us to accept is that beneath all our dreams and disappointments, we live and breathe in abundance. It is hard when in pain to believe that all we ever need is before us, around us, within us. And yet it is true.

Like leafless trees waiting for morning, something as great and as constant as the Earth holds us up and turns us ever so slowly toward the light. Our task is only to be rooted and patient.

Never was this more painfully true for me than during the aftermath of my first chemo treatment. I was in a Holiday Inn at five in the morning after twenty-four hours of vomiting every twenty minutes. I was slumped on the floor, holding the space of a rib that had been removed three weeks earlier. And my wife — in anger, in panic, in desperation — called out, "Where is God?" And from some unknown place in me, through my pale slouched form, I uttered, "Here . . . right here."

The presence of God has never eliminated

pain, only made it more bearable. Now, when things don't go the way I want, I try to kiss what waits beneath all want. Now, when the car breaks down, though I get angry, I try to hear the weeds in the ditch as they point me to the sky. Now, when the vase drops from my hand and shatters, though I whine, I try to see beneath my reflection in the pool of flower water. Now, when hurt, I try to feel my way through the tangle of my very normal reactions into the quiet underlying all experience.

Mysterious as it is — no matter our pain or excitement, our drama or circumstance — all that we could hope for is here. We lack nothing.

The humble challenge of being human is not in agreeing or disputing this truth. That is as fruitless as arguing against gravity. Our humble way, if we can open it, is to root ourselves beneath the thousand dreams and excuses that keep us from the ground we walk. Time and again, we are asked to outlast what we want and hope for, in order to see what's there. It is enough.

- Choose a favorite tree or plant, and though you may not see anything, watch it grow.
- Know that as you watch it grow, the Earth is carrying it toward the sun.
- Imagine yourself as such a tree or plant.

- Close your eyes and know that though you may not see anything, you are growing, and that something larger than you is carrying you toward the light.
- Though none of it is visible, feel this mystery and whisper aloud, "I am growing. . . . I am being carried toward the light. . . . I lack nothing. . . ."

# APRIL 23
# PLAYING SMALL

There will never be an "us"
if I play small.
— SHARON PREISS

In Dante's *Divine Comedy,* the only difference between the lovers who find themselves enduring Hell and the lovers working their way through Paradise is that those in Hell have no individual center, and so they spin in endless identification with each other.

Hard as it is, we cannot shrink from our relationships or we simply become an audience or gofer for the dominant partner or friend. Like most of us, I have struggled with this my whole life: fearful of what might happen if I actually voice my concerns and needs, surprised that doing so — while not always easy or pleasant — always enables me to be myself more fully.

Then, not by chance, I'm always more able to feel and see the world around me. I bring more to the scene and am revitalized more readily by my daily experience.

The great philosopher Martin Buber, who believed that God is most deeply known through relationship, spoke to the heart of this paradox. He said that before there can be a true relationship, there must be two separate beings who can relate. Most of our life experience bears this out. Unless we work to be ourselves, we can never truly know others or the numinous world we live in.

- As you breathe, do not disappear.
- Sit quietly, and as you inhale, realize that the expansion of your spirit is what knows the world.
- During your day, when feeling small, inhale slowly and present yourself again to all that is around you.

# APRIL 24
# LOVE LIKE WATER

Only love, with no thought of return,
can soften the point of suffering.

Water in its clear softness fills whatever hole it finds. It is not skeptical or distrusting. It does not say this gully is too deep or that field is too open. Like water, the miracle of love is that it covers whatever it touches, making the touched thing grow while leaving no trace of its touch. True, the faces of shores and the arms of cliffs are worn to bone. But this is beyond the water's doing. This is the progress of life, of which water is but an element.

Most things break instead of transform because they resist. The quiet miracle of love is that without our interference, it, like water, accepts whatever is tossed or dropped or placed into it, embracing it completely.

Of course, we are human and are easily hurt if not loved back or if loved poorly. But we waste so much of life's energy by deliberating who and what shall be worthy of our love when in the deepest elemental sense, these choices are not in our province, anymore than rain can choose what it shall fall upon.

Certainly, we need to make decisions: Who will I spend time with? Who will I learn from? Who will I live with? Who will I marry? But beneath all that, the element of love doesn't stop being elemental. It does not stop covering everything before it. And over a lifetime, the pain of withholding this great and quiet force is more damaging than the pain of being rejected or loved poorly. For love, like water, can be dammed, but toward what end?

In truth, the more we let love flow through, the more we have to love. This is the inner glow that sages and saints of all ages seem to share: the wash of their love over everything before them; not just people, but birds and rocks and flowers and air.

Beneath the many choices we have to make, love, like water, flows back into the world through us. It is the one great secret available to all. Yet somewhere the misperception has been enshrined that to withhold love will stop hurt. In truth, it is the other way around. As water soaks scars, love soothes our wounds. If opened to, love will accept the angrily thrown stone, and our small tears will lose some of their burn in the great ocean of tears, and the arrow released to the bottom of the river will lose its point.

- Choose a quiet spot, and in a moment of meditation, open to the water of spirit that runs beneath everything.
- Let the energy of love rise from you to the simple objects before you.
- Feel the energy of love in the air surrounding the chair or cup or pencil or piece of broken window.
- Imagine you are the broken window or pencil. Feel the air on your skin of glass or wood. Look upon this one single object the way you would a lover.

- Without naming this, just feel the intensity of attention coming from you with no particular place to go.

# April 25
# The Courage to Join

The real story comes from a love-source that cannot be understood with intellect, but known only as a person is known.
— Coleman Barks

Living in modern times has turned us into watchers, placing a sliver of distance between us and everything we meet. It is this watching that disheartens our days, that takes the color out of the earth and makes the songs of time sound flat.

The Native American view on this is healing. With respect for all aspects of Creation, we are asked to honor whatever we see — rock, rain, fence, or stranger — as a member of our family.

By honoring all things as living, the courage to join with the Universe becomes a manner of being that can happen even while sitting still. In knowing the world this way, there is no such thing as metaphor. The wind is not like God's voice. The wind *is* God's voice. Memories are not images of loved ones returning to us. They are the spirits of loved ones visiting us.

It takes courage to remove the sliver of distance we carry around our necks, but the reward is a world alive and not dead. Such courage lets the juices of the world flow.

- Sit quietly and center yourself.
- After a time, imagine that the things about you — window, tree, rug, bed, door — are alive in the way that plants are alive.
- As you breathe, feel their energies breathe.
- Through your heart's beating, take the chance to welcome them.

# APRIL 26
# THE WAY IS HARD, BUT CLEAR

Though it is the hardest going,
the way is clear.

The naturalist and environmentalist Kevin Scribner tells us that salmon make their way upstream by bumping repeatedly into blocked pathways until they find where the current is strongest. Somehow they know that the unimpeded rush of water means that there is no obstacle there, and so they enter this opening fervently, for though it is the hardest going, the way is clear.

The lesson here is as unnerving as it is helpful. In facing both inner and outer adversities, the passage of truth comes at us with a powerful momentum because it is clear and unimpeded, and so, where we sense the rush of truth is where we must give our all.

As human beings, the blocked pathways of our journey can take on many forms, and — whether it be in avoiding conflict with others, or in not taking the risk to love, or in not accepting the call of spirit that would have us participate more fully in our days — it is often easier to butt up continually against these blocked pathways than to enter fervently the one passage that is so powerfully clear.

In this regard, salmon innately model a healthy persistence by showing us how to keep nosing for the unimpeded way, and once finding it, how to work even harder to make it through.

Some say it is easier for salmon, since the power of their drive to end where they begin is not compromised by the endless considerations that often keep us from the truth. Still, it is the heart's capacity to rise one more time after falling down, no matter how bruised, that verifies that such a drive lives in us too. Like salmon, our way depends not just on facing things head on, but in moving our whole being through.

- Center yourself and bring to mind something you are avoiding. It might be making a life decision or asking for what you need in a relationship.
- Breathe evenly and nose around the energy of the avoidance. What are you butting up against? Identify the resistance. Which part is coming from you? Which part from others?
- Breathe steadily and look for the rush of truth in all this. Feel for the clear and forceful way coming at you.
- For today, simply feel the power of the way that is clear and keep it before you.

# APRIL 27
# LET THERE BE LIGHT

Just trust yourself,
then you will know how to live.

— GOETHE

When Edison was discovering the light bulb, he first engaged in a process of envisioning how an unseeable current of energy could be harnessed and turned into light. Like most of us, the vision came first. Once he understood what came to him, it took quite some time to find the precise material that would work as a filament in the bulb itself.

Later, when asked if he ever grew discouraged or thought he was wasting his time, Edison said no, he learned something important each time he tried. He learned that there was another material not to be used.

The lessons here are very telling and transferable, especially to how we seek our calling in the world and to how we seek out love. To be willing to envision what we need is powerful and real, and just as crucial is the confidence of spirit to know that it will work, even though we haven't found where we belong or whom to love yet. Equally as vital is the perseverance in trying to find precisely what will work.

But perhaps the most inspiring part of Edison's journey is how he didn't view his many attempts as any type of failure on his part, but rather as an inevitable part of the process of discovery.

Finally, after all of this, we are challenged, scientist and lover alike, to use what we discover and live in the light.

- Center yourself, and as you breathe, envision what you need to live more fully.
- As you inhale, commit to trying to find

231

this today without judging what happens.

- As you exhale, commit to making use of whatever it is you discover.

# APRIL 28
# WU FENG

In the end, it is not enough to think what we know. We must live it. For only by living it can Love show itself as the greatest principle.

The way that heat allows ice to thaw and irrigate the earth, so our capacity to embody what we know — our quiet need to bring what lives within into accord with how we meet the days — this ancient act of integrity allows Love to show itself as the deepest sort of gravity.

There was a quiet man whose life-changing moment of such courage is inspiring. He was Wu Feng, a Manchurian diplomat of the 1700s who was posted with an aboriginal tribe in the outskirts of Taiwan. Wu Feng befriended the aboriginal chief, whose tribe beheaded one of its members every year as a form of sacrifice.

Each year Wu Feng pleaded with all of his compassion and reverence for life that the chief put an end to this custom. The chief would listen respectfully as Wu Feng would plead, and then after listening and bowing, the chief would summon the chosen tribe member and without hesitation behead him.

Finally, after living with the tribe for twenty-five years, Wu Feng once more pleaded with the chief to stop this senseless killing. But this time, when the tribe member was called forth, Wu Feng took his place and said, "If you will kill this time, it will be me."

The chief stared long into his friend's eyes, and having grown to love Wu Feng, he could not kill him. From that day, the practice of beheading stopped.

Of course, Wu Feng could have been killed, but his courage shows us that at a certain point, how we live inside takes priority. At a certain point for each of us, talk evaporates and words cannot bring Love into the open. Only the soul's presence coming from us can attract the soul's presence in others.

- As you breathe, be honest with yourself; that is, see things in your life as they are.
- Is there a situation in your life in which a part of you is being sacrificed like the member of the aboriginal tribe?
- Are you repeatedly being asked to deny who you are in some relationship?
- If so, can the Wu Feng in you stop talk-

ing and make itself present?

- If the answer is yes, simply honor that such a spirit of embodiment lives within you.
- Simply ask the question today. Trust your spirit to know when and how to do so.

# APRIL 29
# WITHIN YOUNG LEAVES

Wrapped within
young leaves:
the sound of water.

— SOSEKI

This delicate observation by this Japanese poet is filled with the quiet hope that embedded in our nature, even as we begin, is our gift already unfolded. Embedded in the seed is the blossom. Embedded in the womb is the child fully grown. Embedded in the impulse to care is the peace of love realized. Embedded in the edge of risk and fear is the authenticity that makes life worth living.

Wrapped within young leaves is the sound of water that will nourish them once they have opened. It's already there prompting them to unfold and grow. To believe that this is possible requires a faith in currents larger than any one mind can envision. But that is not such a difficult thing to accept, for as dust owes its path to wind, we, as human beings, are asked to acknowledge that something larger encircles us and prompts us to unfold.

There is a gravity of spirit that pulls the essence of who we are into being. Our job, like all our sister creatures, is to find the abundance of air and water and light, and to unfold what is already within us.

- Sit quietly and imagine your heart is a young leaf, green and tender, wrapped unto itself.
- As you breathe, feel the water of life already in your veins.
- Now, as you breathe, stand and outstretch your arms, and feel who you are unfold.

# APRIL 30
## ONE CONSTANT ARRIVAL

Whether drifting through life on a boat or climbing toward old age leading a horse, each day is a journey and the journey itself is home.

— BASHO

Twelve years ago, as my journey through cancer was beginning, my grandmother was dying. I didn't know I had cancer, but I believe she knew she was dying. I could tell because when I'd visit her in Kingsbrook Medical Center in Brooklyn, she would sit on the edge of her bed and peer off into some distance she alone could see. She was ninety-four, and I had the feeling that she was imagining the other shore the way she did when she was ten, crossing the Atlantic on a crowded steamship that was trudging through the huge waves.

Life for her was one endless immigration, one constant arrival in a new land. Perhaps this is why I am a poet, because immigration is in my blood. Perhaps this is why I understand the world of experience as one vast ocean we never stop crossing, even at death.

I'm asking you to imagine the life of your spirit on earth as such an immigration, as one constant arrival in a new land. Given this, we must accept that no matter the shore before us, the swell and toss of the sea never ends. When brought to the crest of a swell, we can see as far as eternity and the soul has its perspective, but when in the belly of those waves, we are, each of us, for the moment, lost. The life of the soul on Earth has us bobbing on a raft of flesh in and out of view of eternity, and the work of the inner pilgrim is to keep eternity in our heart and mind's eye

236

when dropped in the belly of our days.

- Sit quietly and imagine yourself bobbing safely on the ocean of experience we never stop crossing.
- Breathe deeply and imagine each day is a wave.
- Enter your own rhythms and feel what kind of wave today is.
- If today is cresting, look about you and take in all that you can see of life.
- If today is a belly of a day, acknowledge the hardships you are facing.
- Breathe slowly and remember that another crest is coming. Bring to mind the last rising, remembering what that enabled you to see.

# May 1
## Burying and Planting

---

The culmination of one love, one dream,
one self, is the anonymous seed of the
    next.

There is very little difference between burying and planting. For often, we need to put dead things to rest, so that new life can grow. And further, the thing put to rest — whether it be a loved one, a dream, or a false way of

237

seeing — becomes the fertilizer for the life about to form. As the well-used thing joins with the earth, the old love fertilizes the new; the broken dream fertilizes the dream yet conceived; the painful way of being that strapped us to the world fertilizes the freer inner stance about to unfold.

This is very helpful when considering the many forms of self we inhabit over a lifetime. One self carries us to the extent of its usefulness and dies. We are then forced to put that once beloved skin to rest, to join it with the ground of spirit from which it came, so it may fertilize the next skin of self that will carry us into tomorrow.

There is always grief for what is lost and always surprise at what is to be born. But much of our pain in living comes from wearing a dead and useless skin, refusing to put it to rest, or from burying such things with the intent of hiding them rather than relinquishing them.

For every new way of being, there is a failed attempt mulching beneath the tongue. For every sprig that breaks surface, there is an old stick stirring underground. For every moment of joy sprouting, there is a new moment of struggle taking root.

We live, embrace, and put to rest our dearest things, including how we see ourselves, so we can resurrect our lives anew.

- Try to identify one aspect of your way in the world that has outlived its usefulness — a way of thinking or feeling, of speaking or relating.
- Try to understand why you are still wearing it.
- On loose paper, journal what this outlived aspect is and why you are still wearing it.
- Take the paper and symbolically bury it somewhere special, giving thanks for how this outlived way has helped you to this point in your path.
- Be kind to the new space that burying this has opened in you.
- Water it and keep it in the light.

# MAY 2
## LIVE IN YOUR HANDS

Live in your hands
and your mind will learn
to bow like a root.

Several years ago, while doing a poetry reading in New York City, I encountered an angry young man who had just seen a woman mugged. He was so enraged he wrote a poem on the spot. A pensive voice from across the room called out, "Yeah, it sure beats stopping the mugging." I felt like there was nothing left to say. The story points up, painfully, how living in our thoughts removes us from the very real journey of being alive. To always analyze and problem solve and observe and criticize what we encounter turns our brains into heavy calluses. Rather than opening us deeper into the mystery of living, the over-trained intellect becomes a buffer from experience.

I have a dear friend who has studied almost all there is to study about the heart and the mind and its dance of psychology. This study led her to a very old sage whose last instructions were, "Live in your hands." Once open to this, my dear friend — knowing nothing about stonework — found herself building a stone chapel in the side of a hill. In so doing, she consecrated the chapel that had been waiting in her heart.

I have another friend who, whenever she sees flowers, must gently touch them. I've watched her countless times finger yellow petals. She needs to touch the beauty, and when she does, I can see the beauty touch her. Then something in her opens a little further.

To live in our hands humbles our mind into accepting something other than itself. It is how we heal each other and ourselves. We all come alive through a Braille of heart.

- Choose something small and delicate that fascinates you, and place it before you as you meditate.
- After a time, slowly take it in your hands and carefully examine it with your fingers, feeling its many surfaces.
- Breathe steadily and take the essence of this delicate thing into your mind through your hands.

# MAY 3
## OUR MALE AND FEMALE ENERGIES

As it does no good to harvest if we can't
   eat,
it does no good to act if we can't feel.

There is so much talk these days of masculine and feminine energies and how we've been taught to be one-sided in how we engage the world. I believe most of it to be true. When we are dominated by our male side (overrational and stoic, never showing our feelings), our feminine side (our deeper creative, receptive energies) becomes strident and stifled, explosive when finally allowed to surface.

Not surprisingly, those who are contained

and guarded — male or female — are somewhat frightened by those who are intuitive and expressive; just as those who are more readily impacted by what they feel find the unexpressive quite suffocating. Of course, we find each other, and the stoics grow nervous, while the passionate sweat more. This is part of life: we find each other and pull. The spinning ever want the still to spin. The quiet hush the drums. The crazed are ever fated to entice statues to dance.

We also struggle with these energies inside ourselves. My own experience has been quite telling. As a man who has always been quite active and decisive, I have also, as a poet, been deeply guided by the feminine, directed inwardly by the intuitive life of feeling. But clearly, in the outer world, I was well schooled in being practical, taught never to linger in my feelings long.

It is only after ten years of surviving cancer and a life of overachievement that I have stumbled in and out of joy. In becoming more integrated, more a single wave of masculine and feminine, I can see that I am learning to use my male energies differently, more in concert with my feminine.

Where I was taught to understand and name things, I now experience and feel things. Where I was taught to frame and articulate things at arm's length, I now embrace and absorb what is before me. This

242

framing and naming at arm's length is part of how we have all been encased since childhood in a masculine way of seeing that, out of balance, is dry and uninformed by any passion for life.

The difference is between painting a bird and flying, between understanding the secret positions of love and feeling your heart pound. Too often, under the guise of being asked to be prepared and mature, we are seduced into watching over living, into naming over feeling, into understanding over experiencing. Yet, as two hands cup water to the mouth, we need both male and female energies to drink fully of this life.

- Center yourself and breathe slowly.
- Place one hand before you, palm up, and meditate on all this hand contains — nerves, blood, memory, the power to lift and touch. Meditate on how complete this hand is unto itself.
- Place your other hand before you now, palm up, and meditate on all that it contains and how complete it is unto itself.
- Breathe deeply and bring both of your hands together, and meditate on how much more is possible when both completenesses work together.

243

# MAY 4
## FILLING IN THE DAY

I'm late! I'm late. For a very important date!
No time to say hello! Good-bye!
I'm late! I'm late! I'm late!
> — THE MAD HATTER,
> FROM *ALICE IN WONDERLAND*

I wake clear and rested, light flooding my room. The day seems endless and free. But making coffee, I notice three bills I haven't paid, and after showering, I notice I need a haircut, and since I'll be out that way, I think I might as well pick up my shirts. But I so want to spend time in the sun. So I think, well, after these errands, I'll go to the park, and then I deliberate which park will be just right and decide on one forty minutes away. Finally, wanting to make sure there is some fun in all of this, I call a friend and plan to meet her at a movie at six.

Now I have to hurry along to make sure I can get everywhere on time. But, thankfully, while gassing up, I hear a small bird and lift my head just as a cloud opens and the light floods my mind, and I drop all my plans like change on the ground.

I laugh at myself. I can so easily become a slave to a schedule I create. Not one of these

244

things is necessary today. I drop everything and follow the bird.

- Bring to mind all you have to do today. Feel it crowd you.
- Center yourself and inhale each task slowly and exhale each urgency.
- Rise and enter this day as if it is your first and your last.
- Now drop all that is not necessary.

# MAY 5
## OUR ESSENTIAL CLEARNESS

Like clouds moving in water,
problems make me forget
I am clear.

Water reflects everything it encounters. This is so commonplace that we think water is blue, when, in fact, it has no color. Amazingly, while soft and flowing, water — as ocean or lake or even as the smallest puddle of rain — takes on the image of the entire world without ever losing its essential clearness.

Of course, it is not so easy for us. As emotional beings, we are constantly losing ourselves in the image of everything we experience. But, nonetheless, the nature of water can help us understand our very human struggles.

I began, like so many of us, in a household where it was somehow my job to be the lightning rod for the family's tensions of unexpressed emotion. In this way, I learned to be a problem solver, a rescuer, a caretaker. Through two marriages and countless friendships, I loved by taking on the clouded emotions of those I loved.

The tension of other people's unexpressed emotions kept me from feeling my own depth and clarity. My life became one of turbulence, always struggling to keep my head above the cloudy surface.

But the water, the glorious water everywhere, has taught me that we are more than what we reflect or love. This is the work of compassion: to embrace everything clearly without imposing who we are and without losing who we are.

It is, to be sure, an endless and impossible task. But, though we can never be as clear as water, it helps to remember that while the very real problems we face are the living things we must handle, they are not the essential current of our lives. Beneath the clouds, water desires only to flow, and beneath our tensions and problems, the human spirit wants only to embrace and soften.

- The next time a loved one voices frus-

tration, disappointment, or pain, notice your reaction.
- Are you problem solving or accepting what they are saying?
- Are you trying to cheer them up or bear witness to their experience?
- Are you left holding their pain or deepened for what is shared?
- If you can, receive this pain as if it were a stone dropped into the clear moving depth of who you are.

# MAY 6
## TWIG AND NEST

I think I could turn and live with animals.
They do not sweat and whine about their
condition. Not one is dissatisfied.
— WALT WHITMAN

It was a very small thing, watching a robin carry a twig too big for its nest. It tried once, then twice, to use it, and somehow, with its very small bird brain, it knew it was no good. It simply flew off and picked another.

I went and found the twig. There wasn't a mark on it. I rolled it in my hand and thought of all the times I've labored, trying to make things too big fit. So often what we want is like that twig, too big to be of use, and we stay lodged in an unhappiness created by holding on to something that can't complete our nest.

It was humbling to watch a small bird work, singing as it went, leaving what it couldn't use as it found it. If we could only treat each other with such simple kindness.

- Meditate on your life as a nest that needs to be put together.
- Consider what you are after, what you are carrying — like a stubborn bird — that is too big to be of use.
- Can you put your life together more thoroughly by taking up some smaller version of what you need, something that fits?

# MAY 7
## THE ORDINARY ART

Before fixing what you're looking at,
check what you're looking through.

It was a beautiful sun-filled day. I had driven 300 miles to see her. She was ninety-four and had been in one room for close to eight months. I was her first-born grandson and she was so happy to see me. But after catching up, we sat in silence on the edge of her

248

bed, and finally, she complained how gray a day it was.

I realized then that her one window hadn't been cleaned in almost a year. When I said this, she chuckled, as only someone ninety-four can, and uttered with her Russian accent, "Got a dirty eye, see a dirty world."

It is the same with our minds and hearts. For our very self is the one window we have into this life. And so often, we suffer the mood of a dirty window, believing the brilliant world gray.

Perhaps the purpose of authentic relationship is to help each other keep our minds and hearts clear. Perhaps inner work is the ordinary art of window washing, so that the day is fully the day.

- Sit quietly until you feel centered.
- Now use your breath to wash the ideas from your mind.
- Breathe evenly and wash the film from your heart.
- Breathe deeply and wash the conclusions from your eyes.

# MAY 8
## THE ISSUE OF FAIRNESS

> As long as we see what has come to pass
> as being unfair, we'll be a prisoner of
> what might have been.

This is a very painful issue to discuss for most of us, because so much of how we see the world hinges on a sense of fairness and justice, those truly noble human concepts that govern how we treat each other.

But the laws of experience in the natural world, in which we have no choice but to live, do not work this way. Rather, the larger Universe, of which humankind is a small part, is a world of endless possibility and endless cycle, a world in which life forms come and go, a world itself that has erupted and reformed countless times.

This is why the Hindu tradition has a deity known as Vishnu, who both destroys and bestows life, often in that order. Although fairness and justice are beautiful gravities by which we as human creatures try to live with one another, the storm and the germ, the termites eating the foundation of your home, the errant stone breaking your windshield, the wave swamping your little boat — these molecules of experience do not understand

250

what is fair. They just bombard us in the endless cosmic dance of life that just keeps happening.

When I was struggling with cancer, I was asked repeatedly to release my anger at the injustice of having cancer. Quite honestly, I felt a great many things — fear, pain, anxiety, frustration, uncertainty, exhaustion — but I did not feel that having cancer was unjust. When was I or anyone promised perfect health? An ant can struggle for yards with food in its mouth only to have a dead limb tired of hanging on crush it. What makes human beings presume to be exempt from such things?

I know now that, over the years, my own cries that life is unfair have come from the inescapable pain of living, and these cries, while understandable, have always diverted me from feeling my way through the pain of my breakage into the re-formation of my life. Somehow, crying "Unfair" has always kept me stuck in what hurts.

I offer what has surprised me in my pain: that life is not fair, but unending in its capacity to change us; that compassion is fair and feeling is just; and that we are not responsible for all that befalls us, only for how we receive it and for how we hold each other up along the way.

• Sit outside, if possible, and watch the

pollen carried on the wind. Meditate on how some of these pollen grains will become flowers, and how those flowers will wilt and seed other flowers yet to be.

- Meditate on how the human drama with all its unknown turn of events unfolds in much the same way.
- Breathe deeply and look at the many dreams and mistakes and joys and pains of your life as pollen on a larger wind. Some will grow. Some will not.
- Do not deny your pain in experiencing life, but try not to heighten the hurt by labeling it tragic or unfair.
- Try to hold the pain of your changes with compassion rather than justice.

# May 9
# The Fear of What Is Different

To direct the mind towards the basic unity of all things and to divert it from the seizing of differences — therein lies bliss.
— Tejo-bindu Upanishad

The eye can see what we have in common or focus on what keeps us apart. And the heart

252

can feel what joins us with everything or replay its many cuts. And the tongue can praise the wind or warn against the storm, can praise the sea or dread the flood.

It's not that there are no differences — the world is made of infinite variety — rather it is the seizing of differences, the fearing of differences, that keeps us from feeling grace.

Paradoxically, everything in life touches the same center through its uniqueness, the way no two souls are the same, though every soul breathes the same air.

When we fall into the illusion that one creation is better than another, we remove ourselves from the miracle of being and enter what the sixth-century sage Seng-Ts'an called the mind's worst disease: the endless deciding between want and don't want, the endless war between for and against.

- Light a candle and sit quietly before a window.
- Relax your heart and breathe deeply.
- Notice the many different things that come into view: trees, wind, clouds, the rattle of the window, people walking.
- Notice the candle and the quiet flame rising from it.
- Breathe calmly and imagine the same quiet flame rising within the heart of everything you see.

253

# MAY 10
## THE EDGE OF CENTER

All tempest has,
like a navel,
a hole in its middle,
through which
a gull can fly,
in silence.
— FOURTEENTH-CENTURY JAPANESE,
ANONYMOUS

From across the centuries, this nameless voice tells us that at the heart of all struggle there is a peaceful enduring center, if we can only reach it. All the wisdom traditions affirm this.

Still, a deeper paradox of life is carried here. For the gull flies through the peaceful center; it does not live there. The work, it seems, for us is to draw sustenance from that central, eternal space without denying the experience of the storm.

Repeatedly, we are thrown into the storm and into the center. When in the storm, we are exacerbated by our humanness. When in the center, we are relieved by our spiritual place in the Oneness of things. So to find the center and spread our battered wings is to feel the God within.

254

Our constant struggle is in living both sides of this paradox. For we cannot get to the center without going through the storm that surrounds it. Yet the storm of human experience can only be endured by knowing what the gull knows. The storm can only be survived from the center. In how we pass each other from storm to center and back — there you'll find the trials and gifts of love.

- Close your eyes and let your inhalation call the gull of your spirit to your center.
- Inhale deeply and let your breath call the gull home through your center to the center of All.
- Exhale deeply and feel the edge of storm and the edge of center.
- Know that your breath is the edge.

# MAY 11
## TO SPEAK AND EMBRACE

The dream is awakened when thinking
I love you, and life begins
when saying I love you,
and joy moves like blood
when embracing someone with love.

Though life sometimes begins in the head, the full body of joy cannot be known there.

We all have experienced this difference. Simply recall the first time in adolescence that some other stirred you, the first time the presence of another moved you from being the center of the Universe. Recall the strange but moving sense swimming in your head, leaving you unable to extinguish his or her face from your mind. Like a flicker given air, recall how the real and troubled life of flame began as soon as a word was spoken.

It is the same with how we dream or love ourselves or struggle with our belief in God. Kept swimming in the head, life flickers, never setting us aflame. It has taken a lifetime to learn this. As the fire of music awakens the soul of a composer, love sounds within us where no one else can hear. And just as composers must wrestle out the language by which their songs can be played, we must struggle to pronounce our love. All to have our arms rise like flames off the page.

It is a difficult challenge: to speak and embrace in a world that so thoroughly trains the mind. Yet trouble intensifies if not given air. As we live out our days, the imperceptible breath between thinking and saying, and saying and embracing, can often seem like a canyon, impossible to cross. This is why we have invoked the myth of Cupid for centuries, to remind us of that fluttering presence that somehow pierces our confinement of thinking, forcing us to speak and embrace.

We each carry the bow within us, and while the arrow hurts, our casing of thought is broken, forcing us to tremble. Yes, it is true. I confess: I have thought great thoughts and sung great songs — all of it rehearsal for the majesty of being held.

- Meditate while holding a stone and invite the presence of everything larger than you.
- Breathe slowly and let this presence shape your thoughts.
- Breathe deeply and let this presence now wrapped in thought vibrate in your throat.
- With one word, name this presence. Pronounce it out loud.
- Practice embodiment by feeling the presence of the Universe in both you and the stone as you think and pronounce and touch — all at once.

# MAY 12
## BEING DIRECT

Everyone's bald underneath their hair.
— SUSAN MCHENRY

We waste so much energy trying to cover up who we are, when beneath every attitude is the want to be loved, and beneath every anger is a wound to be healed, and beneath every sadness is the fear that there will not be enough time.

When we hesitate in being direct, we un-knowingly slip something on, some added layer of protection that keeps us from feeling the world, and often that thin covering is the beginning of a loneliness which, if not put down, diminishes our chances for joy.

It's like wearing gloves every time we touch something, and then, forgetting we chose to put them on, we complain that nothing feels quite real. In this way, our challenge each day is not to get dressed to face the world, but to unglove ourselves so that the doorknob feels cold, and the car handle feels wet, and the kiss good-bye feels like the lips of another be-ing, soft and unrepeatable.

- As you breathe, let each breath undress your being — of attitude, of mood, of history.
- As you breathe, feel your skin beneath your clothes.
- As you breathe, feel your being just beneath your skin.

# MAY 13
## FEELING OUR WAY THROUGH

Underneath, there is only one emotion.

I used to struggle, fighting off sadness or trying not to be anxious, but as most of us learn,
once that drop of melancholy or unrest beads
on the heart, trying to feel anything else is
denial. Once the mind like a long guitar string
is somehow plucked with the slightest agitation, there is nothing to do but let it ring itself
out.

We all know of the tears that turn to
laughter. Or the laughing that breaks open to
a cry. Or the anger that crumbles into a
tender loneliness. Or the cool face of indifference that cracks, eventually showing its
adhesive of fear. Amazingly, as the infinite
forms of flowers all rise from the same earth,
the earthly garden of emotions — in all their
delicate shapes and colors — all rise from the
same earth of heart.

What this opens for us is the often hard-to-
accept fact that underneath there is only one
unnamable emotion, which all feelings know
as home. Despite our efforts to be happy and
not sad, to be calm and not anxious, to be
clear and not confused, to be understanding
and not angry; despite all the ways we carve

259

up our reactions to living and then run from one to the other; despite our fear of certain feelings, it is feeling each of them all the way through that lands us in the vibrant ache that underrides our being alive. To reach this vibrant place is often healing.

It is a hard thing, though, to lean into a sadness we don't want, to let the tremor of anxiety work its way through. For myself, my resistance to unpleasant feelings has been my fear that if I give over to the sadness or anxiety or confusion or pain that is upon me, I will drown in it. I fear it will take over my life. I will become nothing but sadness or anxiety or confusion.

But what I discover, again and again, is that feeling any one feeling deeply enough — that is, thoroughly and completely — somehow opens me to the common source of all feeling. And at the source, no one feeling can last by itself. So, through our feelings, not around them, we come upon the unnamable source of all feeling that can heal us of the pain of any one mood.

- Breathe steadily and know that you are safe in this reflective space.
- Once comfortable, allow yourself to feel one moment of sadness or anxiety that you are carrying. Try to stay with the feeling until it begins to pass. Note the lessening of your sadness or anxiety,

however slight, and call this the beginning of peace.

# MAY 14
# A GAME OF SEE-SAW

*The greatest defense is being who you are.*

How often we are drawn into opposition with one another. Certainly, there are times that conflict is inevitable. There is only one parking space. There is only one donut left. There is only one job in view.

But most of the time, on the inner plane, there is plenty to go around, and it is more a game of see-saw: to keep myself up, or to keep my sense of how I see myself up, I somehow feel the need to put you down.

This only diverts me from my path and sucks all my energy into a battle that often doesn't matter. In truth, no amount of rearranging the world will make us feel worthy. The only response to adversity or misunderstanding is to be more completely who we are — to share ourselves more. Otherwise, we are always reacting and countering, and never being.

Just look to the flowers and trees. They do not suppress each other. Even when crowded, they show themselves and grow in all directions and so make it to the light.

- Sit quietly and consider someone who holds a position opposite to yours.
- Breathe evenly and allow yourself to feel the pull to discredit or invalidate this person and their position.
- Now breathe slowly and look for the string of heart that makes you think your opposite views are tied to each other.
- Use your deepest breathing to cut the string.

# MAY 15
## THE RISK TO BLOOM

And then the day came
when the risk to remain
tight in a bud was
more painful than the
risk to bloom.

— ANAÏS NIN

We all face this turning point repeatedly: when resisting the flow of inner events suddenly feels more hurtful than leaping toward the unknown. Yet no one can tell us when to leap. There is no authority to bless our need to enter life but the God within.

How often we thwart ourselves by holding tenaciously to what is familiar. It is instructive, if chilling, that in floral shops the roses that won't open are called bullets. They are discarded because they will never bloom. They have turned in on themselves so tightly that they can never release their fragrance.

Yet as spirits in bodily form, we have the chance to tighten and bloom more than once. But even spirits, if turned in on themselves enough, may grow accustomed to being closed. Unlike roses, however, the human chamber can be shut down for years, and still, it takes but one breath from the true center and we will flower.

It has always amazed and humbled me how the risk to bloom can seem so insurmountable beforehand and so inevitably freeing once the threshold of suffering is crossed.

I have a friend in recovery, and when asked what made him stop drinking, he says, "The pain of drinking became greater than the pain of not drinking." The same can be said for us all. We can flower in an instant, as soon as the pain of not flowering and not loving become greater than our fear.

- Try to identify what scares you most about being who you are in the world.
- As you meditate, imagine the God in you warming your fears open.
- Note what it feels like to have your

263

center safely exposed, even for a moment.
- Without telling anyone, imagine this
moment of opening sometime during
your day: at your desk, on the bus, in
line at the supermarket.
- Note what it feels like to have your
center safely exposed, even for a moment, in the presence of others.
- Repeat this meditation whenever you
start to feel your sense of things tighten.

# May 16
## Not Needing Approval

There are a thousand ways
to kneel and kiss the ground.

— Rumi

I have a young friend who speaks of the time
when he reads stories with his daughter as a
time that needs no confirmation. There is
wisdom in his phrase: a time that needs no
confirmation. We all need to touch down with
the source of life, again and again, in order to
brighten enough to continue. Whether we
make our way in by playing or listening to
music, by meditating, by painting, or loving,
or reading stories to our children, or to our
friends' children, or to ourselves — when we

close our minds like tired eyes and surrender our hearts like mouths thirsted open, we come upon a common source where nothing need be approved or accepted, where no rejection or criticism need be overcome. The experience itself is all the authority we need.

Interestingly, these renewing moments open precisely when we forget about ourselves. Like horses with blinders we can't quite shake, we sniff out our way until we come upon these deep pools to drink from. And for the moment, we are saved.

In truth, we drink from this great paradox daily: though everyone alive shares this moment we are living right now, no one experiences this moment more directly than you. No one can say what it feels like for you to be alive but you. No one needs permission to be alive, to stay alive, to know the joy of touching your unrepeatable hand to the earth.

- Walk beneath a tree and after centering yourself, look up.
- As you breathe, feel the solid burst of the tree up from the earth showering into its leaves.
- The tree grows with no one's consent, with no one's applause.
- Touch the tree, and as you breathe slowly, learn from the tree.

# May 17
## Chasing the Butterfly

In release, we begin.

Once when I was six, I chased a butterfly halfway through the reservoir before cupping it in my boyish hands. I had the beautiful thing, but couldn't see it. To see it, I had to let it go. I kept my hands cupped as long as I could, past nose itch and leg jiggle, and then the dark flitting against my palms made me open and magnificent plates of color lifted against my will.

It was too delicate a story to tell over dinner, and soon there were books and assignments and model cars to glue and arguments and anger, and I forgot there ever was a butterfly. It's only now, some forty years later, that it awakens in me like a revelation placed in the hands of a pilgrim long before he knew enough to believe. Now chasing the butterfly seems a way of life: afraid to lose or be left out, we chase and cling, and clinging, we are lost. It seems so obvious once living it.

Now I can see that during my illness, this was the difference between fear and faith, between terror and the presence of God. Landing in a hospital bed, I chased the beat of everything I faced into my heart and tried to cup it in my boyish hands, burying my head. Of course, I had the beautiful thing beating like that butterfly, now trapped inside me. As long as I kept all of that beauty and power of raw life cupped — in my chest, in my face, in my hands — I couldn't see it. To see it, I had to let it go.

Just as when a boy, I held it as long as I could, until the pounding made me open and this magnificent sense of life lifted out of me against my will. I now know that what I held so tightly within was the presence of God, which held in felt like pain and fear and terror.

Over forty years to learn this vital lesson: that the deepest things beat within, made dark and fearful by our holding, only uplifting the instant we let go.

- Sit quietly and meditate on a particular pain or fear that beats within you.
- Cup your hands on your chest about your heart.
- Feel that pain or fear beating in your chest like a butterfly, like a small thing of beauty waiting to be released.
- As you breathe, open your hands and let it go.
- Let it rise out of you into the open.
- Note how it feels once you stop holding onto it.

# MAY 18
## FRIENDSHIP

Nothing among human things
has such power to keep our gaze
fixed ever more intensely upon God
than friendship.

— SIMONE WEIL

I have been blessed to have deep friends in my time on Earth. They have been an oasis when my life has turned a desert. They have been a cool river to plunge in when my heart has been on fire. When I was ill, one toweled my head when I couldn't stand without bleeding. Another bowed at my door saying, "I will be whatever you need as long as you need it."

Still others have ensured my freedom, and they missed me while I searched for bits of truth that only led me back to them. I have slept in the high lonely wind waiting for God's word. And while it's true — no one can live for you — singing from the peak isn't quite the same as whispering in the center of a circle that has carried you ashore.

Honest friends are doorways to our souls, and loving friends are the grasses that soften the world. It is no mistake that the German root of the word *friendship* means "place of high safety." This safety opens us to God. As Cicero said, "A friend is a second self." And as Sant Martin said, "My friends are the beings through whom God loves me."

There can be no greater or simpler ambition than to be a friend.

- Center yourself and open your heart to the unnamable place of high safety.
- After a time, look around in your heart and see who is there.
- Breathe gently and give thanks for the true friends you have.

# MAY 19
## THE BEE COMES

The flower doesn't dream of the bee.
It blossoms and the bee comes.

At times in my life, I have wanted love so badly that I have reimagined myself, reinvented who I am, in an attempt to be more desirable or more deserving, only to discover, again and again, that it is the tending of my own soul that invites the natural process of love to begin.

I remember my very first tumble into love. I found such comfort there that, like Narcissus, I became lost in how everything other

269

than my pain was reflected in her beauty. All the while, I was abdicating my own worth, empowering her as the key to my sense of joy.

If I have learned anything through the years, it is that, though we discover and experience joy with others, our capacity for joy is carried like a pod of nectar in our very own breast. I now believe that our deepest vocation is to root ourselves enough in this life that we can open our hearts to the light of experience, and so, bloom. For in blooming, we attract others; in being so thoroughly who we are, an inner fragrance is released that calls others to eat of our nectar. And we are loved, by friends and partners alike.

It seems the very job of being is to ready us for such love. By attending our own inner growth, we uncannily become exactly who we are, and like the tulip whose blossomed petal is the exact shape of the bee, our self-actualization attracts a host of loving others more real than all our fantasies. In this way, the Universe continues through the unexpected coming together of blossomed souls.

So, if you can, give up the want of another and be who you are, and more often than not, love will come at the precise moment you are simply loving yourself.

- Identify one trait that makes you feel good about who you are: your laugh, your smile, your ability to listen, or the sound of your voice.

- The next time you exhibit this goodness, notice how who you are affects others.
- These small moments are the beginnings of love. They do not yet have definition.
- Take a moment and give thanks for your small goodness and for the potential love of others.

# MAY 20
## BREAKING PATTERNS

If I contradict myself, I contradict myself.
I contain multitudes.
— WALT WHITMAN

We create patterns that others depend on, and then the last thing we ever imagined happens: we grow and change, and then to stay vital we must break the patterns we created.

There is no blame or fault in this. It is commonplace in nature. Watch the ocean and shore do their dance of buildup and crumble and you'll see this happen daily.

We know we are close to this threshold when we hear someone say, "You're not yourself," or "That was out of character for you." What is difficult at this juncture is to resist either complying with how others see us or withholding who we really are.

The challenge, which I don't do well but stay committed to, is to say to those we love, "I am more than I have shown you and more than you are willing to see. Let's work our love and know each other more fully."

- This is an awareness meditation. As you move through your interactions today, notice whether you are complying with how others see you or withholding who you are.
- After each interaction, simply breathe slowly once or twice and return to the fullness of who you are.

# MAY 21
# WHEN CUT IN TWO

The cut worm forgives the plow.
— WILLIAM BLAKE

The worm is one of the only creatures that grows from being cut. Mysteriously, if you cut a worm in two, each cut half becomes whole, and you have two worms.

What is it in how the worm lives that allows it to grow from its pain, and how might we translate that to being human? Well, without looking too far, the worm is completely in touch with the earth. In fact, it eats earth. It lives in humus — soil — inside and out.

Perhaps the secret to growing from our wounds is to live close to the earth, to live with our hearts and minds and bellies always in touch — both inside and out — with that which is larger than we are.

Perhaps, when cut in two, it is a life of humility, of risking to be at one with the soil of our experience, that allows us to heal into something entirely new.

- Center yourself and meditate with kindness on a place where you feel cut in two.
- Inhale deeply, and bring the Universal air to this raw and tender place.
- Inhale thoroughly, and let the elements infuse your wound with the atoms of a new beginning.

# MAY 22
# FEELING BEYOND THE HURT

Withstanding the tension between opposites until we know it is "enough" releases us from the swing between one extreme and the other.

— HELEN LUKE

Sometimes, when I think of my parents, who have hurt me, I am lulled by a wintering sky to feel for them, to try on their view, but in my empathy an old pattern kicks in and I start to lose the truth of my hurt, as if there's only room for one set of feelings — theirs.

The struggle is a common one. So often we feel for others and lose ourselves, or cut others off to preserve ourselves. Like a radio that can only tune to one station at a time, it seems like only one side of things can be received, though all sides are broadcast.

But compassion is a deeper thing that waits beyond the tension of choosing sides. Compassion, in practice, does not require us to give up the truth of what we feel or the truth of our reality. Nor does it allow us to minimize the humanity of those who hurt us. Rather, we are asked to know ourselves enough that we can stay open to the truth of others, even when their truth or their inability to live up to their truth has hurt us.

This does not remove the emotional facts of our lives, nor does it ask us to remain in a hurtful situation. Rather, compassion asks that we open like mountains to the sky, like mountains that can withstand every kind of weather.

- Sit quietly and bring to mind someone you are at odds with.
- Breathe deeply and allow the truth of your feelings, not just the truth of your position, to rise.
- Breathe evenly and allow the other's person's feelings, not just their position, to rise.
- Let your breathing ease any tension in you that either undermines yourself or undermines this other.

# MAY 23
## TO BE AWAKE

There is always purpose in being,
but not always being in purpose.

How easily we get caught up in defining who we are in relation to those around us. I remember walking home from school in fourth grade, when I noticed Roy, a classmate I didn't really like, walking at the same pace as me on the other side of the street. Until I noticed Roy, I was lost in the joy of walking home, free of school, not yet enmeshed in the anger that waited inside my house. But once seeing Roy, I began, without a word, to walk faster, to try to outwalk him. He, of course, sensed this immediately and picked

275

up his gait. As he strode ahead of me, I felt lacking and so stepped up my gait. Before I knew it, we were both racing to the corner, and I felt that if I didn't get there first, I would be a terrible failure.

I have lived enough in the world to know by now that this is how our ambitions often evolve. We first find ourselves alone in the joy of what we're doing. But somehow, there are suddenly others along the way, and we lapse into the breathless race of comparison, and then we are hopelessly running to avoid being termed a failure.

From here, we often latch onto the nearest goal as a purpose; if we can' t find one nearby, we are thought to be adrift. But our lasting sense of purpose is in our breathing, in our being. As the humanitarian Carol Hegedus reminds us, "Our purpose is that which we most passionately are when we pay attention to our deepest selves."

So underneath all our worries about careers and jobs and retirements, our purpose really comes down to living fully, to being alight with who we are beneath all the names and titles we are given or aspire to.

Imagine Buddha in his moment of enlightenment, of being lighted from within. I doubt if he knew he was aglow. In fact, when Buddha rose from under the Bodhi tree, it is said a monk approached him in utter amazement at his luminosity and asked, "O Holy One, what are you? You must be a God."

Buddha, not thinking of himself as anything but present, answered, "No . . . not a God," and kept walking.

But the dazzled monk persisted, "Then you must be a Deva," and Buddha stopped and said, "No . . . not a Deva," and kept walking.

Still, the monk pursued him, "Then you must be Brahma himself!"

At this, Buddha simply uttered, "No."

The monk, confused, implored, "Then what are you — Tell me, please — what are you?!"

Buddha could not repress his joy and replied, "I am awake."

Can it be that our purpose, no matter whom we run into, no matter what we are told, is simply to be awake?

- Sit quietly and meditate on the things that have come to define you.
- Feel what you do with your days and say, "I am more than my job."
- Feel where you sleep your nights and say, "I am more than where I live."
- Feel who you love and say, "I am more than my relationships."
- Feel all you have suffered and say, "I am more than my history."
- Feel your very name and say, "I am more than my name."
- Feel your breath enter and leave your

277

heart and say, without history or name, "I am the flame of life living in this body."

# MAY 24
## BLOOD REASONS

If you don't know the kind of person I am
and I don't know the kind of person you
   are
a pattern that others made may prevail in
the world and following the wrong god
home, we may miss our star.
— WILLIAM STAFFORD

Like that old saying, "Water fills a hole," the ways of others will fill the space we live in if we don't fill that space with our own authentic presence. For a long time, I thought that keeping who I am to myself was the same thing as being myself quietly. I discovered it is not.

Not that we have to verbalize or shout everything, but we do need to be fully here the way a cliff accepts a wave, the way a stem of clover grows into the one patch of light left in the forest, the way corn sweats its sweet moisture when no one is looking.

In truth, there are always two blood reasons to be who we are. It is how we find love, and

278

it is how we keep the ways of others from sweeping us away.

- This is a walking meditation. During your day, take a slow five-minute walk.
- As you walk, notice the air in the wind move about you and meet it fully with your face.
- As you return to your day, consider how you can meet the wind of others with your heart.

# May 25
## Through the Wall of Flame

As a frightened man in a burning boat
has only one way to the rest of his life,
we must move with courage
through the wall of flame
into the greater sea.

Living long enough, we each find ourselves surrounded by an old way of being, thinking, or loving that is going up in flames. In that unexpected moment, we usually find ourselves full of fear, feeling trapped by an old way of life coming in on us. But this is the passage of rebirth that we must move through if our lives are to unfold. It is the momentary and painful crossing from what is old into

279

what is new.

It is understandable to stall at the wall of flame, not wanting to face all that is burning around us. Yet old ways can burn forever, and waiting for the flames to go out seldom works. We can waste years in the waiting.

Like the frightened man in the burning boat, we must trust that the greater sea we are jumping into will douse whatever catches fire as we move through. This is what faith is all about.

Without trying to be brave and with great fear, I have stumbled and jumped through many walls of flame. The first time, I think, was in leaving home — needing to go, burning at the edge, afraid I wouldn't survive beyond the flame of anger in which I was raised. Not much later, I had to move through the flames of first-love rejection. Here the broken part of me was almost willing to be burned alive. I felt certain there was nowhere to go and nothing that could soothe me. I more fell through this wall than jumped and, of course, once in the sea of life beyond myself, the world continued and I healed.

Perhaps the greatest wall of flame I had to jump through was the pain of cancer and the prospect of dying. It seemed the entire sea was on fire. Even once overboard, drifting farther and farther from the flames, I thought I might drown. How could I know that greater sea was the womb of a deeper life?

I'm sure this is the same for anyone struggling to break out of any form of addiction, illness, or abusive relationship.

But the subtlest ring of fire, it seems, is that self-centered way of thinking that starts to suffocate us with its smoke. For we carry the smoldering of being self-centered everywhere we go. It lives off us and eats up who we are. So, how to jump from the burning boat that is us? Well, it somehow requires jumping from the boat of the ego into the sea of our spirit. This somehow involves the courage to surrender our stubbornness and dreams of control. It means letting the ribs of the ego burn. And jumping through. We will more than survive — we will be carried to an unimagined shore.

- Center yourself and mediate on one way of being, thinking, or loving that stands between you and the fullness of life. It might be a hiddenness you bear. Or a critical/blaming nature you suffer. Or a fear of your own feelings.
- Breathe deeply and imagine what moving through this old way might ask of you. It might be as simple as giving yourself permission to be spontaneous. Or giving yourself permission to break your own routines.
- Breathe slowly and picture yourself moving through the wall of flame burn-

ing about you.
- Breathe steadily and practice making the leap by picturing this again and again.

# MAY 26
## BEING SAD

---

The best thing for being sad, replied
Merlin, is to learn something.
— T. H. WHITE

The idea here is not to divert the sadness, but to give it a context from life other than what is making you sad. Just as ginger can lose its bitterness when baked in bread, sadness can be leavened by other life.

When feeling the sharpness of being sad or hurt, it helps to take new things in. This pours the water of life on the fire of the heart.

So when exhausted from expressing all that hurt, listen to music you've never heard of, or ask someone to tell you an old story from before your birth, or take a drive down a road near a ridge you've always meant to look out from.

Look with your sad eyes on things new to you that will give you something to do with your sadness. Your sadness is the paint. You must find a canvas.

- Sit quietly and breathe evenly and let your sadness rise gently.
- Breathe cleanly and let the things around you that are not sad teach you something.
- Just breathe, and let the chair teach you about wood, let the wall teach you about being bare, let the window teach you how to let light in.

# MAY 27
# OFF THE MERRY-GO-ROUND

No amount of thinking can stop thinking.

Overthinking is an annoying reflex of being human. Often in overanalyzing a problem or replaying what to say or what to do, I feel like a cow shooing a fly that will never go away.

We all do this. No one is exempt. Feeling insecure, I can endlessly repeat the things that should make me feel solid about myself, and all the while my esteem keeps unraveling.

What is there to do? I'm reminded of Einstein's insight that the manner of thinking that creates a problem cannot be the means by which to solve it. In simple terms, when spinning out, the only thing to do, hard as it seems, is to get off the mental merry-go-round.

This is truly the terrain of faith, jumping into the risk to stop in midthought, believing that some deeper knowing will wash over us. In truth, no amount of thinking about yourself will give you confidence, just as no amount of thinking about the sun will warm you, just as no amount of thinking about love will hold you. Confidence and love and the light of the world wait below all the labors of our mind.

- Sit quietly and center yourself.
- Allow your mind to start doing what it does.
- Breathe steadily and with each inbreath, practice stopping your thinking in midthought.
- With each outbreath, practice dropping beneath your thinking into your being.

# MAY 28
## THE RISK OF ATTENTION

For the raindrop,
joy is entering the river.
— THE SUFI PROPHET GHALIB

It is amazing to consider how as infants we

are one with everything. In time, of course, we learn how to distinguish between ourselves and others, between the world we carry inside and the world we move through. But ironically, the sages of all paths are those who, after lifetimes of experience, try to return to this primary state of Oneness.

When I think of the moments I have felt most alive, they all have this quality of joining all-of-what-I-keep-inside with everything-outside-me in a way that makes me forget myself. They all feel timeless and open-ended. Tenderly, the deepest moments of making love allow us to join in that Oneness beyond ourselves, as do certain moments of being immersed in great music or great open spaces. I have also felt this after long periods of swimming or running, or after long periods of being healthfully alone. I feel it when discovering what it is I need to write. Joy, it seems, is the feeling of that Oneness.

Not surprisingly, it is the risk to love — the risk to give our full attention — that lets what-is-eternal-within merge with what-is-eternal-without. In those moments of Oneness, we, as drops of spirit, join the larger river of spirit.

And so, it is the risk to be fully present that opens us to the Oneness that flows through all things, the way a spring brook flows from your acre through my fence, through my land, and on through my neighbor's fence and land. Just as that rush of water ignores all we have built in between, so the wholeness of life moves through us all, undermining all the walls we maintain.

It seems we always have the choice: to remain a builder of fences or to enter the stream that ignores all fences.

- Breathe slowly and meditate on the Oneness of all things.
- Meditate on your breath as the portion of Oneness now flowing through the land of your body.
- As you exhale, let the Oneness, like that spring brook, continue out of you into the life of your neighbor.
- Breathe and realize that in the flow of Oneness, the dearest things move through everything we put in their way.

# MAY 29
# GIVING UP WHAT
# NO LONGER WORKS

Burning your way to center
is the loneliest fire of all.
You'll know you have arrived
when nothing else will burn.

At first this sounds rather somber, but from Moses to Buddha to Jesus, the deepest among us have all shown that living is a process of constantly paring down until we carry only what is essential.

It is the same in the human journey as in the natural world. As the center grows stronger, what once was protective turns into a covering, like tree bark or snake skin, that is now in the way, and, sooner or later, we as spirits growing in bodies are faced with burning old skins, like rags on sticks, to light our way as we move deeper and deeper into the inner world, where the forces of God make us one.

When faced with the need to keep going inward, we are confronted with a very difficult kind of life choice: like carving up your grandmother's table for firewood to keep your loved ones warm, or leaving a job that has been safe and fulfilling in order to feel vital again, or burning an old familiar sense of self because it's gotten so thick you can't feel the rain.

In truth, always needing to stay immediate by removing what is no longer real is the working inner definition of *sacrifice* — giving up with reverence and compassion what no longer works in order to stay close to what is sacred.

- Sit quietly and meditate on the edge of yourself that meets the world. Feel

its thickness.
- As you breathe, feel the inner edge of yourself that meets your spirit. Feel its softness.
- As you breathe, pray for the edge that is you to be as thin as possible and only as thick as necessary.

# MAY 30
# A STRING OF TODAYS

If not now,
when?

Since surviving cancer, there is a burning bit of truth I live with every day. Sometimes it doesn't let me sleep, but most of the time, it brings me great joy. No one uttered this to me, and I didn't arrive at it or work at it. It just revealed itself, the way a broken bone makes us re-feel the immense pressure of air. And this bit of truth is, If not now, when?

It keeps coming down to this: There is no tomorrow, only a string of todays. Still, like most of us, I was somehow taught to dream forward, to fill the future with everything that matters: Someday I will be happy. When I am rich, I will be free. When I find the right person, then I will know love. I will be loving and happy and truthful and genuine then.

But almost dying seared the sense of future from me, and though I expect to live a very long time, though I make plans and look forward to the many things I plan, I have no choice but to dream now.

I start out, as I always have, pouring the best of me into an imagined time yet to be, but then I hear, If not now, when? and the best of me floods back to the only place it truly knows — Now.

This all helps me understand a story about Jesus very differently. I'm thinking of the young, rich merchant who approaches Jesus after his Sermon on the Mount. He admires Jesus so, is truly touched, and wants to join him. So he asks with great sincerity what he needs to do, what arrangements need to be made.

Jesus opens his arms and says, "Come with me now. Drop everything and come."

The young merchant stumbles and cites his many "yes, buts": He can't leave his business so suddenly. He has to leave word. He'll need to gather fresh clothes. How much money should he bring?

With open arms, Jesus simply says one more time, "Come with me now."

How often do we all rehearse this moment, putting off love, truth, joy, and even God, citing our many "Yes, buts" to ourselves, when all we have to do — hard and simple as it is — is to drop everything and Come Now.

- Breathe slowly and meditate on something dear to you that you have been working toward. It might center on being happy, knowing love, finding a partner, or learning how to play music, or how to understand the truth of your experience more deeply.
- Breathe deeply and, for the moment, dream about it now; that is, eliminate the efforts to build it tomorrow.
- For the moment, imagine that whatever portion of this work you are to know or achieve or inhabit can only happen today.
- Inhale deeply and take the energy of everything you've planned and put off back into your life today.
- Rather than feeling overwhelmed with all this, try to let this energy simply fill you as you move through your day.

# MAY 31
# SEEING THROUGH ANOTHER'S EYES

Now, I have no choice but to see with
your eyes, So I am not alone,
so you are not alone.

— YANNIS RITSOS

There is a story of Gandhi that reveals how profound and daring his sense of compassion was. It occurred during one of his famous hunger strikes. A man whose daughter was killed came in anguish, saying to Gandhi that he would stop fighting if the great soul would eat. But Gandhi knew the healing was deeper than just stopping the violence, and so he told the man he would eat only when the tormented father embraced the man who killed his daughter.

It is said that the man collapsed in tears, but did as Gandhi asked, and the larger conflict ended. This is an enormous thing to ask of someone in grief, of someone who has been violated. But beyond the vast courage needed to incorporate this kind of love into our daily lives, Gandhi's request reveals the irrefutable wisdom that only when the broken are healed, no matter what they have done, will we as a people heal.

It is hard to comprehend how this works, yet the mystery of true forgiveness waits in letting go of our ledgers of injustice and retribution in order to regain the feeling in our heart. And so, I am forced to look into my own small life, into my own small and all-consuming pains, and ask, Who am I? Why can't I forgive the wrongs done me? Why can't I, more than forgive, begin to trust again?

291

- Sit quietly, and begin simply by making room in your feelings for other life.
- Now breathe slowly and bring to mind someone you don't understand.
- With each inbreath, let them drift into your heart.
- With each outbreath, try to see with their eyes.

# JUNE 1
## WALKING NORTH

Walk long enough
and we all trade places.

We are always surrounded and carried by the Whole, while we take turns holding and being held, falling and getting up, listening and trying to say what matters. This reminds me of Nur. She too had cancer and was a model of strength, a feisty blessing. I remember when she died. I was so sad. Yet the light was merciless in its beauty that day, forcing me to begin to heal. It made me realize, in those painfully bright hours, that no matter how I turn away, the magnificent light follows, background to my sadness.

It works the other way, too. I have known such moments of complete simplicity that all my problems and limitations seemed, for the moment, to vanish, but they were there, growing like mold in the dark. So I learned that no matter how I lift my heart, my shadow creeps in wait behind, background to my joy.

And when I tried to outrun the fact that I had cancer, it became quite clear that no matter how fast I run, a stillness without thought is where I end. Even when repairing in the quiet of a February afternoon — alone, my ribs all taped — I had to accept that no matter how long I sit, there is a river of motion I must rejoin.

It seems the way of our many lives: wherever we are led, the opposite waits. When I am down, you are up; when you are weak, I am strong. How else to explain that when I can't hold my head up, it always falls in the lap of one who has just opened. How else to understand that when I finally free myself of burden, there is always someone's heavy head landing in my arms.

It's how we grow and heal, again and again, by holding and being held. In my own life, I have been held and dropped, have hurt and soothed others, enough to accept, at last, that the reasons of the heart are leaves in wind. Stand up tall and everything will nest in you.

Yet this is not a complaint. It is as it should be, must be, the way everything natural extends and grows. We all lose and we all gain. Dark crowds the light. Light fills the pain. Living is a conversation with no end, a dance with no steps, a song with no words, a reason too big for any mind.

No matter how we turn or are turned, the magnificence follows. . . .

- This is a walking meditation. Take fifteen minutes during your day and silently walk wherever you are — in the city, in the country, in the parking lot, down the long hall to the one window of light.
- Breathe evenly as you step, feeling your breath in your feet.
- Feel the air that others unknown to you have already breathed.
- Stop in a patch of light, no matter how small. Close your eyes, feel the light on your face, and say to yourself, "This is my home."

# June 2
## Tragedy and Peace

Too many prints in the same place,
because the heart's a narrow path
and our arms its only gate.

At times, so many memories trample my heart that it becomes impossible to know just what I'm feeling and why: my first love laughing in a park whose name I can never recall, my grandmother dying near her dirty bricks in Brooklyn, the dizziness of the Rockies telling me to go back among the living, my ex-wife's shoulders slouching tired in the rain, the old dog I used to live with chasing her tail . . . and a thousand more. . . .

That all the ways we've been touched merge in the ground of who we are is a blessing, a gift of being human. It is what the sages of all traditions have called *peace* — the elusive moment that all things become one. That we can't sort our feelings and memories once the soil of our experience is tilled is the nature of staying alive. That we insist on keeping old wounds alive is our curse.

Yet, as Thich Nhat Hanh reminds us, "Our mind of love may be buried deep under many layers of forgetfulness and suffering." The difference, I'm learning, is in what we focus on. When I focus on the rake of experience and how its fingers dug into me and the many feet that have walked over me, there is no end to the life of my pain. But when I focus on the soil of heart and how it has been turned over, there is no end to the mix of feelings that defy my want to name them.

Tragedy stays alive by feeling what's been

done to us, while peace comes alive by living with the result.

- Center yourself, and as you breathe, feel your heart with its thousand feelings beat within your chest.
- Breathe in a slow rhythm, and let one experience rise that has helped to shape you.
- For the moment, focus on the rake of this experience; focus on the actions you received.
- Now focus on the soil of this experience; focus on the result of being tilled by life.
- Note and feel the difference.

# JUNE 3
## MORE THAN OUR MISTAKES

The buffalo fed on the buffalo grass that was fertilized by their own droppings. This grass had deep roots bound to the earth and was resistant to drought.
— DAVID PEAT

Try as we will, we cannot escape the making of mistakes. But fortunately, the everhumbling cycle of growing strong roots comes from eating what grows from our own shit, from digesting and processing our own humanity. Like the buffalo, we are nourished by what sprouts from our own broken trail. What we trample and leave behind fertilizes what will feed us. No one is exempt.

A pipe falls on a dancer's leg and the dancer must reinvent herself, while the worker who dropped it is driven to volunteer with crippled veterans. A dear friend discovers small bulbous tumors and his tulips begin to speak, and when he dies, his nurse begins a garden. Things come apart and join sometimes faster than we can cope. But we evolve in spite of our limitations, and though we break and make mistakes, we are always mysteriously more than what is broken. Indeed, we somehow grow from the soil of our mistakes. And often in the process, the things we refuse to let go of are somehow forced from our grip.

I have been broken and have failed so many times that my sense of identity has sprouted and peeled like an onion. But because of this, I have lived more than my share of lives and feel both young and old at once, with a sudden heart that cries just to meet the air. Now, on the other side of all I've suffered so far, everything, from the quick song of birds to the peace trapped inside a fresh brook's gurgle, is rare and uncertain. Now I want to stand naked before every wind; and though I'm still frightened I will break, I somehow know it's all a part — even the fright — of the rhythm of being alive.

You see, no one ever told me that as snakes shed skin, as trees snap bark, the human heart peels, crying when forced open, singing when loved open. Now I understand that whatever keeps us from burning truth as food, whatever tricks the heart into thinking we can hide in the open, whatever makes us look everywhere but in the core, this is the smoke that drives us from what is living. And whatever keeps us coming back, coming up, whatever makes us build a home out of straw, out of heartache, out of nothing, whatever ignites us to see again for the very first time, this is the bluish flame that keeps the Earth grinding to the sun.

- Light a candle. Sit quietly and focus on the blue part of the flame as you meditate on one loss you carry within you. It could be a person who has died or left your life. Or a dream that has evaporated.
- Sift through the feelings that surround this loss and find one detail that seems worth saving. It might be represented by a pen or book that someone used. Or a favorite chair. Or a piece of music. Or a gardening tool.
- Holding this detail in your heart, look into the bluish flame and meditate on

the gift you carry from what is gone.
- Now use this detail, if you can, to help you build what is presently before you.
- Try to infuse what is worth saving from what you've lost.
- Use the old to build the new.

# JUNE 4
# HOLDING OUT

Throughout all the ten regions of the Universe there is no place where the Source is not.

— HAKUIN

There's an old story about a young man who's freezing on the side of the road in Alaska. He's hitching a ride to Miami. He's so cold he can barely hold up his handmade sign. After a long wait, a friendly trucker stops and says, "I'm not going to Miami, but I'm going as far as Fort Lauderdale."

Dejectedly, the young man says, "Oh," and turns the ride down.

This is a folk myth of our modern culture that warns us against our want for perfection. How often do we refuse our fate under the guise of holding out for the right thing? How often do we turn down the path presented like a gift because it's not exactly what we're dreaming of? How often do we hold out for the perfect partner, the perfect job, the perfect house? How often do we martyr ourselves to some imagined ideal?

How often do we lose sight of what we're really after, insisting on all or nothing, when there is so much abundance wherever we are and so many opportunities that can help us on our way?

- Sit outside, if you can, and watch the clouds. Search for a cloud that looks like a horse. Whether you find one or not, note what searching-for-one-thing feels like.
- Close your eyes and breathe evenly. Once centered, open your eyes and look to the same clouds. Choose one that compels you, and see what shape is waiting in it.
- Whatever you find, note what finding-what-is-there feels like.

# JUNE 5
## THE SPACES IN-BETWEEN

There's no need to seek the truth —
just put a stop to your opinions!

— SENG-TS'AN

Just as life is made up of day and night, and song is made up of music and silence, friendships, because they are of this world, are also made up of times of being in touch and spaces in-between. Being human, we sometimes fill these spaces with worry, or we imagine the silence is some form of punishment, or we internalize the time we are not in touch with a loved one as some unexpressed change of heart.

Our minds work very hard to make something out of nothing. We can perceive silence as rejection in an instant, and then build a cold castle on that tiny imagined brick.

The only release from the tensions we weave around nothing is to remain a creature of the heart. By giving voice to the river of feelings as they flow through and through, we can stay clear and open.

In daily terms, we call this checking in with each other, though most of us reduce this to a grocery list: How are you today? Do you need any milk? Eggs? Juice? Toilet paper? Though we can help each other survive with such outer kindnesses, we help each other thrive when the checking in with each other comes from a list of inner kindnesses: How are you today? Do you need any affirmation? Clarity? Support? Understanding?

When we ask these deeper questions directly, we wipe the mind clean of its misperceptions. Just as we must dust our belongings from time to time, we must wipe away what covers us when we are apart.

- Meditate on what these statements mean to you, and then speak them to a loved one:
- I appreciate you and your heart.
- I want the channel of heart to be wide open between us.
- I make a promise to you that if misunderstandings or conflicts should grow between us, I will share them with you directly and not let them build or grow in a hidden way.
- I would count the same promise from you as a blessing.

# JUNE 6
## TWO MONKEYS SLEEPING

Tenderness does not choose its own uses.
It goes out to everything equally.
— JANE HIRSHFIELD

We wandered into a corner of the Central Park Zoo, and there, despite the dozens of tourists pointing and tapping the glass, two monkeys were squatting on a perch of stone. To our surprise, they were both in deep sleep, their dark heads bowed to each other, their

302

small frames limp.

What was amazing was that their small delicate hands were touching, their monkey fingers leaning into each other. It was clear that it was this small sustained touch that allowed them to sleep. As long as they were touching, they could let go.

I envied their trust and simplicity. There was none of the human pretense at independence. They clearly needed each other to experience peace. One stirred but didn't wake, and the other, in sleep, kept their fingers touching. How deeply rewarding the life of touch. Each was drifting inwardly, dreaming whatever monkeys dream.

They looked like ancient travelers praying inside a place of rest made possible because they dared to stay connected. It was one of the most tender and humbling moments I have ever seen. Two aging monkeys weaving fingertips, as if their touch alone kept them from oblivion.

I pray for the courage to be as simple in asking for what I need to be.

- Sit with a trusted loved one, a lover or a friend, and open yourself to everything that is older than you.
- Pray this way without touching.
- Now lightly entwine fingers with the simplicity of aging monkeys and open

yourself further to the mystery of tenderness.

- Do not observe or keep track of what happens. Just stay connected and drift in what is unspeakable.

# JUNE 7
# WE ALL SPILL SOUP

Wanting to reform the world without discovering one's true self is like trying to cover the world with leather to avoid the pain of walking on stones and thorns. It is much simpler to wear shoes.
— THE HINDU SAGE RAMANA MAHARSHI

Everyone personalizes and projects. Personalizing is mistaking what happens in the world as always having to do with you. An extreme example would be when a child doesn't do her homework and learns the next day that a plane went down in Dallas; she somehow believes that she was responsible. A more common adult version of this, and less extreme, is when your partner comes home sullen and moody, and you immediately believe it is your fault.

Projecting is the reverse. It occurs when we place the things that happen in us onto the world around us. Often unknowingly, we at-

304

tribute our fears and frustrations to others. Rather than accept my own anger, I see you as angry. A generational example would be that if I am afraid of dogs, I protect my children from dogs and, without asking how they feel, keep them away from dogs too. A subtler example of this is when someone is crying, and we say there is no need to be upset, because we are uncomfortable with all the emotion. Or when we keep asking the other person if they are okay, when it is we who are not.

The truth is that no one can avoid personalizing or projecting. There are only those of us who are aware of it, and those of us who are not; only those of us who own it when it happens, and those of us who don't. But this difference is crucial. Not owning these things can end relationships. Owning them can deepen relationships.

Humans have spilled soup for eternity, and generations have made excuses, saying, "It was the Earth. The Earth shifted," and generations have secretly thought, "He meant to do it."

If you want to save the world, then when you spill the soup, simply say, "I'm sorry I spilled the soup."

- Center yourself, and bring to mind a recent incident in which you have been the spiller of the soup.

305

- Breathe clearly and see with accuracy what you did and how it affected others.
- Breathe gently, and own with kindness your humanness.
- If need be, make amends.

# JUNE 8
# TO REST LIKE A TREE

Praise and blame, gain and loss, pleasure and sorrow come and go like the wind. To be happy, rest like a great tree in the midst of them all.

— *BUDDHA'S LITTLE INSTRUCTION BOOK*

It helps to remember this. Of course, it's hard to remember this when feeling blame, loss, or sorrow. But that's when we need this wisdom the most.

Like everyone, I'd rather not experience the undercurrents of life, but the challenge is not to shun them, but to accept that over a lifetime we will have our share of them.

Avoiding the difficult aspects of living only stunts our fullness. When we do this, we are like a tree that never fully opens to the sky. And dwelling on our difficulties only prevents them from going on their way. When we do this, we are like a great tree that nets the

306

storm in its leaves.

The storm by its nature wants to move on, and the tree's grace is that it has no hands. Our blessing and curse is to learn and relearn when to reach and hold, and when to put our hands in our pockets.

- Stand beside a fully grown tree. Breathe in its wisdom.
- As you watch the tree stay open to wind, feel praise and blame rush you, and try to stand like the tree.
- Breathe deeply, and feel gain and loss circle you and try to open your heart like a branch.
- Breathe slowly, and feel pleasure and sorrow rustle your leaves and try to stand still, holding on to none of it.

# JUNE 9
## THESE ARE THE SIGNS

---

Pain is often a sign
that something has to change.

Our hearts and bodies often give us messages we fail to pay attention to. Ironically, we are all so aware of pain, can hardly ignore it, but we rarely hear what it has to say. It is true that we may need to withstand great pain, great heartache, great disappointment and loss in order to unfold into the rest of our lives. But our pain may also be showing us exactly where we need to change.

If we view our bodies as bridges that carry us from our inner life to the outer world, then pain often gives us insight as to where the bridge is experiencing the most stress. Pain lets us know where we might crack, where our lives need to be reinforced and rested, in order for us to keep bringing our inner and outer lives together.

During my struggle with cancer, I experienced a variety of deep and acute pains. I learned how to hold on and let go, learned how to endure — that is, let the pain go through without denying its hurt. But the most crucial thing I learned was to listen to the pain.

I was being worn down by my chemo treatments, which were very aggressive. I was trying the best I knew how to live through as many treatments as I could manage. Everyone was coaching me to stick it out. "Certainly," I was told by those more afraid than I, "you want to swallow as much poison as you can tolerate, so the cancer will be stricken from your body completely." I remained committed to this approach.

But after four months, I lost feeling in my fingers and toes. The chemo was causing nerve damage, and I had lost my reflexes. I struggled, unsure whether to continue or not. I felt that the cancer was gone, but the chemo was insurance. Endure more, if you can. Hold on.

Within twenty-four hours, I was up in the night with the worst stomach attack I have ever experienced. There I was, pacing the living room floor at three in the morning, trying to endure the pain, asking God for a sign. The chemo had now ulcerated my esophagus. Another attack gripped me. I doubled over: God, give me a sign. What should I do? I want to live.

Another attack. This happened three more times, when I suddenly realized — the pain was the sign. And its message was to stop. It was over. There I stood, hunched over with my windpipe bleeding and numbness in my hands and feet, and God was saying, "These are the signs. Do you want more? I can give you more."

The next day I told my sweet doctor that I would not take that needle to my arm again. And it was over.

- Breathe slowly and meditate on a pain that has been troubling you. It might be physical or emotional or even mental.
- Rather than toughening and resisting the onset of the pain, try to let it move through you.
- Notice where the pain is most acute.

Notice where you first feel it and where you last feel it as it subsides.

- What is the pain telling you about the piece of your body or heart or mind that it is moving through?
- What might you change in how you move, feel, or think that will strengthen this part of you that is hurting?

# JUNE 10
## THE EXERCISE OF GENTLENESS

I have no power of miracle
other than the attainment of quiet
    happiness,
I have no tact except the exercise of
    gentleness.

— ORACLE OF SUMIYOSHI

This Shinto sage from the hills of Japan affirms what we all know in our hearts but seldom honor. I have worked hard to give up attaining a place ordained by others in the world, for this always leads me into noise, confusion, and gruffness. Often it is some grief or pain that halts me, jars me into remembering the exercise of gentleness that opens the quiet world.

The truth is that, more than forgetting this, some unloved part of me whispers insistently that I can have both. Foolishly, I tend to listen, out of pity or pride, only to find out painfully, again and again, that it just doesn't work.

In beautiful mystery, the extraordinary edge to everything is covered over with a current of speed and noise, the way beautiful stones are not quite seeable under the rush of the river's face. Only when we can still the river of the world and the river in our face do things become extraordinary and clear.

- This is a walking meditation. Breathe deeply as you walk.
- As you begin to slow, notice how your field of attention widens.
- Go to the first thing that shows you its quiet happiness.
- Breathe before it slowly, and speak to it with your gentleness.

# JUNE 11
## SHARING THE CLIMB

Those who drink from the one water
gaze at the same stars.

The climb was long. The day was hot. Tom had thought ahead and had frozen his water bottle, so his water would stay cold. But once he drank what had melted, he was left with a small chunk of ice rattling in a plastic bottle. That was when Bill, another climber, who hadn't thought ahead, asked Tom to share his ice. Bill had plenty of water, but it was hot from their climb in the sun.

Tom was glad to share his ice, and tried to break the chunk up so he could pass ice chips into Bill's bottle. After a long frustration, it occurred to Tom to let Bill pour his hot water over the ice and to then let Bill drink from his bottle.

This small moment changed Tom's life. He suddenly realized that if he let things in, he could share more easily than if he kept breaking things down in order to get them out.

As he came back down into the world, he understood the three mysteries of sharing: First, if there's time, let the cold things thaw. But if there is no time, let the warm things in, and only when necessary, break the hard things remaining and pray like hell you can pass them.

- Center yourself, and as you breathe, open your hands, letting the warm things around you in.
- As you inhale, let the energy of life thaw your preparations, making you drinkable.

# JUNE 12
## TO COUNT BY TOUCHING

We need to count by touching,
not by adding and subtracting.

When we count with our eyes, we stall the
heart. For the eyes can see clearly what is
broken without ever feeling the break, and
the mind can calculate the loss without ever
sewing up the wound. Without touching the
life coming apart before us, we can race to
rebuild before the wrecked dream ever hits
the ground. While this makes us resilient and
efficient as ants, it also keeps us from ever
living in what we build.

Alas, what makes us precise and efficient
can also begin a life of neurosis: not touching
what we see, not feeling what we know. This
is how the mind skips the heart's step. How
we forget that blood on the news is real, that
the cry from the street is attached to something living.

I remember waking after rib surgery to find
a dear friend at the foot of my bed. I was
elated to have arrived on the other side and
called to her, but she was staring off. I knew
in that instant she was already mourning me,
and so she missed me coming alive. She was
already preparing for life without me, and so,

the deeper closeness awaiting us was never felt or worn. We think we protect ourselves by taking inventory and moving on, but we only spin our web tighter.

Recently, another friend had a dream in which we were building a home with sturdy shelves for the things we loved. She tried to count the shelves, but couldn't keep the numbers in her head. She had to go over and count the shelves by touching each one. Mysteriously, as she did this, the shelves kept multiplying. Her touch made more shelves possible.

Such a profound and simple lesson: to count with our hands brings us deeper than all counting. Then numbers give way to notes, and sums give way to song.

- Sit quietly and meditate on three things that you hold dear. One might be the love of another; a second, your love of the sea; a third, a special piece of music that makes you feel whole.
- With each breath, let the image and feel of these things rise before you one at a time.
- Keep breathing and count these dear things as they come into your awareness again and again.
- Keep feeling them until the numbers — one, two, three — drop away.
- Keep breathing steadily and let the feel

of these dear things mix and touch each
other.
• Carry this mood of holding what is dear
into your day.

# JUNE 13
# AGAINST OUR WILL

As an inlet cannot close itself to the sea
that shapes it, the heart can only wear itself
open.

One of the hardest blessings to accept about
the heart is that in the image of life itself, it
will not stop emerging through experience.
No matter how we try to preserve or relive
what has already happened, the heart will not
stop being shaped.

This is a magnificent key to health: that,
despite our resistance to accept that what
we've lost is behind us, despite our need at
times to stitch our wounds closed by reliving
them, and despite our heroic efforts to
preserve whatever is precious, despite all our
attempts to stop the flow of life, the heart
knows better. It knows that the only way to
truly remember or stay whole is to take the
best and worst into its tissue.

Despite all our intentions not to be hurt
again, the heart keeps us going by moving us

ever forward into health. Though we walk around thinking we can direct it, our heart is endlessly shaped like the land, often against our will.

- Center yourself, and bring to mind one precious moment you'd like to preserve.
- As you breathe, let in the life that is presently around you — the quality of light, the temperature, the sounds coming and going.
- Breathe steadily and try not to choose one over the other. Simply allow the precious memory and the precious moment to tenderly become one.

# JUNE 14
## SWIMMING IN OUR LOVE

I lose sight of us at times;
the way that fish can't see the ocean;
the price of lovers swimming in their love.

When we first fall in love, the powerful force of possibility grips us and pulls us along deeper and deeper into the days. When first shaping the bonds of love, we look at each other with incredible freshness and appreciate who is before us. We stare into our new lover's eyes the way we might an overwhelming painting in which we imagine the secrets of life have been stroked thickly.

Inevitably, though, as we grow intimate, we begin to lose sight of each other, and there comes a day when we no longer see our loved one as others do. Now we see the *inside* of their face, up close. Now we swim in each other like a mysterious river in which we sometimes see ourselves, and sometimes soothe ourselves, and sometimes drink of each other.

Eventually, we climb *into* the painting we once stared at with our pounding heart, and from inside the painting, we can forget there ever was such a painting. This is how we can take each other for granted. This is how we can imagine that the magic is gone.

But, as the reward for being drawn to the sea is to swim with the waves, the reward for being drawn into the depth of another is to feel each other rather than to see each other. This is the paradox of intimacy. On the way, we see what we dream of feeling, but once there, we feel from the inside what we can no longer readily see.

- Sit quietly with a loved one.
- While holding hands, close your eyes and recall the day you first saw each other deeply. Let that image move through your hands.
- Now, still holding hands, look into each

other's eyes freely, and feel what lives between you now.

- Close your eyes again, and let both the seeing and the feeling flow between you.

# JUNE 15
## STAYING POROUS

Be patient toward all that is unsolved in your heart and try to love the questions themselves.

— RAINER MARIA RILKE

I am jogging in the city on a hot summer day, and my legs are in a rhythm, carrying me without much guidance through small crowds, past roses and bus stops.

I begin to think about my struggle not to give myself away. When growing up, I had to check myself at the door like a coat in order to relate to others. Often, I had to pretend to be less than I was in order to be loved.

For years, I would shelve my light to take care of others. Like a fireman, I'd drop whatever I was doing to rush to the rescue. For so long, the choice seemed only to stay open and lose myself or to close up and cut others off. But today, while running freely through the streets, close to others but not entangled, I realize I am learning after many attempts that I can stay close and porous, caring and present, without holding everyone's anxiety and without going underground. At least I can try.

I am dripping and breathing like a small horse. It is clouding over. It begins to rain slightly. I move through the beautiful people and ask for a hot dog with mustard and sauerkraut. As I chew this simple food, rain from the sky meets rain from my body, and in the rain, sweating, the tang of sauerkraut on my lip, I feel joy. Others shuffle by. Today, there is no room for worthlessness.

- Sit quietly and bring to mind a time when you lost yourself completely in another's problem.
- Center yourself and bring to mind a time when you maintained your sense of self, but cut off another completely to do so.
- Breathe thoroughly and try to let the two feelings coexist: compassion and sense of self.
- Inhale. Sense of self. Exhale. Compassion.
- Inhale. Sense of self. Exhale. Compassion.

# JUNE 16
## THE STEP TO OTHERS

We wander and think
no one will ever find us.
And lifting our sorry head,
we are next to each other.

— MARK NEPO

We imagine that so many conditions are prerequisite to finding love, when all that is required is that, like a man stepping from a boat to a dock, we step over the small gap that exists between us. Often there is nothing to prepare for, nothing to set up in advance — just to step over what separates us and to land in what is before us.

But, giving in to our fears, we widen the gap by creating conditions that must be filled before stepping toward another. This is how we invest in the building of credentials and lifestyles and bank accounts that are often distractions from the simple and essential need to be held. In this way, we move up and down and around, but seldom straight into what will give us love.

To know love we must do more than understand, we must land and enter. Before we step, the gap to others seems like a canyon. But stepping anyway, the separations we

320

move through look so much smaller once crossed. Often the thing feared, once crossed, turns out to be an unexpected bridge from which we can see who we were and who we are becoming.

- Center yourself and bring into focus the gap between you and others.
- As you inhale, bring more of others into that gap.
- As you exhale, extend more of who you are into that gap.
- As you breathe, let the lines of separation blur.

# JUNE 17
## SPIRIT AND PSYCHOLOGY

Even the clearest water
seems opaque at great depth.
— JOEL AGEE

Each of us is like a great, untamed sea, obedient to deeper currents that are seldom visible. Knowing this gives us three insights worth keeping in our awareness. First, we must consider that the deepest patch of ocean is as clear as its surface wave, though it remains unseeable to the human eye that bobs above it. Second, how far we can see into the deep depends on the calmness or turbulence of the surface. And third, just as the depth and surface of the sea are inseparable, so too are the spirit and psychology of each human being.

It is our deep-sounding, untamed currents that cause us to rise and swell, dip and crash. Yet that base of spirit remains unaffected by the storms that churn up the surface. It obeys a deeper order. Still, we as beings living in the world are always subject to both: the depth and the surface, our spirit and our psychology. Though we can never see all the way to bottom, on clear days — when our psychology is calm — we can know the depth that carries us. When free of turbulence and anxiety, we can know the ocean of God that swells within.

So, in love, in relationship, in the brief clarity that living gives rise to, I see all the way through you, as far as my sight can go, and am forever changed. Then the winds come from the east, and suddenly you're all churned up, your depth seems blocked, and I wonder who you are. This happens in the course of knowing one's self as well. It is unavoidable. Watch any patch of sea. It is never completely still. Even when calm, it reflects everything as it spreads and never vanishes. So, too, our feelings, which keep changing in the light.

The degree to which we are clear and seeable depends on how calm we are and how calm the day. But we are never cut off from our spirit, any more than the surface wave is cut off from the ocean floor. Fear of living often comes when we place all our energy into the moment of the wave, into the turbulent moment of our psychology.

If revelation is the brief experience of seeing through the surface, into ourselves or others, then wisdom is the recall of that seeing when the waters are murky.

- Fill a clear dish that is both wide and deep with water. Stir it with your hand, and in silence watch it settle.
- Do this several times while thinking about the storms in your life that are churning up your mind.
- The last two times notice the water at the bottom and how it is less affected by what stirs up the surface.

# JUNE 18
## SURFACING THROUGH

This night will pass . . .
Then we have work to do . . .
Everything has to do
with loving and not loving. . . .

— RUMI

Very often, when hurt or depressed or anxious, we encounter powerful feelings like ghosts without a body, trying to pour themselves into us, trying to dominate our lives. They seem to gather in the cave of our pain, stoking our wounds like stones in a fire that keeps them warm.

After years of struggling to let my painful feelings out, I'm learning that the other side of this, which is just as essential to my well-being, is not to let the hurt or depression or anxiety set up camp inside me.

I must confess it has taken me all this way to fully understand that the purpose of surfacing these powerful feelings is to continually empty my heart and mind of its sediment, so that new life can make its way into me.

There are dangers to not letting such feelings out. But once felt, there are dangers as well to not letting such feelings move on through. For just as our lungs must stay clear for the next mouthful of air, our heart must stay unobstructed for the next feeling we encounter.

There is no freedom until we dance the ghosts from the chambers of our wounds, until we pile our wounds like stones at the mouth of our own quarries.

- Center yourself and call into view a painful feeling that has stayed with you

too long.
- Through your meditation, enter a dialogue with this feeling and ask why it will not go; just what does it need in order to leave?
- Breathe steadily and live with what it says.

# JUNE 19
# A WIDER HORIZON

The eyes experience less stress when they can look upon a wider horizon.
— R. D. CHIN

Whether it be physics or architecture or Eastern forms of meditation or Western forms of prayer, every field of inquiry affirms the fact that the wider our view, the less isolated we are. The more connected we stay to everything larger than us, the less turbulent our time on Earth.

This is why it helps to share our journey with others, because in so doing we become a chorus of voices, and the stress of going solo lessens once we discover that we are not alone.

As light when confined turns to heat, the stuff of our lives when confined ignites brush fires out of our isolation. I felt the difference dramatically when joining a wellness group during my cancer experience. Alone, I was feeling the heat of dying. But once voicing my pain in a circle of others on the same path, my heart relaxed back into the light of living.

So when you see someone stumbling forward with a stone in their heart, simply go near them and listen. When the pains of living feel sharp, open up your attention and give it freely, and the connections will even out the sharpness. When things feel heavy, reach out to whomever is near and distribute the weight.

- Bring into view a situation that is causing you stress.
- While keeping that situation in view, inhale and open yourself to the things around you that are not stressful.
- While keeping both the stressful and the nonstressful in view, breathe slowly and realize that to narrow and to widen is part of being human.

# June 20
## The Air after Pain

Live for the air after pain
and there will be no reason to run.

Hippocrates said that pleasure is the absence of pain. Anyone who has ever suffered knows this is a deep truth. When I fell into the gauntlet of tests that awaited after the pronouncement that I had cancer, I was terrified of being in pain. I introduced myself to every physician and nurse as Mark-*put me out*-Nepo. But with every procedure, there was some medical reason why I had to be awake. I came to realize that there was nowhere to run.

Once I accepted this, which took some time, I understood that what was most terrifying about my pain was the prospect that it would never end, that life would somehow freeze in whatever moment of discomfort I came upon. The terror gained its power from not being able to imagine life beyond the pain.

The breakthrough moment for me came the day I had to have yet another bone marrow sampling. For some reason, these were the worst for me. But with the appearance that day of some deeper grace, I suddenly saw it differently. I recognized that this very uncomfortable procedure lasted at most forty to fifty seconds and I was arranging my entire life and being in anticipation and avoidance of those fifty seconds.

For the first time I realized I had a choice. The pain of those seconds would be the same, but I could ground myself, including my fear, in the very real fact that my life would resume after those fifty seconds. There would be light in the air, once again, after the pain. For the first time, I felt in my soul that I was larger than my pain. This empowered me.

So many times, in our despair, we see our pain as something that will never end. In fact, this often defines our moments of despair: when we believe that our pain contains the rest of us. In contrast, there is this sense of peace to work toward: the belief that our life contains our pain.

- Center yourself and focus on a physical or emotional pain that is with you.
- As you inhale, bring in all that is larger than your pain.
- As you exhale, release the pain into the larger air that is pain-free.
- As you repeat this, focus on the moments that are pain-free, and invite them to expand.

# JUNE 21
## THE PRESENCE OF GOD

I looked a hundred times and all I saw was
dust. The sun broke through and
flecks of gold filled the air.

Consider how the sun continually lights our daily world, yet we cannot see light except in what it touches. Though the sun burns constantly and holds everything living within its pull, though it sends its power across millions of miles, it is unseen for all that way, until it hits a simple blade of grass or makes the web of a spider a golden patch of lace.

In the same way, the presence of God powerfully moves between us unseen, only visible in the brief moments we are lighted, in those enlivened moments we know as love.

For just as we can look at that spider web and never see its beauty until it reveals itself in sudden light, we can look upon the nearest face, again and again, never seeing the beauty in each other, until one or both of us is suddenly revealed. Spirits show themselves in just this way, or rather, our gentleness of heart allows us to see and be seen.

It makes our search for love a humble one. For what is there to do but grow in the open and wait.

- Take something familiar to you, something you see daily — your shoes, your comb, your letter opener — and place it outside in the light.
- Now leave it be for the moment, and meditate on the general presence of love as you experience it.
- After a while, look with your heart's eye on the familiar object in the sun.
- Note how it seems to come alive.
- Realize your heart is now in the sun.
- Feel how it has come alive.

# JUNE 22
## SPIRITUAL FISHING

Honesty is the net
by which we fish the deep.

Though we are taught to make plans and keep to them, and though we work our way through predesigned courses of study to receive credentials and degrees, our attempts at real living don't happen this way.

For me, finding where I fit in the world feels a lot like spiritual fishing. The vast, mysterious ocean of experience keeps calling, and whether it is by buckets of question or nets of honesty, I keep hauling up food from the days. I keep hauling in shells and pearls and

330

seaweed from a common depth that no one can see, and then I spend time cleaning what I've found and hearing what it has to say.

In this way, everyone alive must fish, and this requires stillness and patience and a willingness to drift. For we never know where deep things live. Even our effort to know ourselves resembles this process, for much of who we are lives cleanly below the surface, and we each must be nourished from what lives below, if we are to survive.

Paradoxically, our essential feelings and personal truths live below like fish, not wanting to be caught. But spiritual fishing yields spiritual food, and the secret nourishment of eating what lives within us is that to eat what lives in our shell we must open that shell, and eating what swims below our surface lets us see with the perspective of the deep.

In truth, every person I have ever loved and every path I have been called to has shown itself to me after fishing in the waters of my spirit, which, entered deep enough, is the ocean of all spirit. I believe we are all connected there, and only by this communion — of bringing up and taking in what lives within us — can we hope to uncover our common purpose of being. In committing to this honest practice, wisdom becomes that very good net of mindful heart, through which we rinse and claim the smallest of shells, those hidden casings that hold both food and pearls.

- Find a stretch of running water, and walk along its bank till you are called by it.
- Then reach into its moving clearness as if it were your own soul, and fish with your open hand for what it wants to give you.
- Whether it is a stone or branch or shell or piece of refuse, bring it up and hold it fully in your hand.
- Now meditate and work with this living symbol. Listen for what it knows and how it knows.
- What nourishment is it offering you?

# JUNE 23
## FAME OR PEACE

Rather the flying bird, leaving no trace,
than the going beast, marking the earth.
— FERNANDO PESSOA

Much of our anxiety and inner turmoil comes from living in a global culture whose values drive us from the essence of what matters. At the heart of this is the conflict between the outer definition of success and the inner value of peace.

Unfortunately, we are encouraged, even trained, to get attention when the renewing

332

secret of life is to give attention. From performing well on tests to positioning ourselves for promotions, we are schooled to believe that to succeed we must get attention and be recognized as special, when the threshold to all that is extraordinary in life opens only when we devote ourselves to giving attention, not getting it. Things come alive for us only when we dare to see and recognize everything as special.

The longer we try to get attention instead of giving it, the deeper our unhappiness. It leads us to move through the world dreaming of greatness, needing to be verified at every turn, when feelings of oneness grace us only when we verify the life around us. It makes us desperate to be loved, when we sorely need the medicine of being loving.

One reason so many of us are lonely in our dream of success is that instead of looking for what is clear and true, we learn to covet what is great and powerful. One reason we live so far from peace is that instead of loving our way into the nameless joy of spirit, we think fame will soothe us. And while we are busy dreaming of being a celebrity, we stifle our need to see and give and love, all of which opens us to the true health of celebration.

It leaves us with these choices: fame or peace, be a celebrity or celebrate being, work all our days to be seen or devote ourselves to seeing, build our identity on the attention we can get or find our place in the beauty of things by the attention we can give.

- Sit quietly, and try to breathe at the center beneath your want to be seen.
- Open your eyes and simply give your sweet attention to the things about you.
- Breathe deeply and look at the rug until it becomes fiber. Look at your keys until they become metal. Look at a bird until it becomes song.
- Allow what you see to enter you, and take it with you throughout the day.

# JUNE 24
# QUESTIONS PUT
# TO THE SICK – II

When was the last time you danced?
— QUESTION PUT TO THE SICK BY A
NATIVE AMERICAN MEDICINE MAN

The beginning of dance is giving gesture to what we feel. While this is very obvious and basic to most children, it remains very difficult for those of us schooled to live in our heads.

The ongoing effort to dance, to give gesture to what we feel and experience, is ultimately healing because, as riverbeds are continually shaped by the water that moves through them, living beings are continually shaped by the feelings and experiences that move through them. If there is no water moving through, the riverbed dries up and crumbles. Likewise, if there is no feeling moving through the body, the being at the center of that body will crumble.

More often, though, there is too much to give gesture to, and we fail to move these feelings through our bodies. In truth, much of our inner sickness comes from the buildup and pressure of all that is kept in. The ongoing act of releasing that inner buildup is what spiritual practices call embodiment.

There are many ancient practices intended to help us live more fully in our bodies, including the Chinese art of meditation movement known as *t'ai chi* and the Buddhist art of space awareness known as *maitri,* to name just two. Once unblocked, giving gesture to our inwardness not only frees us from becoming pressurized, but the gestures, once allowed out, teach us how to dance further into our own lives.

Still, most of us learn to feel, trap, and snuff our feelings in our hearts, and if they won't go away, we try to hush them with our minds. If they still persist, we often feel them throb in our temples or burn in our gut.

In contrast to the painful layering of heart,

mind, and body, embodiment itself is nothing more or less than feeling the wound or lip you touch in your hand and mind and heart at once. Embodiment is allowing our heart, mind, and body to exist as one miraculous skin.

* Stand quietly and breathe slowly, feeling your breath move through your heart.
* With each breath, let the feeling of being alive move further into your body.
* First feel it move in and out of your heart, then in and out of your lungs.
* Let the breath of being alive now move up and out your shoulders and hips, and let it extend your arms in whatever gesture happens to come.
* Repeat this process until the breath from heart to fingertip feels like one continuous gesture.

# JUNE 25

## STEMS AND ROOTS

The Love we show saves the Love we
    hide,
the way a sprig in sun feeds its unseen
    root.

Even though I believe in living in the open, parts of me hide. I can't help it. But what I can help is which parts of me — the open or the hidden — run my life. What I can rely on is this inexplicable knowing that when I am in the open, life nourishes even those parts so sorely hidden.

Just as green stems in spring stay connected to their darker roots, just as the roots grow when the stems do, my compassion soothes my fear where I can't see. Unknown to me, my love feeds the underside of my confusion. The light I take in keeps the roots of my soul alive.

We become so preoccupied with what we are not able to address, what we are not able to mend, what we are not able to leave behind, that we forget that whatever we are in the light of day is slowly, but surely, healing the rest of us.

- Bring to mind one thing you feel incapable of solving in your personality.
- Surround it with your breath. Accept that it will be with you for a while.
- Now put it down, and feel the part of you that happens without any work.
- Inhale strongly with this part of your being, and know that its native strength is softening what you can't solve.

# JUNE 26
## THE GIFT OF PRAYER

Prayer is not asking. It is a longing of the
    soul.
It is daily admission of one's
    weakness. . . .
And so, it is better in prayer to have a
    heart
without words than words without a heart.
— GANDHI

This great spiritual teacher reminds us that prayer of the deepest kind is more a pledge of gratitude for what has already been received than a request or plea for something not yet experienced. Such an effort refreshes the soul.

Implicit in Gandhi's instruction is the need to surrender to our lives here on Earth. By admitting our weaknesses, we lay down all the masks we show the world and as we do so, what is holy floods in.

I once saw a blind man rocking endlessly in the sun, an unstoppable smile on his face. Not a word was uttered. To me, he was a priest, a shaman, and his whole being was praying and shouting in silence that the day, beyond his blindness, was happily enough.

This is what the heart knows beyond all

words, if we can find a way to listen: that beyond our small sense of things a magnificent light surrounds us, more than anyone could ask for. This is what prayer as gratitude can open us to.

- Center yourself, and as you breathe, close your eyes and cease all asking.
- Simply breathe with gratitude for the air.
- Relax and feel your frailties and imperfections, and let the simple air fill them.
- Breathe deeply and slowly, and from your tender imperfect insides, ask for nothing and give nothing; just feel without words for your soul's place in the fabric of things.

# JUNE 27
# THE MONKEY AND THE RIVER

It is said a great Zen teacher asked an initiate to sit by a stream until he heard all the water had to teach. After days of bending his mind around the scene, a small monkey happened by, and, in one seeming bound of joy, splashed about in the stream. The initiate wept and returned to his teacher, who scolded him lovingly, "The monkey heard. You just listened."

With the best of intentions, we often build false careers of studying the river without ever getting wet. In this way, we can ponder great philosophy without ever telling the truth, or analyze our pain without ever feeling it, or study holy places without ever making where we live sacred. In this way, we can build a cathedral on the water's edge, spending all our time keeping it clean. Or we can count our money or say our prayers, without ever spending anything or ever feeling God's presence. In this way, we can play music or make love skillfully without ever feeling the music or our passion.

The apprentice was brought to tears because the monkey, slapping and yapping its way in the river, had landed in a moment of joy, and the apprentice knew that all his reverence and devotion and meditation hadn't brought him the joy of a monkey.

The river, of course, is the ongoing moment of our living. It is the current that calls us to inhabit our lives. And no matter how close we come, no matter how much we get from staying close with a sensitive heart, nothing will open us to joy but entering the stream.

I once was on a screened-in porch on a lake I used to visit every summer for twenty years. My friend and I were watching it rain, as we had done countless times over the years. Suddenly, like that simple and beautiful monkey, my friend bounded up, slapped the screen door open, tracked his clothes, and jumped into the rain-filled lake.

I watched like the apprentice, feeling the pain of always being dry, and then I shed my clothes and jumped in too.

There we were: in the center of the lake, water from above in our mouths, in our eyes, pelting us, water entering water, lives entering their living. Each pelt of rain, on us and in the lake, uttering . . . joy, joy, joy.

- As you move through your day, notice your interactions with others and with the life around you.
- Notice if you are watching what is happening or if you are a part of it.
- If you are watching, place your heart in the stream of what is before you, the way you might dip your hand in running water.
- Do this by opening your heart with your outbreath and letting life in with your inbreath. . . . Watch and be. . . . Open and let in. . . . Listen and get wet. . . .

# JUNE 28
## ALL THAT WE ARE NOT

Discernment is a process of letting go of
    what
we are not.
            — FATHER THOMAS KEATING

I can easily over-identify with my emotions
and roles, becoming what I feel: I am angry. . . . I am divorced. . . . I am depressed. . . .
I am a failure. . . . I am nothing but my
confusion and my sadness. . . .

No matter how we feel in any one moment,
we are not just our feelings, our roles, our
traumas, our prescription of values, or our
obligations or ambitions. It is so easy to
define ourselves by the moment of struggle
we are wrestling with. It is a very human way,
to be consumed by what moves through us.

In contrast, I often think of how Michelan-
gelo sculpted, how he saw the sculpture waiting, already complete, in the uncut stone. He
would often say that his job was to carve away
the excess, freeing the thing of beauty just
waiting to be released.

It helps me to think of spiritual discernment in this way. Facing ourselves, uncovering the meaning in our hard experiences, the
entire work of consciousness speaks to a

process by which we sculpt away the excess, all that we are not; finding and releasing the gesture of soul that is already waiting, complete, within us. Self-actualization is this process applied to our life on Earth. The many ways we suffer, both inwardly and outwardly, are the chisels of God freeing the thing of beauty that we have carried within since birth.

- Sit quietly, and as you breathe, feel all that troubles you rise through your body.
- As you breathe, allow these troubles to move away from you.
- Breathe deeply and accept the stillness that comes. It is the skin of your soul, waiting in its completeness for you to carve away the excess of your very human moods.

# JUNE 29
# A LITTLE FISH STORY

The instant fish accept
that they will never have arms,
they grow fins.

I confess I was surprised to wake one day with this knowing about fish. It seems a koan or riddle to decipher. After living with it awhile, I've come to feel that it holds another key to faith: that before we can be what we are meant to be, we must accept what we are not. This form of discernment asks us to let go of those grand fantasies that take us out of our nature, that make us work to be famous instead of loving, or perfect instead of compassionate.

Yet the instant we can accept what is not in our nature, rather than being distracted by all we think we could or should be, then all our inner resources are free to transform us into the particular self we are aching to be.

This act of acceptance is a risk that frees us because we can't find the growth that awaits us until we give up what is against our very nature. It is this surrender, without knowing what will happen next, that allows our lives to truly unfold.

- Sit quietly and allow your true nature to rise within you.
- Without trying to name it or understand it, simply close your eyes and breathe it into your hands.
- Breathe evenly and allow your true nature to find gestures in your hands.
- During your day, play with these gestures.

# JUNE 30
## LOOKING AWAY

In exchange for the promise of security, many people put a barrier between themselves and the adventures in consciousness that could put a whole new light on their personal lives.

— JUNE SINGER

The pull into the truth of things is very strong. Often the only way to resist it is to deny what we are seeing, to pretend our lives do not have to grow or change. Yet when we do this, our spirit, which doesn't know how to pretend, keeps moving. For as the *Isa Upanishad* says, "The Spirit is swifter than the mind." We are then, painfully, like a dog at the end of its leash, staked and running at the same time, pretending we don't know any better.

Interestingly, we tend to think of ignorance as an innocent not-knowing, but the Buddhist teacher Chögyam Trungpa points out that to ignore someone or something is a willful looking away, a grave act of denying what is already conscious. Trungpa suggests that the willful act of looking away is a crime against the essence of things that costs us dearly.

345

When we find our spirit on the move when we are pretending otherwise, the tension can be ripping. It leaves us all with the need to learn how to discern between an innocent not-knowing and a willful looking away. This is an inner knowing that can determine whether we will live like a dog at the end of our leash or whether we will run free through the grasses of life.

- Sit quietly and center yourself.
- As you breathe slowly, try on the in-breath to sense your spirit. Feel where it is living in you.
- On the outbreath, try to feel your place in the world, where you go through the days.
- As you breathe, keep sensing your spirit and feeling your place.
- Simply notice any difference and throughout your day look there.
- Your simple and honest looking will lessen the gap.

# July 1
## The Heart's Blossom

Courage is the heart's blossom.

All courage is threshold crossing. Often there

is a choice: to enter the burning building or not, to speak the truth or not, to stand before oneself without illusion or not. But there is another sort of courage we are talking about here — the kind when afterward, the courageous are puzzled to be singled out as brave. They often say, I had no choice. I had to run in that building for that child. Or I had to quit my job or I would have died.

Despite all consequence, there is an inevitable honoring of what is true, and at this deep level of inner voice, it is not a summoning of will, but a following of true knowing.

My own life is a trail of such following. Time and again, I have heard deep callings that felt inevitable and which I could have ignored, but only at great risk of something essential perishing.

It was this honoring of what is true that guided me through my cancer experience: saying no to brain surgery and yes to rib surgery, saying yes to chemo and no to chemo. Each decision appeared both courageous and illogical to my doctors. Since then, I have been called heroic for surviving, which is like championing an eagle for finding its nest, and I have been condemned as selfish for seeking the Truth, which is like blaming a turtle for finding the deep.

Courage of this sort is the result of being authentic. It is available to all and its reward, far more than respect, is the opening of joy.

- Meditate on a decision that you are struggling with.
- Rather than focusing on your fear of what might or might not happen, try opening to what feels true.
- Without strategizing or imagining the consequences of honoring what feels true, simply let the truth as you know it rise within you.
- As you move through your day, let what is true fill you, even if you don't quite understand it.

# JULY 2
## WRONG VIEW

The mind composed of ignorance or wrong view suffers from spiritual disease; it sees falsely. Seeing falsely causes it to think falsely,
speak falsely, and act falsely. You will see immediately that everyone, without exception,
has the spiritual disease.
— AJAHN BUDDHADASA

In Pali, the ancient source language of Buddhism and Hinduism, the word for mental illness means "wrong view." We must be careful not to interpret this righteously, as in, If you see things differently than I, you are wrong. The wisdom here lies in the revelation that our wellness of mind hinges on how clear and true we remain to the pulse of life itself.

At heart, our mental health comes out of the sacred relationship between our deepest Self and the very source of life. The moment we distort, limit, or rationalize things away from what they truly are, we start to experience the spiritual disease that Ajahn Buddhadasa speaks of.

This Buddhist teacher from Thailand reminds us that these passages of imbalance and blurry thinking are unavoidable. They cannot be circumvented, the way you might drive around a pothole. No, these distortions can only be minimized and repaired. So we must accept that by being human, we will distort the gift of life, and thus we must commit to learning how to refresh our relationship with what is sacred.

Quite often, to uphold "a wrong view," we build and maintain "a wrong way." For example, when younger and sorely in need of approval and love, I hurt so much inside that I assumed that life was somewhere "over there," not where I was. Once believing this, I put all my energy into getting over there. But after a hard journey, I was blocked. The people over there wouldn't let me in. Now I had to figure out who was the gatekeeper and what were his rules, and now there was the doing of all these tasks to satisfy the gate-keeper, so I might be let in. It took me years to realize that no matter the pain, life is always where we are. Nothing is being withheld. All that misguided effort was built on a wrong view. As Buddhadasa says "Everyone, without exception, has the spiritual disease" while underneath, the undistorted life is softly waiting. Given this, we each must make a ritual not of seeing rightly, but completely.

- Sit quietly and bring to mind someone's approval you seek.
- If you can, meditate on why this feels so important to you.
- What is it you need that you think their approval will provide?
- Rather than devise ways to get this approval, try to understand where the need in you comes from.

# JULY 3
## I-ING AND MY-ING

The shore thirsts, but does not own the
    ocean
that keeps it soft. So, too, the heart
and all it loves.

In the ancient Indian language Pali, the word

*ahamkara* means "I-ing," having or making the feeling of "I." The word *mamamkara* means "My-ing," having or making the feeling of "mine." In Buddhism, the feelings of I-ing and My-ing are considered so dangerous and poisonous that they are seen as yet another cause of spiritual disease.

This tells us that as soon as we start to separate what cannot be separated, our mental health will suffer. This tells us that the dearest things in life cannot be owned, but only shared. In truth, we share this mystery called life the way sea creatures share the ocean. While each fish has its nest and small patch of bottom to gum, none can live without the deep that flows through them all.

We are no different. Yes, we can own a watch or a car, but no one can own the love or peace or energy of life that must flow through our hearts if we are to survive.

As soon as we devote ourselves to I-ing and My-ing, we are drawn into a life of distraction from what really matters. Once we commit to making things "mine," we unleash a career of gathering and storing. Now there is the need to wall in and maintain. Now there is an endless sorting through the things of the world that could be mine. Now the attaining. Now the insuring. Now there is possessiveness and jealousy and envy, and the need to protect, and the right to bear arms. Now there is the secret want to get what others have, and the right to sue. This I-ing and My-ing can sicken the strongest soul.

It often contaminates how we love. How many times have we all asked our lovers for the reassurance, "Are you mine?" Even as I write this, I struggle, like you, not to have things, but to make good use of them; not to guard and parcel out my care, but to let the love through. I am, that is for sure. But what is truly mine, beyond this vibrant sense of being alive, that I keep opening to?

- Center yourself, and hold before your mind's eye one thing that you feel ownership around.
- It might be a course you teach or a garden you tend or a child you have raised.
- Breathe deeply, and consider the energy you expend guarding and protecting this special thing rather than enjoying it.
- Breathe steadily, and try to loosen your hold on this special thing and see if it stays close to you anyway.

# July 4
## Here and There

Here is always beneath There.

I remember sitting for a long time on the edge of a summer lake, watching the far shore. I could see early light flood the water in the distance and this somehow made the other side seem exotic. Every morning I'd sit on my small edge of lake and watch the other side, imagining that a certain mystery awaited me. With each day its call grew larger. Finally, on the seventh day, I had to go there, and, up earlier than usual, I rowed across the lake, beached my small boat, and sat in the exact spot I had been watching.

As I looked about, the aura of otherness I had seen from my daily perch was gone. I was somewhat undone, for though this far shore was beautiful and peaceful, the wet clump of shore I ran my hand through was the same as where I'd begun.

I started to laugh at myself. For looking back at where I'd been sitting every day, I saw early light flood the water in the distance, and now where I'd been living seemed exotic. Now a certain mystery called me back to where I was.

So often we imagine that There is more full

of gold than Here. It is the same with love and dreams and the work of our lives. We see the light everywhere but where we are, and chase after what we think we lack, only to find, humbly, it was with us all along.

- Sit quietly with someone you trust and admire.
- Express to each other one point of light you see on the other's shore.
- Meditate on the quality the other sees in you and try to see it yourself.
- Bow to the mystery of where you are.

# July 5
## Beneath False Hope

We need to stay current with each other.
— ANGELES ARRIEN

It has taken a lifetime to understand how easily I can secretly wish for things to change, and in my secrecy prevent true change from happening. For example, I loved a friend for many years who was unable to listen or be kind or patient, and rather than feeling just how much that hurt, I always "hung in there," secretly believing that he would change and grow and one day emerge before my eyes as the friend I always believed he could be.

354

Well, that didn't happen. I am not saying that change is not possible, but more deeply, that true change, the kind that is self-initiated and lasting, has more chance of happening in a relationship that doesn't hide its shortcomings.

As long as I could dream of my friend as I wanted him to be, it softened the true pain of how we were actually living. Without such truth, neither of us could grow — not he, for having to face the effect of his self-centeredness, and not me, for having to risk saying what I needed.

- Center yourself and meditate on the actual truth of a significant relationship.
- Breathe deeply and try to relax the hope of your loved one transformed.
- Breathe steadily and feel the full humanity of your loved one, thorns and all.
- Accept what arises. Honor what you need.

# July 6
## To Witness and Hold

Just as the warmth of summer
can make a cricket sing,
the quality of being held
enlivens the heart.

We have been battered by modern times into obsessive problem solvers, but as life pares us down into only what is essential, it becomes clear that the deepest sufferings of heart and spirit cannot be solved, only witnessed and held.

I have struggled with this constantly. Just recently, after being away for two weeks, I returned to a tender partner who lovingly uttered, "I really missed you." Instantly, I reacted by scanning for ways to solve the feeling — to limit my travel or call more often. I instantly tried to change my patterns of being away from the relationship, rather than just feel the poignancy of being loved enough to be missed.

Frequently, this reflex to solve, rescue, and fix removes us from the tenderness at hand. For often, intimacy arises not from any attempt to take the pain away, but from a living through together; not from a working out, but from a being with. Trust and closeness deepen from holding and being held, both emotionally and physically.

I'm learning, pain by pain and tension by tension, that after all my strategies fail, the strength of love waits in receiving and not negotiating; in accepting each other and not problem solving each other; in listening and affirming each other, not trying to change or fix those we love.

- Sit quietly and bring to mind the situation of a friend or loved one that you would like to change.
- Breathe deeply and accept that you cannot live their life for them.
- Instead, exhale slowly and be with your heart's knowledge of what it means to love this person.
- Exhale cleanly and release your want to fix their pain.
- Inhale cleanly and simply hold them, pain and all, in your center.

# JULY 7
## PATIENCE

---

I have just three things to teach:
simplicity, patience, compassion.
These are your greatest treasures.

Patient with both friends and enemies,
you accord with the way things are.

— LAO-TZU

Patience is the second of Lao-tzu's central teachings, and it is a hard bit of wisdom to accept, for the place of waiting is always trying and very difficult to live out. Yet, quite honestly, it is waiting that saved my life — clearly the most demanding and rewarding practice I have encountered.

Had I not withstood the confusion and indecision and ambiguity and the pain and alarm of imagining the worst during the endless diagnostic gauntlet, I would never have made it to the right course of treatment that carried me through my experience of cancer. Had I not waited — which is different than avoiding what needs to be done — I would not be able to write these very words to you. For I would have undergone unnecessary procedures that would have severed me from my memory and my ability to speak.

Fear wants us to act too soon. But patience, hard as it is, helps us outlast our preconceptions. This is how tired soldiers, all out of ammo, can discover through their inescapable waiting that they have no reason to hurt each other.

It is the same with tired lovers and with hurtful and tiresome friends. Given enough time, most of our enemies cease to be enemies, because waiting allows us to see ourselves in them. Patience devastates us with the truth that, in essence, when we fear another, we fear ourselves; when we distrust another, we distrust ourselves; when we hurt another, we hurt ourselves; when we kill another, we kill ourselves.

So when hurt or afraid or confused, when feeling urgent to find your place on this Earth, hard as it is, wait . . . and things as you fear them will, more often than not, shrink into the hard irreplaceable beauty of things as they are . . . of which you have no choice but to be a part.

- Sit quietly and bring to mind a situation, now resolved, that required you to be more patient than you were prepared to be.
- If you can, recall how you viewed the situation and the people involved: when it first presented itself, when your patience ran out, when the situation resolved itself.
- How did waiting change you?
- What, if anything, did waiting give you?

# JULY 8
# MOMENTS, NOT WORDS

Like the moon,
come out from behind
the clouds! And Shine!

— BUDDHA

When I think of those who've taught me how to love, moments come to mind, not words. As far back as grade school, when Lorrie wouldn't stop spinning when recess ended. Spinning to a deeper, higher call, she laughed,

359

her little head back, her arms wide, trying to hug the world.

Then, the day Kennedy was shot, there was my choir teacher, Mr. P., crying for a man he didn't know, letting us go home, but I came back to hear him play a sad piano to what he thought was an empty room. And Grandma holding my little hands open on her basement steps, saying, "These are the oldest things you own."

Or the changing faces I would wake to at the foot of my bed while recovering from surgery. Or my father-in-law watering black walnuts six inches high that wouldn't be fully grown for a hundred and fifty years. Or my oldest friend who always listens like a lake.

Though words can carry love, they often point to it. It is the picking up of something that has dropped, and the giving of space for someone to discover for themselves what it means to be human, and the forgiving of mistakes when they realize that they are.

- Center yourself and bring to mind three people who have taught you how to love.
- As you breathe, recall the moment that revealed each lesson.
- Discuss these teachings with a loved one.

# July 9
## The Surface and the Deep

When under, remember the surface.
When on the surface, remember the deep.

When our days are turbulent and troubled, our challenge is to remember that the wave is not the sea. Though it pounds us, the pounding will pass. Though it tosses us about, the tossing will pass, if we don't fight it.

Often our fear misleads us to stay in close to shore, when the safest place is in the deep, if we can get there. Any swimmer knows: Stay too close to shore and you will be battered by the surf and undertow. We must swim out past the breakers if we are to know the hammock of the deep.

Stay on land or make it to the deep. It is the in-between that kills.

- Sit quietly and practice entering the deep.
- Imagine each breath is a stroke.
- Breathe slowly and stroke your way past all distraction.
- When you feel the swell of life around you, simply drift. . . .

# July 10
## The Ring of Safety

Who sees all beings in his own Self
and his own Self in all beings,
loses all fear.
— The Isa Upanishad

I was sitting on a bench in the sun, waiting for Robert, when a yellow jacket landed about four feet to my left. I watched its striped anterior pulse and protract, the sun making its black rings blacker and its yellow rings almost orange.

It made me think of my mother and how if that yellow jacket were within yards of her, she would have rolled up the nearest magazine and with trepidation tried until she swat it. Her fear of being stung made her kill many a small thing. She couldn't tolerate the uncertainty that something living might hurt her, and in her deep fear of being hurt, she walled herself in, swatting everything away.

Almost forty years later, I realize that we all suffer the uncertainty of being hurt by the life that surrounds us, and we all have a changing ring of safety beyond which we are likely to hurt other living things in the guise of self-defense.

I sat on the bench and the yellow jacket

flitted closer. But having almost died from cancer, feeling blessed to be here at all, I let the little insect come much closer than I used to. With a softer, more truthful eye, I could see it had little interest in me, and I am ashamed to admit just how many times I have harmed others because, like my mother, I couldn't tolerate the unpredictable nature of their advance.

How often we imagine things are dangerous when they are only doing what comes naturally. The yellow jacket came closer still; when it was almost on my arm, there was time enough to gently shoo it on its way. It flirted with me for quite some time, coming close till I would shoo it on, buzzing at a distance, then coming close again.

This is so much like the dance we do with strangers and loved ones alike. How often we murder parts of ourselves by not letting things advance or come close. How often we let fear and the swat rule our emotional lives. How often we kill or chase away everything that moves.

I think of Francis of Assisi, who held so still the birds landed on his branchlike arms, and we wonder why we are so lonely when we won't let anything full of life come near. If we could only see the bee, or the bird, or our enemy as a brief living center like ourselves, we could let them go on their way without pulling us into opposition.

363

- Close your eyes and meditate on someone who feels intrusive or annoying to you. Note what you feel, but assess, if you can, exactly what feels intrusive. Is the sense of intrusion coming from your fear, or is the person being truly intrusive?
- Consider precisely what must be done to keep yourself safe. Adopt only that action, and if you can, engage the intrusion, the fear of it, and the fact of it no further.
- Note how far your fear would have you keep others away. Note how much closer things can be if you let things do what they do outside your actual boundary of safety.

# July 11
## The Moon and the Dewdrop

Enlightenment is like the moon reflected in a dewdrop on a blade of grass. The moon does not get wet, nor is the drop of water broken. . . . And the whole moon and entire sky are reflected in even one drop of water.

— Dogen

The mystery — in love, in work, in any moment of oneness — is that, like the dewdrop and the moon, we are briefly ourselves and everything at once. Our essential nature is not changed, only enhanced.

The lovers and friends that have helped me stay alive and be more fully alive have come into my life like Dogen's moon — all of their love, as big as the sky, fills my heart and yet I do not become them, but only more myself.

Anything or anyone that asks you to be other than yourself is not holy, but is trying only to fill its own need.

In truth, the smallest stem of a damaged heart, like a single blade of grass, holds the essence of everything alive. Enlightenment is the kiss of anything — moon, storm, or kindness — that opens us to that essence.

- Center yourself and bring to mind one moment in which you felt touched by life other than your own. It might have been in nature or in the arms of a loved one.
- Breathe deeply and consider how that touch has affected you.
- After a time, ask yourself, Where do you keep that touch of life? When do you need it most?

# July 12
## Making Waves

I would do anything for you.
Would you be yourself?

In the Hans Christian Anderson classic, *The Little Mermaid,* Ariel gives up her beautiful voice in exchange for legs. This is a seemingly innocent fable that captures our deal with the modern devil. For aren't we taught that mobility is freedom, whether it be moving from state to state, or from marriage to marriage, or from adventure to adventure? Aren't we convinced that upward mobility, moving from job to job, is the definition of success?

Of course, there is nothing inherently wrong with change or variety or newness or with improving our condition. The catch is when we are asked to give up our voice in order to move freely, when we are asked to silence what makes us unique in order to be successful. When not making waves means giving up our chance to dive into the deep, then we are bartering our access to God for a better driveway.

As a story about relationship, the lesson of Ariel is crucial. On the surface, her desire for legs seems touching and sweetly motivated by love and the want to belong. Yet here too is another false bargain that plagues everyone who ever tries it. For no matter how badly we want to love or be loved, we cannot alter our basic nature and survive inside, where it counts.

- Sit quietly and consider your own history of love.
- As you exhale, consider a time when you gave up some aspect of yourself in order to be loved.
- As you inhale, allow yourself to reconnect with this silenced part of your nature.

# JULY 13
# NOW YOU SEE IT, NOW YOU DON'T

God leads me to still waters
that restore my spirit.
— PSALM 23

It doesn't take very long for each of us to accumulate an emotional history. A child burns her hand on a stove and a fear of fire begins; in a tender moment, a hand is slapped and a fear of love begins. Our emotional associations and reflexes run deep. Often, the heart breathes beneath all our associations like a soft, sandy bottom waiting underwater.

Thus, to see ourselves clearly, we must try to still our associations till we are as transparent as a calm lake. When still enough and clear enough, others can also see through to our bottom. It makes love possible again. But paradoxically, when someone is moved to reach for us, their fingers stir things up, sending ripples everywhere, and we and they can often lose sight of what matters.

All this affirms the need to stay with our feelings long enough for the emotional associations — the ripples — to settle. No one can escape this. No matter how young or old you may be, no matter how innocent or experienced you are, if you've been awake and alive and in any kind of relationship that has in any way been real, your waters will stir, your emotions will ripple. It seems the only way we can truly know our own depth is to wait for our associations and reflexes to subside, till we are clear as a lake again. Only when what gets stirred up settles can we see ourselves and each other clearly.

- Breathe slowly, and allow your agitations of heart to come and go with each breath.
- Breathe steadily, and try to outwait your reflexes to be angry or anxious or envi-

ous or resentful.
- Breathe evenly, and with each exhalation try to feel the depth of heart that waits below.

# July 14
## To Know Someone Deeply

To know someone deeply
is like hearing the moon through the ocean
or having a hawk lay bright leaves at your
    feet.
It seems impossible, even while it happens.

Discovering who we are is like breaking a trail up the side of a mountain. Yet the deepest friendships begin when we look into the eye of another and discover that they have been there too. It is always astonishing to me to find out that someone else sees what I have seen, and always humbling to learn that what I thought was my path and my mountain is everyone's.

We carry whole worlds within us as we brush by each other in the supermarket to read mayonnaise jars. The entire drama of life churns in our blood as we rush underground to catch a train. We are always both so known and so unknown.

This is why knowing someone deeply is

such a treasure. It opens the sky of all time. It lets the song come out of the sea. It lets the heart like a photograph be developed for being touched by another.

And though we may find someone along the way who's been where we are going or going where we have been, we must never stop breaking our own trail up the mountain. For only by daring to be ourselves can we deeply know others.

- This is a walking meditation. As you make your way to work or the store, walk steadily and breathe slowly.
- As you breathe, feel the inwardness that is you.
- As you walk and breathe, notice others doing the same.
- As you meet the eyes of others, realize that they are just as deep as you.

# July 15
## The Risk to Be Touched

Touch bleeds the heart of its pressure.

There are many reasons why we want to be touched. The simplest and most profound is that touch heals us. The way a drop of water spreads when touched, the pains of living that

370

we carry spread when we are held and comforted. The buildup of bearing things alone is released for being touched with sincerity and love.

Beneath all language, touch is the common gesture, the energy that connects all that lives inside us with all that lives outside us. We can disagree — be Catholic or Muslim or Jewish, be conservative or liberal, corporate or rural — and all the stern walls created by what we think will crumble for the gentle reach of a compassionate hand.

Often, we are frightened to let others in, afraid of being hurt, and, sometimes, once knowing the salve of being touched, we seek that comfort for pains we can only heal ourselves. I, repeatedly, have found myself doing both. But these are problems of when and how to open ourselves to touch. The need to be touched is never really in question, anymore than we question the need to breathe.

When my grandmother was dying at ninety-four, I felt crippled at heart because she had reverted to speaking the Russian of her childhood, and I feared we wouldn't be able to understand each other. But an old friend took me aside and said, "You both can understand touch." With this, I stroked her face and arms in silence and she rubbed my wrists, and, even when she couldn't open her eyes or speak any longer, we had a language of

371

comfort that carried us to the moment of her passing.

Sometimes we would do better to admit the heart works best in mime. For beneath the worries and fears of being hurt or rejected or taken advantage of, beneath the avalanche of excuses and explanations, there waits a deep and simple pulse that we need from each other in order to be whole.

- Enter a meditation with a loved one you feel safe with.
- Focus on a pain that has been difficult to bear alone.
- Now take turns. Have one of you express, as directly and simply as possible, not the circumstances of this pain, but the feeling of bearing it, while the other listens in silence.
- Now, using only your fingertips, have the listener comfort the speaker through the gift of touch.

# July 16
## THE MAGIC OF PEACE

As the lungs remember
to breathe, even when we sleep,
the spirit keeps us alive
through the dream of our will.

372

It is said that Merlin, when training young Arthur in the woods of Camelot, told him that the only difference between magicians and the rest of us is that magicians accept that our will is but a dream. Certainly, we decide what clothes to buy and what car to drive and even how to spend our days. But these are like the stones a hungry fish mouths along the bottom as the river sweeps its small life along.

Still, we devote ourselves to these small things, for that is what we do, and it is true, God is inside every particular. Yet often, we survive, and even thrive, not because of our endless schemes but in spite of them.

But what I need to tell you is that I met Merlin in a dream, and I asked him about being alive. He wanted to know if I knew Arthur and, after a time, he whispered, "Go beneath the many languages of desire . . . for our peace depends on whether we fight or ride the stream."

- This is a bedtime meditation. As you settle into sleep, breathe steadily, and just as you entrust your need for air to your lungs throughout the night, entrust your need for peace to your spirit and lean into the depth that surrounds you.

# July 17
## The Impulse to Love

If somebody were to cut me into a
  thousand
pieces, every piece of me would say
that it loves. . . .
                       — CHRIS LUBBE

The man who said this is a deeply spiritual
person who is a native of South Africa. He
like many others grew up under apartheid.
He told me that he was taught by his ancestors not to stay bitter or vengeful, for hate
eats up the heart, and with a damaged heart,
life is not possible.

In a way, we are each confronted with the
same dilemma that Chris faces: how to feel
the pain of living without denying it and
without letting that pain define us. Ultimately,
no matter the burden we are given — apartheid, cancer, abuse, depression, addiction —
once whittled to the bone, we are faced with
a never-ending choice: to become the wound
or to heal.

Terrible things are hard enough to experience the first time. Beyond their second and
third and fourth experience as trauma, their
impact can easily make us become terrible if
we do not keep our want to love alive.

Perhaps the most difficult challenge of being wounded is not turning our deepest loving nature over to the life and way of the wound.

This touching statement by this South African man affirms that the nature of the human spirit is irrepressible. Just as a vine or shrub — no matter how often it is cut back — will keep growing to the light, the human heart — no matter how often it is cut — can reassert its impulse to love.

- Center yourself and bring to mind someone you admire who is still loving despite the pain they've experienced.
- Breathe slowly and open your heart to the wisdom of their being.
- Breathe deeply now, and let your heart-breath wash over your own pain, the way that surf softens footprints in sand.

# JULY 18
# A FIREFLY OF LOVE

Who knows
that in the depth of the ravine
of the mountain of my hidden heart
a firefly of my love is aflame.
— ABUTSU-NI

This quiet Japanese woman's confession to

herself almost a thousand years ago tells us that the most important things begin so far inside we can hardly hear them ourselves at first. Or that we keep the most important things so tucked away that they barely have a chance to grow. Probably her sigh of heart bears witness to both. Please. Read her lines again. Now.

These are not just words, but the heart-cloud of a living being, catching herself alive in a moment that has repeated itself in everyone who has ever known or wanted to know love. And, though I'm not sure how, we can, in the snap of a guarded moment, in the wince of an unexpected hurt, be a mountain away from what we feel. But if we own the separation, we then begin the arduous pilgrimage back to Oneness.

Somewhere along the way and often with good reason, we learn to fear putting our feelings out in the open, out in the weather of ordinary air, as if our small piece of love will die for exposure to the elements, as if our true feelings will not survive the gaze of others. Yet we all know so very well that without air nothing can grow. So what are we to do with our tiny little firefly?

It is a beautiful irony that in confessing her hiddenness, Abutsu-Ni has given us a way. For isn't it her firefly that has fluttered all the way up from the ravine, up from the mountain of her hidden heart, flitting to moisten her eye and wag her reluctant tongue? Isn't it her little firefly of love that has kept its tail lit for more than nine hundred years?

It doesn't have to be pretty or smart, just honest and true. For many a dance starts with a trip, and many a song finds its opening through a cough.

- Breathe deeply into your own heart.
- Once there, breathe slowly and repeat Abutsu-Ni's words aloud as if they are your own.
- Breathe deeply, and feel the small firefly of your love flitting inside the mountain of your heart.
- Breathe slowly, and with each breath, let the firefly flit up your ravine, up your mountain, and up your throat.

# JULY 19
## THE WISDOM IN BLINKING

Asleep too long, we need to wake.
Awake too long, we need to sleep.

We blink a thousand times a day. A thousand times a day the world goes dark. A thousand times a day we wake. We can't escape this opening and closing. It's a reflex we can't control. Even as you read this, your eyes,

377

along with your heart and mind, are blinking — opening and closing repeatedly, no matter what you do. It is part of being human.

Yet so much depends on which you see as home — being open or closed. Do you see life as one stream of light interspersed with nights of dark, or as one stream of darkness interspersed with days of light? Though there will never be an answer, what we believe about the nature of life matters. It lifts or burdens our days. So ask yourself, more than once, Is life one long miracle of feeling interspersed with moments of breaking? Do we repeatedly fall in our humanness from a never-ending light? Or is life one long painful breaking interspersed with moments of wonder? Do we struggle up from the unending dark briefly into glimpses of light?

Obviously, there are times we feel one way and times we are certain it is the other. There are even times we know it is both. But how we allow for both — how much we make the light our home and how much we settle into the dark — determines the personal alchemy of our hope and despair, our optimism and pessimism, our belief and doubt.

My journey has been mixed. Entering surgery, I was certain life was dark and I couldn't keep my eyes open. But waking from surgery, I was certain that all that had changed while I was under. Now everything was buoyant and I could barely close my eyes to rest. The same thing has happened when losing love. I felt closed and dark and unable to open. Yet falling in love has always made life one singing interval of light during which I can barely sleep.

Perhaps the wisdom in blinking is that it keeps us in the middle, keeps us from drowning in the dark and from burning up in the light. Perhaps this is the reflex that lets us make sense of being human.

- Meditate with your eyes closed, and keep them closed until you feel the need to open them.
- Now meditate with your eyes open, and keep them open until you feel the need to close them.
- Repeat this, and accept your very human need to wake and rest.

# JULY 20
## LEARNING HOW TO FLOAT

When we stop struggling,
we float.

When first learning how to swim, I didn't trust the deep. No matter how many assuring voices I heard from shore, I strained and flapped to keep my chin above the surface. It exhausted me, and only when exhausted did I relax enough to immerse myself to the point that I could feel the cradle of the deep keep me afloat.

I've come to understand that this is the struggle we all replay between doubt and faith. When thrust into any situation over our head, our reflex is to fight with all our might the terrible feeling that we are sinking. Yet the more we resist, the more we feel our own weight and wear ourselves out.

At times like this, I remember learning to float. Mysteriously, it required letting almost all of me rest below the surface before the deep would hold me up. It seems to me, almost forty years later, that the practice of finding our faith is very much like that — we need to rest enough of ourselves below the surface of things until we find ourselves up-held.

This is very hard to do. But the essence of trust is believing you will be held up if you let go. And though we can practice relaxing our fear and meeting the deep, there is no real way to prepare for letting go other than to just let go.

Once immersed, once below the surface, it is not by chance that things slow down, go clear, feel weightless. Perhaps faith is nothing more than taking the risk to rest below the surface.

That we can't stay there only affirms that

we must choose the deep again and again in order to live fully. That we must move through the sense of sinking before being upheld is what trusting the Universe is all about.

- Fill your bathtub with warm water.
- Hold your hand open, palm up, with the back of your hand on the surface of the water. Feel the effort required to keep your hand on the surface.
- Breathe slowly and relax, letting your hand enter the water. As your hand relaxes, feel yourself meeting the deep.
- While breathing slowly, keep placing your hand in the water, and practice entering the deep and resting below the surface.
- Practice moving beyond the sense of sinking.
- Practice the soft attention needed to realize when you are beginning to be upheld.

# July 21
## Revealing Who We Are

No bird can fly
without opening its wings,
and no one can love
without exposing their heart.

It is perhaps the oldest of inner laws, as inescapable as gravity. There is no chance of lifting into any space larger than yourself without revealing the parts you hold closest to your chest.

Any time you hesitate revealing who you are, picture yourself as a bird perched on a roof, wings tucked at your sides. To enter a relationship without opening your heart is to jump off that roof without spreading your wings.

It's true that baby birds hesitate the first time out of the nest, but once tasting the air, it is in their nature to open and rise, and close and land. This is their life. It is ours too.

The paradox, of course, is that we must trust that the power to lift and land, for us, is in revealing what we hide. Once revealed, these tender things become our wings.

- Sit quietly outside, if possible, and watch the birds open, lift, and land.
- Breathe freely, and as the birds take flight, practice opening and resting your heart.

# JULY 22
## UBUNTU

Ubuntu — I am because you are,
you are because I am. . . .
— A DEEP AFRICAN WAY OF BEING

In the winter, I met a man in South Africa. After several days together, I asked him about Ubuntu. He said, "It is a deep African custom." He did not explain, but rather repeated its meaning, more slowly and with deeper reverence, "It means . . . I am because you are; you are because I am . . . Ubuntu."

It is something I have always believed in, that in the ignited space of our deepest suffering, in the release of our deepest fears, in the familiar peace of our deepest joys, we are each other. I felt it in the cancer rooms, in the eyes of burdened mothers sitting across from me, none of us wanting the dark things growing inside . . . Ubuntu.

I have been finding it in every path, in every way . . . in Martin Buber's sense of I-Thou, where only in keeping what-is-between-us real can God appear . . . in the gift of Jesus, where two or more of you come together, there I am . . . in the one compassion of Buddha . . . in the numinous love that ancient stones emanate if we are still enough to bow to them. Ubuntu . . . I am because you are, even in how we live off the breath of plants; you are because I am, even in how plants live off our exhalations.

I remember — years after Robert helped me survive cancer, after I helped him survive alcohol — I remember the two of us in a small park eating sandwiches with numb fingers, like little damaged birds, and Robert raised his head suddenly and said, "I have had cancer," and I took his hand and offered in return, "And I have been an alcoholic." Ubuntu . . . how we need each other to be complete.

- Sit quietly in a public place until your breath and the air you are breathing feel like one.
- Breathe steadily until your heart and the hearts of those around you feel like one.
- Keep breathing slowly until you feel, with each breath, the interconnected-ness of all life.

# COMING TO TERMS

---

We are the stage
and all the players.

One of the great contributions of psychology has been to help us understand how we replay our hurts and affections with people other than those who have hurt or touched us. There are many names for this, the more well-known being "projection" and "transference." In essence, we play what has been said or done, or what hasn't been said or done, over and over, until we come to terms with it. The coming to terms is called *healing, surrender, letting go,* or even *forgiveness.*

Being yelled at and then later kicking the dog is the stereotype of this. Yet more often, we replay the styles of clumsy love we experience. For example, while growing up, I endured the cold dismissal of my truest feelings. When I would show my hurt, I was seen as trying to weaken my parents' resolve. They then turned their backs on me, as if by showing my pain, I was trying to trick them.

Having experienced this, I am especially sensitive to the pains of those close to me, yet there are times when I catch myself holding firm, just out of reach, replaying my parents' role as well as my own. This is humbling and upsetting, to say the least.

But just as germs must run their course, all the players in our dramas must be voiced before they will leave us be. Just as we keep trying to get what we never got from someone else who doesn't know our game, we also keep the trespass alive by reenacting it on others nearby until we can humbly know what it is to be hurtful — the first step toward forgiveness.

I have seen myself doing what was done to me, never as cruel or as harsh. But it has been enough to make me tremble at how easy it is to be cruel when afraid, and how difficult it is to accept that we are all capable of terrible things, and how cleansing it is to realize that true kindness breathes just beneath this acceptance.

- Meditate on an insensitivity you have suffered, either in childhood or in friendship or in relationship.
- Breathe slowly, and let the person who carried this insensitivity drop away and focus on the nature of the insensitivity itself. It might have been a turning away, a rejection, an indifference, a harsh criticism, a rush of anger, or a steeling of feeling toward you.
- Breathe deeply, and recall the last time you carried a semblance of this same

insensitivity to another. Try to recall what led you to do this.

- Breathe fully now, and let all semblances of insensitivity go.

# JULY 24
## OUT FROM UNDER

---

All the darkness! I'm going to walk into the light!

— JOB

Sometimes there's just too much to consider, too much to understand and analyze, too many consequences to play out in our mind, too many things to clean, unpack, or repair before we can go out and play.

Sometimes the simplest and best use of our will is to drop it all and just walk out from under everything that is covering us, even if only for an hour or so — just walk out from under the webs we've spun, the tasks we've assumed, the problems we have to solve. They'll be there when we get back, and maybe some of them will fall apart without our worry to hold them up.

Wouldn't that be nice?

- Sit quietly and try to stop working your problems.

- With each breath, put a concern down and feel your being intact without it.
- Breathe freely and realize that your being is whole whether you solve your problems or not.

# JULY 25
## CRACKS OF LIGHT

The human soul is to God is as the flower to the sun; it opens at its approach, and shuts when it withdraws.
— BENJAMIN WHICHCOTE

God, like the sun, emanates on all: on the hill exposed in the open, on the plant growing in the window, even on the weed getting cracks of light under the porch. The same source of spirit emanates on our different lives, regardless of our circumstance. Thus our experience and perception of God in the world may be limited and different, may even change, but that doesn't define or limit the Source.

And though the sun appears to disappear every day, it is the Earth that turns away, causing night. Likewise, when it appears that God is nowhere to be found, it is we, in the turmoil of our lives, who turn away or are turned away and back, again and again.

But unlike weeds that grow under the

porch, we can move back into the light.

- This is a daytime meditation. Sit quietly in your room and watch the light outside move through the trees.
- After a time, keep breathing deeply, and slowly rise and go outside into the light.
- Walk directly into a patch of light.
- Inhale cleanly and feel its warmth all over.
- Stay there.

# JULY 26
# HOUSE OF CLAY

The only reason we don't open our hearts and minds to other people is that they trigger confusion in us that we don't feel brave enough or sane enough to deal with.
— ANE PEMA CHÖDRÖN

There was a clay house near Puhaditjhaba in Qwa Qwa, South Africa. The roof was flat, made of loose sheets of corrugated iron, held in place by a taut length of wire that ran across the entire roof. Each end of the snug wire was tied to a huge bag of sand, and both hung heavily on opposite sides of the house. It appeared as if the bags of sand were a saddle of heaviness that kept the roof from flying away.

At first, I thought, no nails or screws, how precarious. But for some reason, the scene stayed with me, until I realized that the people who lived there could open their home to the sky when things turned glorious. Now this simple clay house seemed an image of adaptability and balance: a way to make it through the storms and a way to open to the heavens. Now the heavy bags of sand were an honest and removable grounding.

It makes me wonder, how much do I nail down prematurely? How much of my pain comes from ripping up what I've overfastened on days I need to see the sky?

- Sit quietly in your home and imagine the room you are in without its roof, with the raw light pouring in.
- Breathe slowly and bring to mind the roof you carry above your heart as you move through the world.
- Imagine what the clear days would feel like without this emotional roof.
- As you inhale, try to feel the pull where your protective roof is fastened.

# July 27
## Allowing Pain In

I am becoming water:
I let everything rinse its grief in me
and reflect as much light as I can.

Another paradox I continually struggle with is how to let others in without becoming them. How to open the door of compassion without the things and people we feel for overpowering us.

It goes as far back as Jesus and Buddha, and the miracle of such spirits is that they show us that there is some basic clear element in each of us, like water, which can glow without a name, which can allow the pain and grief of others in without turning us into just pain and grief.

Many traditions speak to this. We call it love when we do this for another and compassion when we hold this intention for all living things. The Tibetan Buddhist tradition has a meditation practice called *tong-len* that asks us to breathe in the suffering of the world, to hold it in that unbreakable place of compassion, and to then breathe back light.

The beauty of such a practice is that it assumes and affirms that there is something timeless and indestructible within each of us that can heal us and the world if we can just open ourselves to it.

- Sit quietly until you feel centered.
- Breathe steadily, and bring to mind and heart the pain of someone dear to you.
- Breathe deeply, inhaling their pain to that center of compassion we all carry.
- When you feel their pain, you have transformed some part of it.
- Now exhale light.

# JULY 28
## GRACE COMES TO THE WAVE

Enlightenment for a wave is the moment the wave realizes that it is water. At that moment, all fear of death disappears.
— THICH NHAT HANH

Much like the life of ordinary waves, we as human beings are gathered in our passion out of a larger home, that sea of infinite spirit, and propelled from an unfathomable depth, we mount and curl and crest and spray, only to subside back into that from which we come.

Profoundly, grace comes to the wave when it realizes what it is made of. Since it has risen from the very same water into which it will crash, its fear of ending is somehow lessened. For it is already a part of where it is going. Can it be that you and I, like simple waves, experience such an enlightenment the instant we realize that we are all made of the same water? Can truly knowing this, the way that waves know wind, lessen our fear of death?

I think I experienced something like this while healing from my rib surgery. I was broken of all difference, dashed of all the ways I could distinguish myself from others. In this tired and dizzied state, I could see that we are all made of the same stuff and that life before me and after me is probably no different than the lights and shadows flickering off my cells right now. Like the wave, aware that it is water, I realized briefly that my skin is a very thin boundary and that wherever I am going is the same as where I am. As a human being now aware of this larger sea of spirit, my fear of death has lessened, though, even as I write this, I don't want to die.

I think now that the other way to read all this is to say that enlightenment is the moment we realize that we are made of love. At that moment, all fear of living disappears. For grace comes to the heart when it realizes what it is made of and what it has risen from. In that moment, grace comforts us, that no matter the joy or pain along the way, we are already a part of where we are going. Enlightenment for a heart on Earth is the moment we accept that it is the loving that makes waves of us all, again and again and again.

- Breathe slowly, and meditate on the nearest window. Note how the same air gathers outside the window and inside the window.
- Breathe slowly, and meditate on how your mouth is like that window. Note how the same air gathers outside of you as well as inside of you.
- Breathe deeply, and feel the essence of everything move in and out of the window that is you.

# July 29
## Live Humble as a Dog

Live humble as a dog
and the world will come alive
in your mouth.

The day I brought my golden retriever home as a pup, I had no idea that she would become my teacher. She was seven weeks old and slept in my shirt the whole way home. I could feel her small rhythmic exhalation like a tiny animal wind warming my heart. Day by day, I came to understand her sheer, complete, and constant presence. I never knew anything to be so thoroughly involved in the moment at hand, so innocently devoted to whatever was before her. If she was rolling in grass, the world was the grass and the feel of the roll. If she was circling the rug to lie down, life was solely the want to curl and sigh. I came to envy my puppy's ability to be completely wherever she was.

I also came to understand how she knew the world through touch, primarily through her mouth. Without the hesitation that plagues humans, she stuck her snout in everything, and this immediate knowledge of things gave her joy.

This little dog, incapable of words, taught me that there is an inexpressible feeling of foundation that comes from staying directly connected to the earth, a humility that comes from directly touching whatever we are experiencing. This direct connection helps bring things alive; it is refreshing. In this way, the energy of the world floods through whatever moment we dare to enter fully.

- This is a walking meditation. Center yourself and walk in rhythm with your breathing.
- As details come alive for you — the light on a branch, the slickness of a puddle, the moss growing from a stone — try to touch the simple things that call to you.

- Breathe deeply and nose your heart into the day.

# JULY 30
# WHEN THE PATH IS BLOCKED

When the path is blocked,
back up and see more of the way.

We are each a mountain for the other to climb, and often our path to love is interrupted by a mishap or a problem or something unexpected that needs attending. We tend to call these unexpected things in life "obstacles."

Often the thing in the way comes from another person: a stubbornness falls like a tree blocking where we want to go, or a sadness comes like a flash flood to muddy the road between us, or just as we go to rest in the clearing we have prepared, we are bitten by something hiding in the undergrowth. Thus, in daily ways, we have this constant choice: to see each other as the stubborn, muddy, biting thing that blocks our way, or to back up and take in the whole person as we would a mountain in its entirety, dizzy when looking up into its majesty.

When we are blocked in our closeness with another, we have this constant opportunity: to raise our eyes and behold each other completely, then to kneel and lift the fallen tree, or cross the flooded path, or pluck and toss the biting thing. We have the chance to keep climbing, so we might cup the water that runs from each other, so we might quench our thirst as from a mountain stream, knowing that love like water comes softly through the hardest places.

- Center yourself and bring to mind a loved one — a friend, a partner, or a family member — and focus on the one stubborn thing coming from them right now.
- Without denying this difficulty, inhale and widen your heart's view. Back up, if you can, and see the whole person, stubbornness and all.
- Breathe deeply and feel both the difficulty that is theirs, as well as the entirety of their spirit which causes you to love them.

# JULY 31
## THE EYE IS THE LAMP

The eye is the lamp of the body.
If your eye is sound, your whole body
will be full of light.

— JESUS

Jesus implies that the eye that is clear lets light in. Considering the eye as something that lets light in and not just something that observes light outside itself opens the heart of the matter. To make it through the days, we must consider our heart as something that lets the reality of others in, and not just something that maps its way through the desires and fears of others. To let others in as well as to let ourselves out seems essential to staying authentic.

There is a liberating paradox that often cripples our hearts when seen as either/or. It involves the tension between risk and safety. Often risking openness is seen as a dangerous way to lose all safety, and keeping closed is seen as a way to stay safe. This reflects a walled-in, walled-out sense of being in the world. Within the wall is safe; outside the wall is not. This belief, of course, never acknowledges the suffocating dangers of the wall itself. The mask worn after the face has grown becomes a wall that rubs and cuts.

The paradox is that in true interior ways, the only path to deep safety, that sea of inner peace, is through the shifting sands of risk. Risk opens safety. It doesn't shut it down. Only through the risk to open can we inhabit and receive the strength and fullness of what is whole.

This raises the very profound question of how to define self-protection. Is it hiding who

you are or is it being who you are? Is it guarding yourself with all that you see or is it clearing yourself to let light in? Is it preparing
yourself against all that can hurt you or is it
opening yourself to all that can heal you?

- Close your eyes and erase the blackboard of your mind with the sponge of
  your breath.
- Now look out and note the first instance
  of light and what it illumines.
- Hold that object before you and realize
  that the light it has absorbed is now
  moving through your screen of risk and
  safety.
- Feel it enter. Accept the light.

# AUGUST 1
# THE PAIN OF BECOMING

For the flower, it is fully open
at each step of its blossoming.

We do ourselves a great disservice by judging
where we are in comparison to some final
destination. This is one of the pains of aspir-
ing to become something: the stage of development we are in is always seen against the
imagined landscape of what we are striving
for. So where we are — though closer all the

time — is never quite enough.

The simple rose, at each moment of its slow blossoming, is as open as it can be. The same is true of our lives. In each stage of our unfolding, we are as stretched as possible. For the human heart is quite slow to blossom, and is only seen as lacking when compared to the imagined lover or father or mother we'd like to become.

It helps to see ourselves as flowers. If a flower were to push itself to open faster, which it can't, it would tear. Yet we humans can and often do push ourselves. Often we tear in places no one can see. When we push ourselves to unfold faster or more deeply than is natural, we thwart ourselves. For nature takes time, and most of our problems of will stem from impatience.

Before my experience with cancer, I was sorely driven as an artist. I pushed myself greatly. I think the creative impulse was deep and irrepressible in me, and ultimately healthy, but it was my secret need to achieve some sort of greatness that made me press until something began to rip. It was the unending, relentless push to measure up — and quickly — against some imagined form of myself that made the flower of my mind tear.

I do not believe that people bring cancer on themselves, but I do believe that wherever we weaken ourselves, that part will give way to illness first. It was not by accident that the cancer struck the creative side of my brain.

Perhaps one of the hardest remedies to accept for our pain of becoming is that wherever we are in our path — no matter how flawed or incomplete — is a blossoming unto itself. However much we've done at the end of the day is more than enough; it is dream becoming truth.

- Close your eyes and meditate on a simple yellow rose that is budding.
- Breathe fully, and do not wait for the rose to fully open to see its beauty.
- Rather, focus on the yellow petals about to open. See their beauty now.
- Breathe deeply, and look upon yourself as such a rose; do not wait for some imagined end to see your own beauty.
- Rather, inhale and appreciate the beauty of yourself about to open.

# AUGUST 2
## THE MERMAID

A mermaid found a swimming lad,
Picked him for her own,
Pressed her body to his body,
Laughed; and plunging down

Forgot in cruel happiness
That even lovers drown.
— WILLIAM BUTLER YEATS

We want so badly to share our innermost experience with our loved ones, but often, like the mermaid, we forget that not everyone can go where we go. Indeed, we all share this mysterious fact — that no one else can go into our depth completely. We must travel there alone. It is where we commune with God.

The lad can visit the mermaid's depth, but can't live there or he will drown. And the mermaid can visit the lad's life on land, but can't stay there or she will suffocate. We must, each of us, return to our inmost element in order to survive. Frequently, we judge each other for not coming along, even take such an inability as rejection, when in fact, if we are kept out of our native element too long, we will suffocate or drown.

The living terrain of relationship actually exists in the overlap of our inmost natures. The mermaid and lad return to embrace where the deep and air meet. It is the mermaid's responsibility of love to bring her treasures to the surface where they can be shared, and the lad's obligation to rinse his treasures in their common surf. In this way, every authentic relationship becomes a home where we return from our solitary communions with God.

Never was this clearer to me than when wheeling Anne, my partner of twenty years, to the operating room where she would have surgery for cancer. I went as far as I could and watched her grow smaller through the glass doors. I realized then, that whether it be our quarrel with God or with dead parents or with the limitations of our humanity, each of us must go beyond the glass doors of our experience alone. And the work of compassion is to guide our dear ones as far as we can and to be there when they return. But no one can go beyond the glass doors for us or with us.

On land or at sea, entangled in community or independent in isolation, we all share this essential aloneness. And in the journey between the depths and heights that nourish our souls and the touch of others that keeps us sane, we are humbled into the miracle of love.

- In dialogue with a trusted loved one, identify one thing you wish you could share more completely.
- Discuss if this is possible, discerning, where you can, what efforts can be made to share more completely, and what aspects of you are simply out of reach by the nature of who you are.
- Now, in meditation, dive into that place

where no one else can go, and bring back to the surface a small treasure, and try to share it.

- Switch positions, and repeat this process.

# AUGUST 3
## THE STRIPPING OF OUR WILL

These bodies are perishable,
but the Dweller in these bodies is eternal.
— BHAGAVAD-GITA

Most vegetables and fruits grow within a covering that must be peeled away if the sweetness and ripeness is to be eaten. There are many ways this speaks to the human journey, but perhaps one of the most important involves the way in which who we are grows within the covering of our will.

We often protect our little seeds of effort, desire, passion, and curiosity by wrapping them in grand designs and ambitious plans that in the end rarely have anything to do with the sweetness and ripeness of what finally grows within us. However, it is important to remember that, just as corn cannot mature unless it is covered for months by its husk, we need to incubate who we are within layers of who we might yet become.

There is nothing wrong with this. Most things in life need a protective container in order to grow. We can hurt ourselves, though, when we keep the fruit that is us covered too long. We can go bad, can begin to spoil within, if we stay encased in old plans once who we are inside has matured. Perhaps when we move or change careers or relationships, we are trying to free ourselves of all that has covered us, even if it has helped us grow. Although, we may come to realize that it may be our way of loving that needs to be shed and not who or what we care for.

The most humbling part of this is that, though we need to make plans and work toward goals and imagine possible futures, none of it can prepare us for the moment that we ripen. Once the soul fills out like mature fruit, all of our fantasies, ambitions, and deep complaints turn to useless skin. Once ripe, once able to feel compassion and joy, all forms of sacrifice and postponement for the future begin to make us decay inside. Like the silk that keeps the corn shiny, all our delicate dreams of tomorrow have served their purpose when the heart pops up like a kernel.

Since none of us can control or time the ripening of our sweetness, we can only try not to define ourselves by all that covers us, even if it has helped us grow. In this way, we can strive hard and long, wanting to be the

405

sun itself, only to ripen and burst with our little bit of sun exactly where we are. So dream, as you will, plan to build your version of the pyramids, scheme to make and spend several fortunes. For nothing matters but the sweetness, the sweetness incubated in our dreams and sufferings, finally brought to air.

- Choose a piece of fruit, perhaps an apple or an orange.
- Breathe slowly, and feel the skin that keeps you from the fruit.
- Thank the skin for bringing the fruit to you.
- Now peel some of the skin and eat some of the fruit.
- Do this again while meditating on some covering — a plan or dream or desire — that has helped you be who you are.
- Now close your eyes and peel some of your own covering, giving thanks for being brought this far.

# AUGUST 4
## AGITATIONS OF THE DARK

When the dark is at rest,
the light begins to move.
— *THE SECRET OF THE GOLDEN FLOWER*

Just how do we deal with agitations of the dark? How do we make our way through the tangle of being confused or sad or blocked in understanding a way to tomorrow? It seems natural enough to treat our problems like an overgrown path and go hacking our way through, doing small violence to ourselves. Yet this insight from an ancient Chinese text implies something harder and simpler. It implies that agitation itself is dark, that only when we can keep our hands off will there be room for light.

How many times have I examined and reexamined the words of another in my mind, growing dark vines by going over and over what was said: What could it mean? What could all that wasn't said mean? What must I now do in response or in non-response? The thought-weeds grow, blocking the light.

I laugh when I think of how many hours I have spent in my life weaving storylines that never came true until, like weeds, they covered my heart. It is as if the light, in infinite patience, won't force itself into our hearts. No, it seems to wait and wait for us to open, content to fill whatever small space we can clear in ourselves.

It seems that agitations of the dark always cover over. For myself, I worked for years covering over sore lesions of esteem with agitations of accomplishment, till my heart was covered over with a thicket of achievements. Only when I put the achievements aside did the light begin to move. Only then did a Universal warmth reach my sore center. Only when I let the dark energies rest did I begin to heal.

- Consider something you are reexamining in your mind.
- Breathe deeply, and if you can, stop thinking about it.
- Let your breath part the dark thoughts, so the light of being can reach the sore center that wants to be held.

# AUGUST 5
## THE CHICK BEING BORN

Every crack is also an opening.

When in the midst of great change, it is helpful to remember how a chick is born. From the view of the chick, it is a terrifying struggle. Confined and curled in a dark shell, half-formed, the chick eats all its food and stretches to the contours of its shell. It begins to feel hungry and cramped. Eventually, the chick begins to starve and feels suffocated by the ever-shrinking space of its world.

Finally, its own growth begins to crack the shell, and the world as the chick knows it is coming to an end. Its sky is falling. As the chick wriggles through the cracks, it begins to eat its shell. In that moment — growing but fragile, starving and cramped, its world breaking — the chick must feel like it is dying. Yet once everything it has relied on falls away, the chick is born. It doesn't die, but falls into the world.

The lesson is profound. Transformation always involves the falling away of things we have relied on, and we are left with a feeling that the world as we know it is coming to an end, because it is.

Yet the chick offers us the wisdom that the way to be born while still alive is to eat our own shell. When faced with great change — in self, in relationship, in our sense of calling — we somehow must take in all that has enclosed us, nurtured us, incubated us, so when the new life is upon us, the old is within us.

- The next chance you get, watch something being born.
- If moved by this notion, actively pursue this. Go to a zoo. Or a farm. Or a nursery. Or an aquarium. Or walk the floor of newborns at your local hospital.
- As you witness birth of some kind, note what detail touches you.
- Take it as a teacher and see if it de-

scribes something struggling to be born in you.

# AUGUST 6
# THE HEART'S PLEASURE

We are born with this need
to cry our naked cry
inside each other.

We are so shy about our sexuality that we often miss the quiet teachings that overcome us in moments of true intimacy. The deep intensity of sensitivity during orgasm, for instance, is a sweet paradox in how we all cherish that moment and want to return there, over and over, and yet none of us can endure that ecstasy for very long.

This heightened moment reveals a great deal to us about both our very human limitations and our deepest moments of being alive. It is not by chance that we feel compelled to be naked and vulnerable in the presence of another, that despite all our fears and defensive styles, we want to be held and touched completely just at the moment when we are unbearably sensitive.

This is the heart's definition of pleasure, and though we need this moment of exposure and release to feel complete, we also must

410

accept that we cannot bear it for very long. This is why the cries of ecstasy and agony often sound the same. That we need to feel such complete sensitivity and vulnerability in union with another is proof that no one can live this life alone. In this way, true intimacy cannot happen without trust. When we let our bodies become this sensitive while holding back the heart, we forego ecstasy and experience its smaller echo, climax.

In actuality, this moment of ecstasy, of holding nothing back, can be experienced not just during sex, but in the being and doing and truth telling of all our relationships — in the ecstatic moment when we allow ourselves to be completely revealed and held at the same time. In this daring and fragile moment, the heart rehearses all its gifts: being who we really are, holding nothing back, trusting another, being complete, and witnessing the completeness of another.

- This is a meditation on intimacy to be shared with a loved one.
- Sit facing each other and breathe slowly until you find a natural common rhythm.
- Maintain eye contact and gently hold each other's face.
- Trace each other's features slowly and lightly with your fingertips, letting the walls between you thin.

411

# AUGUST 7
## WHAT WE BRING ALONG

A river doesn't hold all the water
that passes through it.

In our journey through time, we all struggle
constantly with what to bring along and what
to leave behind. It feels so hard to throw
anything away, but if we don't, we will drown
underneath a weight of our own making.

The river is a good model. It doesn't own
the water that rushes by, yet it couldn't be in
more intimate relationship to it, as the force
of what moves through shapes it. It is the
same with everything we love. In truth, there
is no point to holding on to the deepest
things that matter, for they have already
shaped us.

The purpose of sentiment, then, is to
release the powerful feelings that sleep in us.
Sometimes books and cards and shells and
dried flowers do this. But often we carry
more than we need, seldom trusting that what
these small treasures represent is already living within us. Often the most useful gift we
can give ourselves is to lay our lives open like
a river.

• Hold a memento that has meaning for

you and meditate on the feeling it
releases.
- Be aware of where this feeling lives in
you.
- Consider how alive or not this memento
is for you.
- Consider why you keep it.

# AUGUST 8
## SURRENDER LIKE A DUCK

Beneath what I try to see
is all I need.

It was years ago, but I remember it clearly. I
was walking along the shore of a lake in the
middle of the day, and there in the sun, a
good ten yards out, was a duck curled into
itself, asleep. With its slick tufted head tucked
into its body, it bobbed peacefully in the lapping of the water.

This little scene undid me, for here was an
ultimate lesson in trust. Without any intent
or knowledge of itself, this little duck, asleep
in the womb of the world, was a deep and
wordless teacher. If only I — if only we —
could surrender this completely to the mystery of life, we would be carried and renewed.

It was obvious that the duck would wake
and swim its little patterns on the water, but

413

this little creature's ability to let go so completely allowed its time on Earth to be filled and saturated — if just for a few minutes — with a depth of peace that only surrender can open us to.

Only rarely have I let go this completely, yet those moments of total surrender have thoroughly changed my life. When struck with cancer, I somehow fell from the ledge of my fear and entered the operating room like this little duck. It was the threshold to the other side. When lonely and afraid to reach out, I have somehow collapsed repeatedly into the ocean of another's love, and it has cleansed my weary heart. And in my search now for wisdom to live by, I stumble at times and surrender what I think I know, so completely, that I find myself adrift in a deeper way that is neither wise nor unwise, but simply life-affirming.

- When you are tired, sit quietly and breathe away the heaviness of the day.
- With each breath, release a thing undone, a bruise encountered, a worry or fear that has been fed.
- Do not analyze or solve these things, just breathe them away.
- Once light enough, see yourself as that little duck, and feel the lapping of the mystery all around you. Feel its buoyancy.

- For just ten seconds, surrender — that is, soften all resistance — and let the water of life carry you.

# AUGUST 9
## PREPARING THE WAY

So long as you haven't experienced
this: to die and so to grow,
you are only a troubled guest
on the dark earth.

— GOETHE

To die is not a bad thing. Cells die every day. Paradoxically, it is how the body lives. Casings shed. Coverings fall away. New growth appears. It is how we stay vital. Likewise, ways of thinking die like cells, and we suffer greatly when we refuse to let what's growing underneath make its way as the new skin of our lives. It is the stubbornness with which we refuse to let what's growing underneath come through that pains us. It is the fear that nothing is growing underneath that feeds our despair. It is the moment that we cease growing in any direction that is truly deadly.

When resisting this process, we become a troubled guest, moaning like a human crow. We double the pain of living when we try to stop the emergence that all life goes through.

Imagine if trees never shed their leaves, or if waves never turned over, or if clouds never dumped their rain and disappeared.

I say this as much to remind myself as you: Little deaths prevent big deaths. What matters most is waiting its turn underneath all that is expending itself to prepare the way.

- Sit quietly and consider the many selves you have been. As you breathe evenly, consider how the new self has always been growing underneath the old.
- Now close your eyes and meditate on the newness growing within you right now.
- As you breathe steadily, relax your grip on the habits of your mind that might be blocking your growth.

# AUGUST 10
## AT RANDOM

Random is the instant a horse at full speed has all four hooves off the ground.

This is the original meaning of the word. It refers to the mystery of unbridled passion, to the lift that results from total immersion and surrender. In our age, however, *random* means without design, method, or purpose.

It refers to utter chance. It helps us dismiss whatever appears to be beyond the control of our will. If we didn't author it, it must be accidental.

Yet our lives are full of unexpected surges of kindness that seem to come from nowhere. Just when you're thirsty, a cup is gathered and passed around. Just when you are lonely to the point of snapping that bone way inside that you show no one, someone offers you a ride or steadies the grocery bag about to drop from your grip. Just when you feel nothing can raise your sad head from the lonely road, the deer stutter across the road in exact rhythm with Handel.

So what might we learn from the horse at random? Consider how all of its energy and desire mounts for the brief moment it inhabits itself fully, and in that moment, it flies. Only to touch down again. And to fly again. And touch down again. For us, the moment at random is the moment of holding nothing back, of giving our all to whatever situation is before us. In that charged moment, we come as close to flying as human beings can — we soar briefly with a passion for life that brings everything within us to meet our daily world.

I experienced this again and again in the many hospital beds I lay flat in while going through cancer. When I could hold nothing back — not tears, not pain, not frustration or anger — I found myself at random, off the

417

ground, though I couldn't get out of bed. And remarkably, it put me in the flow of the lives around me.

For just as pain in the body signals other cells to flood the injured area, our honest experience lived at random calls other lives to our aid. Just as blood flows from healthy parts of the body to those that are injured without either part knowing they will meet, so too in the Universal body. We flow to each other's aid, often without knowing where we are headed. Mysteriously, the life force heals itself this way. And what we call "chance" or "luck" or "coincidence" is the circulation of life healing itself through us and in us.

- Do one thing at random today.
- If a patch of sun catches your eye, hold nothing back. Go stand in it and raise your face to the sky.
- If you're caught in the rain, open yourself to it, however briefly.
- If you hear live music on the street, seek it out and listen quietly for a moment.
- If you see something beautiful, smile slowly. If it still seems beautiful, allow yourself to laugh that you have the privilege to see it twice.
- Hold nothing back. Allow what touches you to change your path.

# AUGUST 11
## WHILE RUNNING

To see takes time.
— GEORGIA O'KEEFFE

While running in May, I saw a neatly trimmed hedge, and sprouting briskly through its symmetry were scraggly blue flowers wildly obeying no form. It made me smile, for I have spent many years resisting being pruned and shaped. I loved how the wild blue just hung there above the hedge.

While running in June, I saw an older man out pruning that hedge. He was so involved: clipping gingerly, then backing up, sweating through his eye, as if the world depended on his diligence. I was touched by his care. We nodded briefly, and without a word, it was clear that it wasn't the hedge, but that he needed something to care for. I realized this is how I've lived since surviving cancer.

While running in August, I came upon a slim fountain gushing from an unseeable center, as high as it could, reaching without arms until it ran out of reach, and at its closest to the sky, it began to fall back on itself; always what was rising up replacing what was falling away. Sweating and heaving, I realized that this is what it means to be free.

- Sit quietly, and call to the part in you that resists being pruned. Affirm it.
- Breathe deeply, and call to the part in you that needs to care. Embrace it.
- Breathe freely, and call to the part in you that after reaching falls back on itself. Bless it.

# AUGUST 12
# TO LIVE OUT LOUD

We are here to live out loud.

— BALZAC

Early on, we know enough to cry and sound our way into the world; this is the primary purpose of voicing ourselves. Whatever comes out becomes a lifeline, a vein of expression by which we affirm, again and again, that we are vital, a quickening part of all the majesty and variety of life.

But soon — perhaps in school, or at home, or when first venturing after a sense of love we somehow think is not within us — too soon, we start believing that we cry and sound in order to be heard. And everything changes.

Then we become anxious to be received, to be accepted, and approved. But imagine if birds only sang when heard. If musicians only

420

played when approved of. If poets only spoke when understood.

There have been many times I've struggled through the expectation and disapproval of others to refind my voice and rejoice as a living piece of things. Certainly, there is a particular joy and nourishment in being heard. But I have come to realize that sounding my way into the world, to express who I am, must always come first. Since wanting to be thought well of never goes away, I always have to keep the reactions of others at bay long enough for my voice to make it to the light.

I must tell you of an old man I know who came here from Italy. He's spent his life working as a plumber. He is a good, sweet man, and when he laughs, which is often, he cries, no matter who's around or whether or not anyone understands. He keeps his pipes clean. He lives out loud. Unknowingly, he has shown me how to love the world.

- Go outside, if you can, and listen to the birds. Hear the clearness of their song.
- Note how there seems to be nothing between their impulse to sing and what they sing.
- As you breathe, note what you are feeling and note whatever hesitation keeps you from sounding it out loud. This is a human malady.

- Work on removing your human hesitation. As you inhale, feel what rises in you. At the top of your breath, blink the mind shut like an eye. As you exhale, let the feeling sound from you, no matter how softly.

# AUGUST 13
# BIRD-ROCK

Maybe that's why I want to touch people so often — it's only another way of talking.
— GEORGIA O' KEEFFE

I was aching and vulnerable, feeling far from home, when, through the harsh shore wind, I saw a large rock surrounded by the rough churned-up sea. The rock was covered with all kinds of animals: willet, gull, cormorant, sea lion, seal, pelican, otter. All had found refuge from the hammering of the sea; climbing, winging, hauling themselves on the rock; living together, laying on each other; finding this rock-oasis of wind and sun; too tired once on the rock to fight, each having been wrung out by the pounding of the wet, wet hours.

I realized this is how the wounded find their way, how we have found each other, even in this book. Every survivor, regardless of what they survive, knows the hammering of the sea, and the rock we find refuge on is an exposed place where we finally accept each other — too tired from swimming to think any longer about territories, too tired to talk except through simple touch.

The wellness group I attended weekly was such a rock. The meeting rooms of recovery are such a rock. The thousand quiet rooms of therapy are such a rock. For those who have suffered, tolerance is not a political position or even a principle. For those of us who have suffered, who have hauled ourselves into the sun, anything exhausted beside us is family.

- Center yourself, and imagine this moment as a rock you've climbed on out of your suffering.
- Breathe deeply, and feel the momentary peace from the hammering of your days.
- Open your heart to see if others you know spend time here.
- If someone in particular comes to mind, be open to talking with them about all this.

# AUGUST 14
## THE PUYE CLIFFS

I thought I could become wise, but it is much beyond me. Far away is all that has come into being and very, very deep. Who can find it?
— ECCLESIASTES, 7:24–25

Humility, which comes from the word *humus,* the soil, offers more than a bowed head. It gives us a connection with everything older than we are and so, provides us with a calming perspective outside of our daily worries, and often beyond our understanding.

I felt this deeply one day when visiting a friend in New Mexico. We drove an hour north of Sante Fe, where we found the Puye Cliffs, dwellings cut in stone where fifteen hundred Pueblos lived for twelve generations. We climbed the top, and, winded by what seemed the edge of the world, Carol said, "How beautifully insignificant we are. . . ." We imagined the elders choosing this site 800 years ago because the vastness would keep everyone aware of the Creator.

The wind grew stronger, whipping in the little holes where native spirits lived, and they began to sing beneath the wind, and I thought of Carl Jung confessing that only in terms of the centuries did his life have meaning, and I realized that everyone who ever sought the truth of spirit has lived like this, looking out from their dark hollowed cave onto the majesty of all there is.

How we all climb through the trials of our outer life to the precipice of humility and in-dwell there on the edge of mystery. How we climb through our suffering to a place where we can carve out a tiny home from which to dizzy ourselves with the knowledge that we are small and the Universe is big.

Oh, I have suffered the climb, like climbers before me, to live high on the wall and wait. There we stood together and alone, worn by the days to exactly what we are. There, on the inner cliffs where humbled creatures meet to see what can't be seen and know what can't be known, we spread our arms like hawks to taste the ancient air. We spread our minds like trees rooted on the edge to accept the end of knowledge arriving like sun, not to instruct us but to warm us and help us grow.

Oh, we leaned into the vastness and spread our hearts in our simple chests, pounding beneath the wind, like a human thing three inches from its song.

- The next chance you get, travel to an open natural space — a mountaintop, an ocean shore, the bank of a wide lake,

425

or the center of an open field.
- Meditate there in silence, letting the wind surround your tiny breath with the feel of everything older than you.

# AUGUST 15
## BEING HELD

Perhaps the shortest and most powerful prayer in human language is help.
— FATHER THOMAS KEATING

A hardness we can't see, cold and rigid, begins to form between us and the world, the longer we stay silent about what we need. It is not even about getting what we need, but about admitting, mostly to ourselves, that we do have needs.

Asking for help, whether we get it or not, breaks the hardness that builds in the world. Paradoxically, asking even for the things that no one can give, we are relieved and blessed for the asking. For admitting our humanness lets the soul break surface, the way a dolphin leaps for the sun.

One of the most painful barriers we can experience is the sense of isolation the modern world fosters, which can only be broken by our willingness to be held, by the quiet courage to allow our vulnerabilities to be seen. For as water fills a hole and as light fills the dark, kindness wraps around what is soft, if what is soft can be seen.

So admitting what we need, asking for help, letting our softness show — these are prayers without words that friends, strangers, wind, and time all wrap themselves around. Allowing ourselves to be held is like returning to the womb.

- As you breathe, try to relax and soften your guard for these brief moments.
- Breathe slowly, and feel your pores open more fully to the world.
- Inhale deeply, and let the air and silence get closer.
- Inhale cleanly, and allow yourself to be held by what is.

# AUGUST 16
## DUMP YOUR POCKETS

Please remember, it is what you are that heals, not what you know.
— CARL JUNG

This is very difficult to remember. I struggle with it daily. Even when I understand this enough to open my heart like a sponge to the day, someone I love comes along in pain and

I start dumping my pockets, looking for the one thing I know that will help them. But time and time again, the only thing they want is for me to open my heart like a sponge to them. They only want to be heard and held.

This is so easy to see in other forms of nature. Stars hold the dark by being light. Rivers keep the Earth alive by being wet. Wind clears our heads of clouds.

These are the teachers that open the heart, the things that wait in our nature for us to bring them alive. These are the things that heal ourselves and each other.

When my pockets are empty and I've dumped all I know, I often end up shrugging, admitting my ignorance of what to do. Humbly, it is then that the real work of love begins.

- Once during the day, think of who you are as living energy and not as a goal to be achieved or an obstacle to be overcome. Feel yourself without inventory.

## AUGUST 17
## EACH IS A LIVING FLUTE

Suffering makes an instrument of each of us,

so that standing naked, holes and all,
the unseen vitalities can be heard
through our simplified lives.

Sometimes we can't get what we want. While this can be disappointing and painful, it is only devastating if we stop there. The world thrives on endless possibilities. It is what makes nature a reservoir of health. Yet if the heart is cramped or the mind locks on to its pain, we can narrow wonder to a thread. In contradiction to the endless number of eggs that spawn a fish and the endless number of cells that blossom to heal a wound, we can hold out the one thing we want as the only food. From here, crisis and desperation are a short step.

It becomes a sorry occupation, beating oneself up for the one seed that didn't take. It is an insidious way: the more we refuse mystery, the more we feel responsible for all that befalls us. Indeed, the more we distract ourselves with analyzing strategies that failed, the more we avoid the true feelings of loss that no one can escape en route to a full and vital life.

Even if we can accept this, none of us is exempt from the turmoil and pain that arises when what we want is love. For once we pour ourselves into loving another person, it seems as if they take who we are with them when they go. In truth, they take a deep part of us, but what feeds the heart from within is endless, and everything that is living heals.

Nowhere is this more evident than in the beauty of trees. Their endless turns of bark and nubs of trunk make each look like a sage. Yet, amazingly, the skin of an old tree is no more than a living map of its scars. Can it be that the cuts turn scars and the scars turn into beautiful quiet notches in which things that fly can nest?

In every space opened when what we want gets away, a deeper place is cleared in which the mysteries can sing. If we can only survive that pain of being emptied, we might yet know the joy of being sung through. Strangely and beautifully, each soul is a living flute being carved by life on Earth to sound deeper and deeper song.

- Sit quietly and meditate on a relationship in which you feel you have lost a part of yourself. It might be a romantic relationship, a friendship, or a family tie.
- Breathe steadily and contemplate how this happened. By rejection? Or submission? Or by giving away your ability to choose what your soul needed? Or did your loved one move away or die?
- Breathe deeply, beneath all right and wrong, and along the hurt, underneath the loss, see if you can feel what has

been opened and exposed for this tearing away.
- Even if you can't name it, take this new
presence with you and spend the day
getting to know the deeper song waiting
to be played through you.

# AUGUST 18
## SETTLING INTO THE WAIT

Be serene in the oneness of things
and erroneous views
will disappear by themselves.

— SENG-TS'AN

I am sitting in Bryant Park in New York City
as I write this. It is summer and the tall oaks
all lean south for some reason. It is midday
and everyone is slouching in the heat. There
are professional lunchers, German tourists,
old men dozing, and the homeless muttering
to themselves as sparrows flit, their chirp
some message no one can decode.

At times life seems an enormous waiting
room with no destination, in which some
walk stiffly to and fro, waiting for the pain to
stop. Others wait for something good to happen. Still others fear that something bad will
begin. The driven plan while they wait. I am
each of them.

431

It is such a struggle — has always been — for each of us to settle deep enough into the wait, into the weight till we discover that there's nowhere to go.

Perhaps the greatest challenge, once fully awake, is to drop all reaching and simply open like a clam waiting in the deep until life in all its guises floods through the half-closed center that is us.

Then God enters us like a brilliant stone falling in a lake, and the past ripples behind us, and the future ripples before us, and we are breathing in eternity.

- This meditation may take some time. Sit quietly, and try to meditate until your sense of time starts to fall away.
- As you breathe, allow your images of the past and your hopes for the future to rise and pass.
- As you slow beyond waiting, allow the past and the future and your sense of time to merge.
- As you enter your day, try not to reach for life. Try not to leave or arrive. Try to let life enter you.

# AUGUST 19
## THE NECESSARY PRIVILEGE

Not to feel is to stop the heart from
breathing.

So often, we war against sadness as if it were
an unwanted germ, and pine after happiness
as if it were some promised Eden, whose gate
is keyed to the one secret flaw we need to
rectify in order to be worthy. Even our
Constitution attempts to rescue us from the
hard full journey of individuation, ensuring
what no government can ensure, the soul's
contentment; suggesting that happiness is our
inalienable right, while implying that to
experience sadness leaves us somehow de-
prived.

Yet it is no mistake that to suffer means to
feel keenly. For to feel deeply and precisely
with full awareness is what opens us to both
joy and sorrow. It is the capacity to feel keenly
that reveals the meaning in our experiences.

If you are thirsty, you can't dip your face to
the stream and say, "I'll only drink the
hydrogen and not the oxygen." If you remove
one from the other, the water cannot remain
water. The life of feeling is no different. We
cannot drink only of happiness or sorrow and
have life remain life.

433

The truth is, that as the lungs make use of the air we breathe, the heart makes use of the things we experience. Thus, to be alive is to feel. This is our right. To feel keenly is our necessary privilege.

- Recall your most recent moment of happiness and what opened you to it.
- Recall your most recent moment of sadness and what opened you to that.
- Let each quiet breath bring these feelings together the way rivers merge into a sea.
- Without trying to keep them separate, feel your happiness and sorrow merge in the depth of your being.

# AUGUST 20
# HOLDING IN THE BELLY

The inward battle — against our mind, our wounds, and the residues of the past — is more terrible than outward battle.
— SWAMI SIVANANDA

I saw a sea otter rolling in the bay. It held a crab or small turtle against its belly, and on its back, it would eat a piece, then press the crab or turtle to its belly and turn over and swim some more.

This stayed with me for days until I realized that I have been living like this otter; holding the uneaten part of my shell to my belly as I roll through the deep, and, of course, it is impossible to swim freely while holding dead shelled things so tightly.

Indeed, trying to move on and eat the past at the same time is the cause of many ulcers. Realizing this made me stop and face the sadness of old wounds that I was holding tightly in my belly.

It made me understand, yet again, that while we try to integrate inner and outer experience, while we aspire to such a oneness, the work is often one at a time: facing ourselves without going anywhere, not nibbling at the ailing soul on the run.

- Still yourself and see if there is a strain between your doing and your being, a strain from tending something in your life while on the move.
- If so, stop and face what is in your belly. Make what you need to tend where you are going.
- Breathe deeply and let your inner and outer attention go in the same direction.

## Teachers Are Everywhere

> Teachers arise from somewhere within me that is beyond me, the way the dark soil that is not the root holds the root and feeds the flower.

So often we think of ourselves as freestanding and in charge, because we have the simple blessing of being able to go where we want. But we are as rooted as shrubs and trees and flowers, in an unseeable soil that is everywhere. It's just that our roots move.

Certainly, we make our own decisions, dozens every day, but we are nourished in those decisions by the very ground we walk, by the quiet teachers we encounter everywhere. Yet in our pride and confusion, in our self-centeredness and fear, we often miss the teachers and feel burdened and alone.

In trying to hear those quiet teachers, I am reminded of the great poet Stanley Kunitz, who as a young man struggling darkly with how to proceed with his life, heard geese cross a night sky and somehow he knew what he had to do. Or how a man I know was slowly extinguishing himself, sorely depressed, when, finally exhausted of his endless considerations, he heard small birds in snow in unexpected song. He realized he was a musician who needed to find and learn the instrument he was supposed to play.

From the logic of being freestanding and in charge, experiences of this sort seem crazy-making and untrustworthy. But the soil of life in which we grow speaks a different language than we are taught in school. In actuality, truth and love and the spirit of eternity are rarely foreseeable, and clarity of being seldom comes through words.

In my brief time on Earth, I have felt the light of ageless spirit fill me unexpectedly when I thought I would die, and as water pumps its way up a slim root making that plant leaf out toward the light, I have found myself, against all fear and will, flushed with possibility in the direction of dreams I had hardly imagined.

Whether through birds in snow, or geese honking in the dark, or through the brilliant wet leaf that hits your face the moment you are questioning your worth, the quiet teachers are everywhere. When we think we are in charge, their lessons dissolve as accidents or coincidence. But when brave enough to listen, the glass that breaks across the room is offering us direction that can only be heard in the roots of how we feel and think.

- Breathe evenly, and accept that there is no way to prepare for unexpected teachings other than to keep your heart and mind quiet and receptive.

- Breathe deeply and slowly, knowing that as the body must be stretched to do exercise, the heart and mind must be stretched to stay open to the spirit of life.
- Breathe fully and steadily, stretching the passageways of your heart and mind, accepting that you are a flower yet to open.

# AUGUST 22
## BENEATH ARRIVING

I'm only lost if I'm going someplace in particular.

— MEGAN SCRIBNER

A friend was traveling around Europe, training from city to city. Despite her plans, her interest drew her in different directions, and a path unfolded that she couldn't have foreseen. Each point of discovery led to the next, as if some logic out of view were guiding her. During this phase of her journey, though she often wasn't sure where she was, she never felt lost. It was when she needed to arrive at a certain station at a certain time that she felt she was off course, astray, and at the fringe of where she was supposed to be.

All this led her to realize that the more narrow her intentions on any one day, the more she felt behind, late, and lost. In contrast, the wider her net of designs, the more often she felt a sense of discovery. Regardless of where she had to be, it seemed that the more open to possibility and change she was, the more she felt like every moment she came upon was holding a treasure she was supposed to find.

Of course, there will always be times that we need to find our very precise way. But more often than not, our image of a destination is only a starting point that we cling to needlessly. When we can free up our sense of needing to arrive in a certain place, we lessen the weight of being lost. And once beneath arriving and beneath our fear of failing to arrive, the real journey begins.

- This is a walking meditation. Choose somewhere nearby you'd like to walk to — a bench in a park, a coffee shop downtown, or a schoolyard not too far away.
- Choose a simple route and begin your walk.
- As your walk unfolds, be open to what catches your interest — a bird song, a ripple of light, or maybe the sound of children playing. Follow that interest.

- Practice letting go of your plan and discovering the path of interest that waits beneath your plan.

# AUGUST 23
# THE TASTE OF SKY

Of magic doors there is this,
you do not see them even
as you are passing through.

— ANONYMOUS

Often as we are being transformed, we cannot tell what is happening. For while in the midst of staying afloat, it is next to impossible to see the ocean we are being carried into. While struggling with the pain of change, it is often impossible to see the new self we are becoming. While feeling our hand pried loose by experience, we seldom can imagine what will fill it once it is opened. As the days rinse our heart, we can feel something unseeable scour us through, though we can't yet imagine how much fresher milk and sky and laughter will taste once we are returned to the feel of being new.

- Sit quietly and bring to mind a struggle you are now experiencing in your life.
- Breathe through this struggle and bless

the buried part of you just waiting for its turn in the world.

# AUGUST 24
## ENTHUSIASM

We are human beings:
our being infinite as wind,
our human house full of holes.

As difficult as it is to accept that there are no answers in life, it is even more difficult at times to accept that no one holds what we presume are the answers. No one. There is only, it seems, the returning glimpse of wholeness in which all is seen and felt, and the frequently muddled aftermath when clarity is gone and all speech fails.

In essence, as we must blink a thousand times a day, what is human in us blinks continually over our essence. In this way, our limitations humble us, covering our gifts repeatedly, blinking away: there, then not; there, then not. There is no escaping the mix of all this. There is only holding the mystery of truth in view, even when we're in the dark, the way we can feel the warmth of the sun when our lids are closed.

So what are we left with? Well, we are each faced with the endless and repeatable task of discovering, or uncovering, our enthusiasm, which means in essence being at one with the energy of God or the Divine. The word itself comes from the Greek *en* (one with) and *theos* (the divine).

Despite our endless limitations, it seems that the qualities of attention, risk, and compassion allow us to be at one with the energy of the Whole and the result is enthusiasm, that deep sensation of Oneness.

As such, enthusiasm is not a mood that can be willed or forced. Rather, it is the ripple that follows the stone. It can only be felt after we immerse ourselves in life.

Like a bird gliding on the current of air it cannot see, or a fish swimming with the tide of deep it cannot see, or a note being sung as part of a song it cannot see, we are all left with the necessary risk to starve the ego — that in us which believes it can control the world — so that the unseeable music of being may rise and carry us. In recurring humility, our enthusiasm, our momentary oneness with the energy of the Universe, is the sound of God moving through the harp of the soul.

It is a mysterious and strenuous and simple practice: to walk when we are able and be still when we are not, to bleed the dark that builds within us, and trade it for the light which is always waiting. Despite all our limitations, the most crucial challenge of being human is to show up like a rose.

- Take a moment during your day and sit quietly outside with your eyes open.
- As you breathe, be aware of the times you must blink.
- Be comforted by the fact that, even when you blink, the sun does not stop shining, the birds do not stop singing, and the flowers do not stop opening.
- As you breathe and blink, be comforted by the fact that even when you can't see, your spirit does not stop shining, your heart does not stop singing, and your life does not stop opening.

# AUGUST 25
## LOVE IS IN THE BEING

---

The center I once glimpsed is all around
    me,
a landscape I now live in, and I will not
pretend any more.

If those I love can't recognize me
with my soul out in the open,
I will no longer retreat
and show what is familiar.

You do not have to do anything to be loved. You do not have to perform, or achieve, or earn a merit badge, or be witnessed doing good. It has taken me almost half a century to learn and believe this. It is my work to this day. For our messages to the contrary are deep.

Growing up, I heard my father say a thousand times, "Don't tell me how hard you try, just show me what you accomplish." But my life has shown me that the opposite is true. In my heart, where the spirit of the world really comes alive, it doesn't matter what I accomplish. The only thing that matters is how deeply I try. For out of this trying comes sincerity and love.

This has led me to another realization of heart: Being who we are does not let others down. For much of my adult life, I've heard the message, "You must consider others," offered as a caution against following your heart because it might upset others. Certainly, true compassion begins with the consideration of others, but the displeasure of others is no reason to muffle your love.

You do not have to do anything to be loved, and being who you are does not let others down. This needs to be repeated, and often. Simply be who you are, and love what is before you.

- Center yourself, and with each breath, put aside your accomplishments.
- Breathe deeply, and with each breath, put aside the things you haven't ac-

complished.

- Sit in the center of your being without these uniforms of goodness and know that you are as beautiful as a mountain or a river.

# AUGUST 26
# THE RABBIT AND THE GARDEN

The real voyage of discovery
consists not in seeking new landscapes
but in having new eyes.
— MARCEL PROUST

In the movie *Phenomenon,* John Travolta's character has done everything he can think of to keep this pesky rabbit out of his garden. He's even put in fencing that goes three feet underground, and still everything he plants is nibbled through.

Suddenly one night he wakes and realizes he's been going about this all wrong. In the moonlight, he quietly goes to his garden and opens the gate, then sits on his porch and waits.

To his surprise, as he begins to fall asleep, the rabbit scurries out the gate. While he'd been trying to keep it out, the rabbit was trapped in his garden, and he was inadvertently keeping it in.

How often do we barricade and fence up our lives against hurt and loss, thinking we're keeping the painful things out, when they're already trapped inside us eating at our roots, and what we really need to do is to open the gate and let them out?

- Center yourself, and consider what you are currently trying to keep out of your heart. It might be a fear of what's to be, or a memory of what has been, or the truth of a situation you are living right now.
- Close your eyes and open the gate to your heart and wait. Breathe and wait.
- Breathe slowly and give the rabbit a chance to leave your garden.

# AUGUST 27
## KEEP THE COLORS WET

I cannot tell if the day
is ending, or the world, or if
the secret of secrets is inside me again.
— ANNA AKHMATOVA

The longer I live, the harder it is to discern between the stronger emotions. They all spill into each other where they begin. The longer

I go, though, the more I can tell between not feeling and feeling. For this is all that seems to matter. Not feeling puts me on the sideline, makes the world black and white, and me, a dry shade of gray. Only feeling keeps me in the scene, keeps the colors wet.

The other day was very wet. I went for groceries and the old man packing bags was staring off. I knew by his heavy, silver eyes that he was a widower, and just as he lifted my no-fat cottage cheese, he was seeing her floating somewhere before him, and the soda and the swordfish and the English muffins were piling up as the black belt kept moving, and I gently took the cottage cheese from his hand, and he returned, looking at me, a bit dizzy to still be here.

I've worked so long and hard to be able to feel my way into the lives of others, only to realize we are all this way, and it is not just sad, it is more than sad. It is the ground of heart where we all meet. Sometimes the skin of mind is torn and we are no longer separate beings. When the talking's done, we become still proofs of love. I left the store that day feeling more than one heart should and couldn't tell if I was in trouble or on holy ground.

- Sit quietly, and breathe your way beneath the names we give to our emotions.

- Breathe slowly, and try to feel the stirrings that rise within you without calling them happy or sad.
- Breathe evenly, and try to feel the place of spirit where they all begin.

# AUGUST 28
## IN THE OCEAN OF SPIRIT

Though the wind enlivens the tree,
the tree is not the wind.
And though life enlivens us,
we are not the Source.

Everywhere we are given examples of how the life-giving elements move through us and bring us to life. Consider how fish make up the sea, in fact depend on the sea, and yet the sea, though found in each fish, can not be contained in any one fish. Consider how the tree has no control over the movement of the wind, any more than the fish has control of the movement of the sea.

Humbly, this gives us a way to understand the vast life of spirit. For like the tree and the fish, we as human beings have no control over the movement of grace. Souls, like fish, make up the ocean of all spirit, depending on that element, and yet the ocean of grace, though found in each soul, cannot be contained in any one soul.

If we understand this, it affects the way we live. For no matter your spiritual lens or the names you prefer for the mystery, human beings make up the world of God, depend on the world of God, and yet the world of God, though found in each being, cannot be contained in any one life.

When we refuse this truth, we begin to self-destruct, because in our pride and will we try to contain and control more than any one human being can. Only when we recognize the elemental relationship of soul to spirit — of individual life to the stream of life — only then do we paradoxically have the blessing and energy of all life.

If I am honest in looking at all my attempts to love and be loved, I must admit that this also holds true in matters of the heart. For aren't all our passions and yearnings little fish that make up a greater sea of Love? Don't we depend on the Love that surrounds us to bring us alive within? And yet the ocean of Love, though found in each heart, cannot be contained in any one heart. In truth, the essence of Love, as Jesus affirms, is greater than all the hearts that claim to have it.

But how does knowing all this help us live? For myself, I can only offer that I often feel like a tree standing up to wind. And just as we can only hear a great wind for the trees that stand against it, we can only know God by leaning our soul into the wind of our experience.

- Watch the wind move through a familiar tree.
- Watch until the wind has left, and notice how even when still the branches sway slightly.
- Notice how even what seems like still air is just a subtle wind.
- Meditate on how similar the life of spirit is as it moves through us.
- Feel the force of life like a subtle wind move through you as you breathe.

# AUGUST 29
## LIVE YOUR WORRIES THROUGH

Live, I say, live your worries through
and your spirit will wake from its fever,
and you will want others like soup.

During my struggle with cancer, the endless medical gauntlet of going through procedures and tests and then waiting for the results gave me a lot of practice in dealing with worry.

I quickly realized that fear gained its power whenever I would leave the moment at hand to imagine bad things descending in the future, like pain and loss and grief. Even

450

when realizing this, I was hard-pressed to stop it, and soon I discovered that worry was the mental echo of fear, the replaying in detail of all the bad things that might or might not come into being.

Finally, through exhaustion, I dropped my fear and worry for a moment, and found that I landed back in my life as it truly was, laced with difficulties and joys alike. I found that the moment I was living, no matter my circumstance, was the only safe place. From here, I could truly reach for others whose love and care fed me. In large measure, it was the moment after fear and the reaching for others after worry that kept me well.

- Take one thing that is worrying you, and use your breathing to make a flag of yourself.
- With each exhalation, shake your hands open, letting the gust of worry move through you.
- Feel the moment your worry has left your hands, no matter how brief it seems.
- If you feel worried or fearful during your day, exhale slowly and open your hands.

# STEPPING OUT OF FEAR

> I will always have fears, but I need not be
> my fears, for I have other places within
> myself from which to speak and act.
> — PARKER J. PALMER

No feeling takes over our lives more suddenly or more completely than fear. It seems to come up from nowhere and, in a blink or swallow, can infect everything.

The blind Frenchman, Jacques Lusseyran, describes how fear was the only thing that truly prevented him from seeing: "Still, there were times when the light faded, almost to the point of disappearing. It happened every time I was afraid. If, instead of letting myself be carried along by confidence and throwing myself into things, I hesitated, calculated, thought about the wall, the half-open door, the key in the lock; if I said to myself that all these things were hostile and about to strike or scratch, then without exception I hit or wounded myself. The only easy way to move around the house, the garden or the beach was by not thinking about it at all, or thinking as little as possible. Then I moved between obstacles the way they say bats do. Otherwise what the loss of my eyes had not accom-

452

plished was brought about by fear. *It made me blind.*"

More than anything, fear blinds, and only by stepping without hesitation into the next inch of the unknown can we build confidence in the life we are about to live.

- Sit with three small items before you. Close your eyes and center yourself.
- Practice moving through the unknown by reaching without hesitation for each of the items before you.
- With each breath, pick one up and place it somewhere else nearby.
- Keep doing this until your reach feels as smooth as your breathing.

# AUGUST 31
## IN YOUR VEINS

Forget about enlightenment.
Sit down wherever you are
And listen to the wind singing in your veins.
— JOHN WELWOOD

When starting out, I wanted so badly to become a poet that I held it in view like some hill I needed to climb to see from. But getting to the top, something was missing, and so I had to climb the next hill. Finally, I realized I didn't need to climb to become a poet — I was a poet.

The same thing happened with love. I wanted so badly to become a lover, but climbing through relationships like hills, I realized again that I was a lover all along.

Then, I wanted to become wise, but after much travel and study, it was during my bedridden days with cancer that I realized I was already wise. I just didn't know the language of my wisdom.

Now I understand that all these incarnations come alive in us when we dare to live the days before us, when we dare to listen to the wind singing in our veins. We carry the love and wisdom like seeds and the days sprout us.

- Sit down wherever you are, and simply breathe.
- With each breath, put down the names of what you aspire to.
- Breathe steadily, and put down the names of relationship too: lover, father, mother, daughter, son.
- Sit where you are without any names covering you, and listen to the wind in your veins.

# SEPTEMBER 1
## KIKAKOU AND BASHO

We shouldn't abuse God's creatures.
You must reverse the haiku, not:
a dragonfly;
remove its wings —
pepper tree.
but:
a pepper tree;
add wings to it —
dragonfly.
— THE JAPANESE MASTER BASHO IN
   RESPONSE TO KIKAKOU'S POEM

The destruction or healing of the world
hinges on which way this thought unfolds.
Whether we pull things apart or put things
together makes all the difference. Indeed,
Basho's small instruction reveals to us how
human history has unfolded, with one pilgrim
taking things apart and another putting them
back together, and on and on.

As an example, let's look at two very different explorers who both shaped the world as
we know it: Christopher Columbus and Carl
Jung. While Columbus crossed the ocean with
the intent of breaking things down and
retrieving whatever treasures he could find,
Jung crossed an interior ocean with the intent

of putting together whatever he might find to make treasures of what he already had. We must ask what made one explorer set foot on a continent he'd never seen and proclaim, This is Mine!, and what made the other bow and utter in humility, I belong to this. . . .

Perhaps the difference is that Columbus was searching outwardly with a predetermined sense of conquest when he reached the New World, and Carl Jung was searching inwardly with an undetermined sense of love when he reached the Unconscious. Both were clearly devoted to their search, but where Columbus was intent to separate and own, Jung, like Basho, was intent to unify and belong.

We must be watchful, for we suffer both the impulse to separate and own and the impulse to unify and belong. As our eyes shut and open repeatedly, we as builders take things apart and put them together repeatedly. Yet as wakefulness depends on keeping the eyes open, healing often depends on keeping things joined.

In love, in friendship, in seeking to learn and grow, in trying to understand ourselves, how often do we, like Kikakou, remove the wings of the thing before it has a chance to free us?

- Sit quietly and meditate on a quest you are currently involved in. It might be a

456

quest for self-understanding, for a deeper relationship, or for a home or better job.

- Look closely at how you are working at this quest.
- Are you taking things apart or putting things together?
- Are you trying to separate and own or to unify and belong?
- Are you removing wings or adding wings?

# SEPTEMBER 2
# WHERE LOVE IS DEEP

Where love is deep
much can be accomplished.
— SHINICHI SUZUKI

Despite our culture's over-emphasis on doing, there is a rightful place and time to get things done. In truth, there is very little we can *not* do. Much of the time we just lack either the ability to envision the dream built or the confidence that we can build it.

I remember early on how my grandmother would encourage me to envision even the smallest dreams down through my hands into the world. She would say, "See it here," pointing to my forehead, and then she would take both my little hands and say, "Now see it here." Then she would laugh and say, "And soon, it will be here." With this, she would look around the room.

It is an amazing thing about being human that we can feel something inside and then build it in the world. It seems we have this inborn need to love and to create. At their deepest, these drives of spirit appear to be the same. For through her love, wasn't Grandma creating me? Don't we help birth another the instant we encourage them to see with their heart? Don't we help birth the world each time we give someone confidence to build what they see with their heart?

Somehow we are meant to wrestle the earth — wood, clay, marble — into forms; to seize the air — notes, words, color — into signs; meant to hold other breathing questions like ourselves and shudder as we part. I go on and on as if to declare that life is worth living. It makes me ask with joy, What shall we fall in love with tonight? To what color shall we devote our being? What instrument shall we be next?

- Close your eyes and envision some becoming that you dream of. It might the dream of a solid relationship or the dream of a home or the dream of building something lasting with your hands.
- Breathe deeply and envision the dream

458

fully completed, existing in the world.
- Breathe slowly and spend time with this vision. Enter it and circle it.
- Now open your eyes and look to your hands.
- Feel the completed dream move into your open hands.
- Feel your hands pulse with the energy of the dream waiting to be built.

# SEPTEMBER 3
# THE UNWATCHED SPACE

I tried so hard to please
that I never realized
no one is watching.

I imagined, like everyone else at school, that my parents were sitting just out of view like those quiet doctors behind clean mirrors, watching and reprimanding my every move. As I reached adulthood, the habit continued. I walked around constantly troubled by what others must be thinking of what I was or was not doing. In this, we are burdened with the seeds of self-consciousness. From this, we trouble our spontaneity and the possibility of joy by watching ourselves too closely, nervously unsure if this or that is a mistake.

It is from the burden of others watching

and judging that the need to achieve gets exaggerated into the want for fame. I remember at different times fantasizing the future gathering like an audience, ready to marvel at how much I had done with so little. It didn't even matter for what this attention might come. Just let some form of watchfulness be approving, and I would know relief.

It wasn't till I woke bleeding after surgery, with all those mothlike angels breathing against me, that I realized that the audience was gone. I cried way inside, not because I had just had a rib removed and not because I was in the midst of battling cancer. I cried because I had not only been physically opened, but also opened beneath my sense of being watched. Somehow the unwatched space was given air. Though I could explain it to no one, my sobs were sobs of relief, the water of a de-shelled spirit soaking ground.

Years have passed, and I wait long hours in the sun to see the birch fall of its own weight into the lake, and it seems to punctuate God's mime. Nothing sad about it. Now the audience of watchers is gone and I can feel life happen in its quiet, vibrant way without anything interfering. Now, sometimes at night, when the dog is asleep and the owl is beginning to stare into what no one ever sees, I stand on the deck and feel the honey of night spill off the stars, feel it coat the earth, the trees, the minds of children half asleep, feel the stillness evaporate all notions of fame into the unwatched space that waits for light. In this undistorted silence, the presence of God is a kiss. It is here in this unwatched space that peace begins.

- Sit quietly, and breathe away the many eyes that seem to watch you.
- Center yourself, and breathe away the opinions of your coworkers and friends.
- Focus on the unwatched space within, and breathe away the judging eye of your parents or grandparents that you keep so alive in you.
- Inhale from the unwatched space, and even breathe away your dreams of recognition and fame.
- Inhale from the unwatched space, and feel the attention of life connect you to everything.

# SEPTEMBER 4
## GROWING INSIDE THE SONG

What lies behind us
and what lies before us
are tiny matters
compared to
what lies within us.
— RALPH WALDO EMERSON

I saw a woman singing while pregnant and imagined how the rhythms of song affected the life forming within her; imagined the song drawing her unborn child's soul closer to its time in the world, the way light works on a root strengthening underground.

I watched her sing and realized that the life within her was growing inside the song. I looked around the room, for we were in a circle of song, and everyone's singing was bringing their soul closer to its time in the world. The nervous man was less nervous while singing, and the insecure woman next to me was relaxing her unworthiness as she sang, and I was able to drop my replaying of wounds while my mouth was open and my eyes were closed.

It was then I realized that regardless of the words or the melody, this effort to sing is a way to open the passageways between what is growing within and what is growing without.

I now believe it is important that we sing while pregnant with our dreams and troubles and want of truth and love. Important that we attend our little seed of spirit with the same care we would offer an unborn life forming within us. Essential that we care for our unique body as a carrier of life magically forming within us as we make it through our days.

• Center yourself and meditate with your

hands on your belly, imagining that you are pregnant with a form of yourself growing within you.
- Breathe deeply, and when comfortable, give voice to your breath, letting your breathing have whatever sound it will.
- Breathe slowly and fully, knowing this simple voiced breath is a song.
- Breathe-sing while your hands hold your spirit forming within you.

# SEPTEMBER 5
# THE GROUND WE WALK

Walker, there is no path,
you make the path as you walk.
— ANTONIO MACHADO

I listened carefully as he described his little girl's first steps. He encouraged her to keep her eyes on him, and only when she didn't, did she stumble. Only when she lost her focus, when she became too conscious of the steps she was taking, did she fall.

I was afraid he was going to declare some parental primacy, that without his loving presence, his little girl wouldn't be able to make her way. But to my surprise, he understood her first steps more deeply as a wisdom that effects us all.

He stared off, offering slowly, "She made me realize that when I stop looking for a sense of truth, I stumble. When I lose my focus on what really matters, I fall."

This small story has stayed with me. For aren't we forever taking first steps, again and again? Don't we uncover a mystery of strength by looking out before us and bringing into focus a deeper sense of truth? Isn't balance, in reality, the ability to step quite naturally, like this little girl, without too much thought into everything larger than our fear?

- Sit quietly, and imagine one aspect of yourself as you would like to be: more loving, less afraid; more confident, less distrusting; more understanding, less critical.
- Breathe evenly, and without troubling yourself with how, step with your heart into the field of this growth.

# SEPTEMBER 6
## IN OUR OWN ELEMENT

A fish cannot drown in water.
A bird does not fall in air.
Each creature God made
must live in its own true nature.
— MECHTHILD OF MAGDEBURG

Somewhere in the Middle Ages in a remote part of Germany, this introspective seer came upon the wisdom that living in our own natural element is the surest way to know the inner prosperity of health, peace, and joy.

Her examples are striking; all we have to do is put the fish in air and the bird in water to see the dangers of being what we are not. Of course, it is very clear and obvious for both the fish and the bird where they belong. Not so for us humans.

Part of the blessing and challenge of being human is that we must discover our own true God-given nature. This is not some noble, abstract quest, but an inner necessity. For only by living in our own element can we thrive without anxiety. And since human beings are the only life form that can drown and still go to work, the only species that can fall from the sky and still fold laundry, it is imperative that we find that vital element that brings us alive.

I vividly recall my struggles as a teenager when my mother wanted me to be a lawyer and my father wanted me to be an architect. Somehow I knew I needed to be a poet; something in it brought me alive. The only one to understand was my boyhood friend Vic, who in the midst of qualifying strongly for pre-med studies, realized he needed to be a florist. For something in working with flowers brought him alive.

This is not about being a poet or a florist or a doctor or a lawyer or an architect. It is about the true vitality that waits beneath all occupations for us to tap into, if we can discover what we love. If you feel energy and excitement and a sense that life is happening for the first time, you are probably near your God-given nature. Joy in what we do is not an added feature; it is a sign of deep health.

- Sit quietly, and inhale your God-given nature. It is as near to you as air is to a bird.
- Inhale and meditate on what you must be involved in to feel your own true nature.
- Regardless of the job you're in, how can you be more completely who you are in a daily way?
- As you move through your day, involve yourself in one gesture of vitality that puts you in touch with your own true nature.

# SEPTEMBER 7
# THE DAILY EXPERIMENT

You are the laboratory
and every day is an experiment.

Go and find what is new
and unexpected.

— JOEL ELKES

Every time we talk to someone, there comes back to us a map of expectation as to how we should respond. We share a confusion; we are often given a direction. We share a pain; we are often given an instruction. We share a desire; we are often given a plan. The power of these unspoken maps should not be underestimated. For the endless gravities of expectation we move in and out of govern most of our thinking and summon most of our energy in denying them or complying with them.

In actuality, underneath all the plans, pressures, and expectations, underneath all the subtle guidance and nudging we receive from almost everyone, the next step is truly unknown and has never been taken by anyone. Thus, our spiritual charge is to maintain the wonder of the singular explorer that each of us is.

Though I treasure that wonder, I have been obedient for most of my life, doing what was expected of me and more, in hopes of being loved. And I have been rebellious, doing the opposite of whatever was mildly implied, ready to break any hold another might have on me. But the freshest step has always come when I've been brave enough to land at the end of what little I know, breathing new air

467

and feeling new feelings, in reaction to no one, in wonder at what is always possible.

- This is a standing meditation. Center yourself, and though everyone who's ever lived has walked, realize that no one has ever taken the step you are about to take.
- Inhale slowly and breathe in this paradox.
- Exhale all your thinking about taking steps.
- Simply breathe and practice what is new by taking the step before you.

# September 8
# Outlasting the Fog

To be near something beautiful or precious but to be unable to experience it is the subtlest possible form of torture.
— Robert Johnson

We all have these moments when the rose loses its color for some reason, or the music no longer stirs us, or the sweet, gentle soul across from us no longer seems to soften our heart.

To move in and out of meaning is as natural as moving in and out of light because clouds form and dissipate. It becomes torture, though, when we believe that the rose is no longer colorful, or that the music is no longer stirring, or, worst of all, when we conclude that the person across from us is no longer gentle or sweet.

In truth, worse than not seeing at all is seeing but not being touched by what we see. Certainly, things and people change — the simpatico of our needs can shift — but we have no chance of recognizing real change or loss if we cannot recognize and accept our inability at times to feel what we see.

Often, the emotional tragedies of life begin when we rearrange our lives — changing partners, religions, and jobs — in an effort to find a sense of meaning that is sleeping numbly within us.

It reminds me of a man who built a home on a cliff by the sea, only to have a month-long fog roll in. He cursed the place and moved away, but a week after he'd gone, the fog cleared. Being human, we all have fogs roll in around our heart, and often, our lives depend on the quiet courage to wait for them to clear.

- Sit quietly with one thing in your life that appears to have lost its meaning for you.
- As you breathe, let your inbreath freshen your heart.

- As you breathe, let your outbreath freshen your eye.
- Enter your day, keeping the thought of this one thing near, and from time to time, look at it freshly.

# SEPTEMBER 9
## YOU KNOW TOO MUCH

Two scientists traveled halfway round the world to ask a Hindu sage what he thought about their theories. When they arrived, he kindly brought them into his garden and poured them tea. Though the two small cups were full, the sage kept pouring. Tea kept overflowing and the scientists politely but awkwardly said, "Your holiness, the cups can hold no more." The sage stopped pouring and said, "Your minds are like the cups. You know too much. Empty your minds and come back. Then we'll talk."

— LEROY LITTLE BEAR

Knowing everyone's birthday is not the same as feeling the wonder of birth. Nor is being accomplished in the many positions of love-making the same as being passionate. It was the great Canadian scholar Northrup Frye who pointed out that understanding the principles of aerodynamics has nothing to do

470

with the experience of flying.

If at times you feel numb or distanced from the essence of what you know, perhaps your mind, like the sage's teacup, is too full. Perhaps, like a bowl too full of fish, your deepest thoughts have no room to move. Perhaps we all need from time to time to dump out all that doesn't stick. To let God like a great wind rim our head like an empty bowl.

Information is not wisdom. The mind, while a great and irreplaceable tool, can store instead of feel, can sort instead of understand, can, like a beaver, build a dam of everything precious. If you cannot speak when your mouth is stuffed with unchewed food, how can you think clearly if your mind is stuffed with undigested information?

But how do we empty the mind? By not overthinking. By not storing or sorting. By not replaying fears or dreams or doubts or praise. By choosing the most important thing on our endless list of things to do and doing it fully after tearing up the list.

All the wisdom traditions say to be still — that the stillness will bore holes in our useless knowing. But how do we begin? Every time you find yourself sorting life in your head, stop and notice what the brightest spot of light around you is touching. After a week of this, make a deal with yourself: trade five facts about how to live for one hour of unplanned living. Then have some tea.

- If your mind were a suitcase and could only hold five things, what would they be?
- When experiencing something troublesome, how many times do you go over it in your mind? Why? What would happen if you only went over it once?
- When going to sleep, does your mind sort and file and replay information?
- When waking, does your mind more easily experience what's before you?
- If so, try to give life to the sensation of waking twice during your day.
- Bring only one thing from your suitcase with you today. Leave the suitcase home.

SEPTEMBER 10
WHO WE ARE AND
WHAT WE KNOW

To arrive at understanding from being one's true self is called nature. To arrive at being one's true self from understanding is called culture.

— CONFUCIUS

It seems we all learn in two ongoing ways:

472

being who we are helps us know more about this life, and what we learn helps us be who we are. If we look at how we move through our days, we can see that we are all made of different mixtures of nature and culture. As a boy, I burn my hand on a stove and understand the dangers of heat. When experience is the teacher, I am a child of nature. As a teenager, I listen to others about their failures in love and this knowing shapes how I try. Here, understanding is the teacher and in this moment I am a child of culture.

I must confess that encountering these definitions changed how I see myself. For instantly, I realized that though I prided myself on being deeply natural and experiential, I was, in fact, very cultural, mostly a watcher. It has since become clear that the danger for a natural learner is avoiding the need to turn one's experience into understanding. At these times, we become the flighty one who never strings the hurts and joys together into a lesson — the one who repeats everything. The danger for a cultural learner, however, is avoiding the need to turn one's understanding into experience. At these times, we are the weighty one who considers everything but never acts — the one who never engages anything. Either way, when we falter in applying who we are to what we know, we experience a lapse in being real. This is a chronic condition that I, for one, have experienced often.

Indeed, as birds fly and molt, as spiders spin and trap, as snakes slither and shed, humans care and know. And as the bird can't find much to do with its fallen feathers, as the spider spins and gets stuck in its web, as the snake ignores its already forgotten skin, we are left with our knowledge, intent that it be useful. But the use, it seems, is in the caring.

- Center yourself, and as you breathe, look over your life and try to discover whether you are more natural or cultural in how you learn.
- Breathe steadily and ask yourself who is your primary teacher: experience or understanding?
- Note which is your strength and which you could invite more fully into your life.

# SEPTEMBER 11
# THE DISCOMFORT OF NEWNESS

Anxiety is the dizziness of freedom.
— KIERKEGAARD

Perhaps the first time we experience such a disorientation is when we learn how to walk,

474

when we move away from the wall or chair, away from the guiding arms of Mommy or Daddy. Certainly, the ability to walk is worth that discomfort in transition.

It happens again when we first fall in love, when we first move our care beyond the walls we are so accustomed to. Likewise, the ability to love beyond our walls is well worth the dizziness of taking new steps.

The truth is that every fresh experience has this dizziness of freedom that we must move through. Every time we reach beyond what is familiar, there is this necessary acclimation to what is new. It is the doorway to all learning. We needn't be afraid of it or give it too much power. We simply have to keep leaning into what we are learning.

- When you can, watch small birds fly. Note how sudden winds cause them to dip and swerve and how they adjust and keep flying.
- Breathe deeply, and know that your heart is such a bird, and that its dips and swerves create a discomfort of newness that you have no choice but to experience, if you are to keep flying.

# IN AN EAGLE'S EYE

The vastness of this endless sky
is reflected in the corner of an eagle's eye.
In just this way, the heart
when lifted up, reflects the Universe.

As the moon brings sun to those turned from the light, the opened heart brings love to those struggling through darkness. It is important to remember here that the moon is not the source of light but a reflection; and likewise, as magnificent as the heart is, it is not the source of love, but a conveyer of forces often out of view when we are struggling.

I have come to realize that the people I've admired throughout my life, the ones I've tried to emulate, were all like the moon appearing in the night, and though I secretly wanted to be like these wonderful people, it was their openness that allowed them to shine in the middle of my darkness, an openness I didn't need to copy or envy, just uncover in myself.

I think of my grandmother, whose huge immigrant warmth enabled me to see myself, the way a full moon lets you see your hands in the dark. And there was the one teacher with the golden eye who held truth in the air before our confused young egos, and somehow it relaxed me into finding what really matters. And there was the seventy-year-old priest who led my wellness group, so genuine in his love that his heart reflected everything with equal detail and compassion: our pain and grace, our fear and hope, our confusion and certainty.

All this to somehow say that to care is to rise above things without leaving them. When we care, we receive the truth that lives beneath words, and the sense of what is too much to say then reflects off our hearts, soothing those around us.

- Sit with a trusted loved one and describe the heart of someone you admire.
- How have you benefited from this person's grace?
- Where does this grace live in you? Can you benefit yourself?
- Meditate together on the quality of heart you admire and invite it to show itself through you.

# SEPTEMBER 13
## WISDOM-CREATURES

Show yourself
and I will swim to you.

As spirits in bodies we live like whales or dolphins, always swimming near the surface, forever compelled by a light from above that we can't really make out. And just as the water brushes against the eyes of these fish as they make their way in and out of the deep, the days shape how we see.

So much is going on at any one time beneath what we show the world that all our feelings, all our thoughts and expressions, splash like water on those we surface before. In this way, every person when looked squarely in the eye is a wisdom-creature, full of things that cannot be said. Each of us a spirit-fish breaking through for love and air.

We often don't take the risk or time to stand before another long enough for their truth to surface. This is what I need, for you to wait till I can get there, all fresh from the deep. After all the trouble we go through to find each other, we must wait over and over for our loved ones to break through with their wisdom.

478

- Sit quietly with a loved one and facing each other, center yourselves with your eyes closed.
- When ready, look into each other's eyes in silence.
- Inhale the wisdom of the other. Then bow to each other.

# SEPTEMBER 14
## SIMPLE AS A FISH

I've been a fish: in search of bottom when I've surfaced, in search of surface when I've bottomed, and the ribbon of God's sea passing through my gills is what I've felt and thought and spoken.

A simple fish nosing its way along the bottom is in itself a profound teacher, and like the deepest teachers, it doesn't even know it is teaching. Yet in its tiny, efficient gill lives the mystery of how to live as a spirit on Earth.

As we all know, by swimming, the smallest fish takes in water, and its gill turns that water into the air by which it lives. Though there are biological details that explain the mechanics of this, it is, in essence, a mystery.

The question is, What in us is our gill? Our heart, our mind, our spirit, a mix of all three? Whatever it is, like the smallest fish, we must turn water into air in order to live, which for us means turning our experience into something that can sustain us. It means turning pain into wonder, heartache into joy.

Nothing else matters, and just like fish we must keep swimming to stay alive. We must keep swimming through the days. We cannot stop the flow of experience or the need to take it in. Rather, all our efforts must go into learning the secret of the gill, the secret of transforming what we go through into air.

So, what is your gill? For me, it is my heart, and love becomes the unseeable trail I leave behind. But whatever it might be for you, it is more important to swim through the days and honor the gill inside you than to figure out how it all works.

- Sit quietly and breathe slowly.
- As you breathe, notice how turning air into breath is what keeps you alive.
- Keep breathing slowly, and as you breathe, open your heart to the mystery of turning experience into feeling and pain into wonder.
- Inhale deeply, and let the gill inside you work.

# September 15
## Questions Put
## to the Sick – III

When was the last time you told your
   story?
      — QUESTION PUT TO THE SICK BY A
      NATIVE AMERICAN MEDICINE MAN

Stories are like little time capsules. They carry
pieces of truth and meaning over time.
Whether it is a myth from 4,000 years ago or
your own untold story from childhood, the
meaning waits like a dry ration; only by the
next telling does it enlarge and soften to
become edible. It is the sweat and tears of
the telling that bring the meaning out of its
sleep as if no time has passed. It is the telling
that heals.

Often we repeat stories, not because we are
forgetful or indulgent, but because there is
too much meaning to digest in one expression. So we keep sharing the story that
presses on our heart until we understand it
all. I remember my first fall in love, how deep
the fall and how painful the landing. When it
was over, when she left me for other loves, I
was devastated. Throughout my college days,
my sadness was a wound that needed air, and

each telling of my story — though even strangers grew tired of hearing it — each telling of her sudden eyes and her sudden leaving was a stitch that healed the wound in my heart.

And when my mother-in-law lost her husband of fifty-five years, when I sat with her two weeks later, after all the flowers and speeches, she stared into that moment of his passing and told me over and over of his last breath and of finding him slumped in his chair. At first I thought her adrift, but realized this was how she was trying on the meaning of her grief. Like a shaman or monk, she was chanting the mantra of her experience until its truth was released.

Imagine how many times Paul told the story of being knocked off his horse by God. He did so, most likely, because with each telling, he was brought deeper into revelation. Or how many times Moses told of his meetings with God. He did so, I imagine, because, with each telling, he saw God more clearly. Or how many times Lazarus told of being brought back to life by Jesus. He did so, no doubt, because with each telling, he was brought deeper into his reawakening.

The truth is that though we think we know what we are about to say, the story tells us and saves us, in the same mysterious way that breathing is always the same but different.

- Sit with a trusted loved one, and take turns:
- Meditate on the markings on your heart.
- Pick one marking and watch how it changes as you breathe.
- After a while, tell the story of how you came to have this mark on your heart and how it affects you today.

# SEPTEMBER 16
## WHERE WE'VE BEEN

I have been born again and again
and each time, I have found something
to love.

— GORDON PARKS

Our ability to find something to love, and to love again for the first time, depends greatly on how we resolve and integrate where we've been before. A great model for us exists in the chambered nautilus, an exquisite shell creature that lives along the ocean floor. The nautilus is a deep-sea form of life that inches like a soft man in a hard shell finding his prayers along the bottom. Over time it builds a spiral shell, but always lives in the newest chamber.

The other chambers, they say, contain a gas

or liquid that helps the nautilus control its buoyancy. Even here, a mute lesson in how to use the past: live in the most recent chamber and use the others to stay afloat.

Can we, in this way, build strong chambers for our traumas: not living there, but breaking our past down till it is fluid enough to lose most of its weight? Can we internalize where we've been enough to know that we are no longer living there? When we can, life will seem lighter.

It is not by accident that the nautilus turns its slow digestion of the bottom into a body that can float. It tells us that only time can put the past in perspective, and only when the past is behind us, and not before us, can we be open enough and empty enough to truly feel what is about to happen. Only by living in the freshest chamber of the heart can we love again and again for the first time.

- Center yourself and close your eyes and imagine the passages that have brought you to who you are.
- Inhale evenly and see which passage holds the most feeling.
- Breathe steadily and ask yourself, Is the past living in me, or am I living in this passage of the past?
- Do nothing today; simply be with what your heart answers.

484

- Tomorrow, share the feeling with a friend.

# SEPTEMBER 17
# THE LAZY SUSAN SELF

The God in us is not a half-presence.
There is no screening who we are.

For years I lived this way: turning the side of me to others that they could understand, spinning the aspects of my true self like a lazy Susan, offering only what others wanted or needed or felt most comfortable with.

I became very good at this, could spin in a crowd of loved ones, accommodating many needs at once. I came to believe that I was being selfless, an agile listener, reliable and giving. I thought I had found a way to be both who I am and considerate.

What I didn't realize was that more and more of who I truly am was being hidden, and that showing only the part of me that others found acceptable was not being true to my self. Over time, I became a spy with my deepest feelings and beliefs. The cost eventually was a subtle, but ever-present spiritual suffocation.

No one asked me to do this. Certainly, I have had wounds in my history that conditioned me to hide myself at times. But it was my own misperception of how to negotiate the world that made an art form of changing faces, even though all the faces unto themselves were true.

Fear of conflict. Fear of rejection. Fear of not being loved. Fear of showing what I believed no one else could possibly understand. A lack of trust and faith that the flower inside me could survive the elements out here — all this stayed unaddressed for years while I spun my lazy Mark self.

As we live it, the line between privacy and hiddenness is very thin indeed. I have learned, painfully and thoroughly, that each of us is an entire symphony, and though there are times when all of us will not be heard, disease begins the moment all of us is not played.

- Sit quietly and meditate on one aspect of who you are that you turn away from others. It might be your gentleness or your silliness or your sense of doubt or your sense of dream.
- Breathe slowly, and ask yourself, what is it you fear might happen if you let this part of you be seen?
- Breathe deeply, and lower yourself into the center of your heart, into the place where this precious aspect lives.

486

- Breathe freely now in the safety of this moment.
- Be still and try to breathe this precious part of you out into the room.
- Note how it feels to have such a precious part of you move through you, from your heart into the air.

# SEPTEMBER 18
## GOD'S HELP

---

We don't let go into trust
until we've exhausted our egos.
— ROB LEHMAN

There's an old story about a man who was caught in a flood. First he was called and told to evacuate his home. He calmly refused, saying God would save him. The waters rushed the streets, climbing the foundations of the homes. When the streets were filled, a rescue team in a rubber raft called to him, and he again refused, saying God would save him. The power of the water deepened and the flood was crashing through the windows of his home. He was now perched on his roof. A helicopter came and he still refused, saying yet again that God would save him.

The flood did what floods do and he drowned. On the other side, he was angry and bitterly questioned God, "Why didn't You save me?! I kept my faith till the end!" And God, perplexed, replied, "I tried. I called and sent a raft and a helicopter. But you wouldn't come."

Like the thought of love, God starts in everything unseeable, but comes to us plainly in the things of this world.

- Close your eyes and pray for one thing you need.
- Breathe deeply until the prayer loses its words.
- Open your eyes and enter your day listening to the things around you, for they carry what you need.

# SEPTEMBER 19
## BEYOND ALL ASKING

If you try to understand love
before being held,
you will never feel compassion.

There was a boy who knew how to make others relax by his friendly talk, and once they relaxed, he'd ask his many questions. But he always went home alone. The next day he'd talk some more, and sooner or later, he would always get to questions of love, colorful questions that would stretch and spread and fall, just like leaves.

He lived this way for many years and the deep asking opened his heart. The space of his heart grew very wide and people would come and go like birds in the orchard of questions that was his heart. But once everyone left, he was alone with all he knew.

One day there was a vibrant being who would not enter the orchard of his questions. No matter how friendly he was, she wouldn't answer him. She simply fluttered close and held him, then waited in the world. It took the boy a long time, for he was now covered with the bark of a man, but he wanted to be held, and so, uprooting himself, he left the shade of his own heart and began to live.

- While breathing deeply, consider the ways you prepare yourself to be loved.
- With each inbreath, lift up your prerequisites to being held.
- With each outbreath, let go of all that is unnecessary.
- Breathe slowly, and begin by allowing yourself to be held by the very air.

# SEPTEMBER 20
## UNCONDITIONAL LOVE

> Unconditional love is not so much about how we receive and endure each other, as it is about the deep vow to never, under any condition, stop bringing the flawed truth of who we are to each other.

Much is said about unconditional love today, and I fear that it has been misconstrued as an extreme form of "turning the other cheek," which to anyone who has been abused is not good advice. However, this exaggerated passivity is quite different from the unimpeded flow of love that carries who we are.

In truth, unconditional love does not require a passive acceptance of whatever happens in the name of love. Rather, in the real spaces of our daily relationships, it means maintaining a commitment that no condition will keep us from bringing all of who we are to each other honestly.

For example, on any given day, I might be preoccupied with my own needs, and might overlook or bruise what you need and hurt you. But then you tell me and show me your hurt, and I feel bad, and you accept that sometimes I go blind to those around me. But we look deeply on each other, and you accept my flaws, but not my behavior, and I am grateful for the chance to work on myself. Somehow, it all brings us closer.

Unconditional love is not the hole in us that receives the dirt, but the sun within that never stops shining.

- Center yourself and consider a relationship in which you have recently endured some pain in the name of love.
- As you inhale deeply, consider the conditions that keep your pain unexpressed.
- As you exhale deeply, consider "being unconditional" as a bringing forth from within, rather than the enduring of what comes from without.
- Enter your day and consider "bringing forth who you are" in the name of love.

# SEPTEMBER 21
## A SILENT TEACHER

Only when I stop collecting evidence
do the stones begin to speak.

I want to speak to something very dear and obvious that has taken me my whole life to truly learn. We have touched on it elsewhere. More than knowledge, which I believe in, it involves knowing.

I have always been a reader. The worlds opened by honest voices throughout the ages have saved me from confusion and loneliness, time and time again. I have also spent roughly forty of my forty-nine years in school either as a student or a teacher. Not by chance, however, the classroom has enlarged over time to the living of life itself, and the teaching has involved less and less instructing and more and more the asking of simple things the secret of their simplicity.

But what I really want to say is that, astonishingly, the reward for truth, after all this way, is not justice or knowledge or expertise — though these things may happen — but joy; and the reward for kindness is not goodness or being thought well of or even having kindness returned — though these things may happen too. No, the reward for kindness, as well, is joy.

After the hard years of getting a doctorate, after studying on my own hundreds of sacred texts from so many different paths, I have learned that the blessing for experiencing oneness is not the strength or clarity that arrives with it, but, more deeply, a peace from dividedness.

Whether resting in a hospital bed when the pain has stopped, or waking in my lover's arms as her fingers ease the worry from my head, or falling asleep with the words of someone long dead lying open on my lap, the bareness of truth and compassion is the same. It returns me to a simple if rare moment in which thinking and feeling and knowing and being are all the same. It is this enlivening moment — so hard to find and so elusive to hold — that is my silent teacher.

- Close your eyes, and bring into focus one thing you know from reading or studying that has helped you. Note where it comes into your awareness. Does it come alive in your head, in your heart, or in your stomach?
- Bring into focus one important thing you have learned from living. Note where it comes into your awareness. Where does it come alive?
- Without judging either, note the sameness or difference in how these knowings live in you.

# SEPTEMBER 22
# FACING SACRED MOMENTS

The higher goal of spiritual living is not to amass a wealth of information, but to face sacred moments.

— ABRAHAM HESCHEL

493

Maybe it's part of being American, this want to build on things instead of facing them. After all, our ancestors believed it their manifest destiny to keep moving on until they ran out of land. But now that there's nowhere left to go, a different sense of exploration, that has waited centuries, is calling.

Instead of building a road to somewhere other than where we are, the life of the spirit requires us to open doors that wait before us and within us. This is what Abraham Heschel calls "facing sacred moments": the opening of doors into the life we already have.

The effort to build our way elsewhere can be admirable and even heroic, but it often distracts us from inhabiting the life we are given.

Certainly, there is nothing wrong with bettering our outer circumstances, but these constructions mean nothing if we never face the very pulse of life that waits like a kind mother at the edge of our exhaustion.

- Sit quietly, and bring to mind a sacred moment you have known.
- Breathe your way back to it, and as you inhale, face it. Let its light warm you from within.
- As you exhale, face your life today and let what's sacred find you.

# SEPTEMBER 23
## REPETITION IS NOT FAILURE

Repetition is not failure.
Ask the waves, ask the leaves, ask the
   wind.

There is no expected pace for inner learning. What we need to learn comes when we need it, no matter how old or young, no matter how many times we have to start over, no matter how many times we have to learn the same lesson. We fall down as many times as we need to, to learn how to fall and get up. We fall in love as many times as we need to, to learn how to hold and be held. We misunderstand the many voices of truth as many times as we need to, to truly hear the choir of diversity that surrounds us. We suffer our pain as often as is necessary for us to learn how to break and how to heal. No one really likes this, of course, but we deal with our dislike in the same way, again and again, until we learn what we need to know about the humility of acceptance.

• Sit quietly and bring to mind one learning that keeps returning to you. It might be about giving yourself away repeatedly, or your struggle to trust, or about a particular way you hurt others repeatedly.

- Sit quietly, and as you breathe, try not to resist what this recurring piece of life is trying to teach you.
- Sit quietly, and as you breathe, see yourself as a shore and this recurring piece of life as a wave whose job is to make you smooth.

# SEPTEMBER 24
# THE WAY OF INDIVIDUATION

Far out at sea, a tuna fleet surrounded a group of spinner dolphins swimming over a school of tuna, catching them in a gigantic net. Small, powerful speedboats circled the animals, creating a wall of sound that disoriented and terrified the dolphins, who sank down silently into the net, only the movement of their eyes showing signs of life. But when a dolphin crossed the corkline at the edge of the net, it knew it was free. It burst forward, propelled by powerful wide tail strokes. . . . It then dove, swimming at full speed . . . down and away into the dark water, only to burst from the surface in a high bounding series of leaps.

— JEFFREY MOUSSAIEFF MASSON

This dolphin moment reveals a recurring sequence for us as human beings. Confined against our will — or even sometimes confined with our own consent — we go lifeless as we feel the need for space. Feeling confined, fearful, enervated, not sure where the edge of the net is — this is the depressive, confusing struggle that always precedes freedom.

But like these magnificent dolphins, we know the instant we are free, as an inner power overwhelms us, and we are compelled with joy to explore the deep which gives us the grace to break the surface, bounding briefly into a Oneness that is hard to imagine.

This whole process describes in a moment of nature what Carl Jung called "the way of individuation": how a divided individual sorts through their deepest confinements in order to pursue a wholeness of being.

If we have a call, it is to outlast the net so we can dive and break surface.

- Center yourself and picture your spirit as a powerful dolphin.
- Breathe fully and try to feel the net that is confining you.
- Bring into view the edge of that net.
- What must you do to swim past the net?

# SEPTEMBER 25
# TO HUNT OR HIDE

If to hunt or hide is twin-edged madness,
then faith's the courage to risk and receive.
I close my eyes and am impaled by
    light. . . .

                — ROBERT MASON

We spend so much of our time on Earth running after or running from. In our want of love, we chase after someone or set ourselves up as bait. In our dreams of success, we hunt after goals and hide from what we or others perceive as failure. And none of it — none of the strategizing to land a job or the hiding in order to prevent being hurt — can reward us with peace or protect us from life.

I wasted so many hours not just in trying to get published, but in hunting for the right publisher that would make me feel worthy in the eyes of others. None of that effort, even when successful, brought me any closer to the pulse of life that writing uncovered for me in the first place.

We often fantasize in secret, imagining that life is better elsewhere if we could just get there. We often work harder in our dreams than in our life. We tend to do this with our want for a more satisfying relationship. We

498

imagine that somewhere outside of the life we are living there waits a man or woman who will alleviate all our pain and all our numbness. So we hide our dissatisfaction with the life we've created and secretly hunt for an imagined cure for what it means to be who we are.

As Robert Mason so wisely infers, our recourse to complacency and unhappiness is not to hunt for bigger game or to hide our deepest hurts. Nor is it to move our inner furniture to another town or bedroom. Our greatest chance to change our life is to close our habits of mind and to open our ever-virgin hearts.

- Close your eyes and breathe slowly.
- Imagine that what wakes in you has lived forever, and that it wakes within a soft and resilient casing of tissue that will take you wherever you want; that you have these delicate surfaces through which to feel wind and see light and sense the spirit of everything else that has lived forever.
- Imagine that once awake you walk in a world where small creatures fly about our heads and sing, where colorful, juicy things grow on trees, that you can eat what grows from dirt. Imagine that there is always water running nearby, that you can wash the tiredness from

your face as often as you like.
- Imagine that once awake you live in a time where there are others you can talk to about this miracle of being alive, others you can laugh with and cry with, others you can love.
- Imagine you can open your eyes and dance in a world where water can fall from the sky, that you can open your throat and song can come from it, that you can find the sun and let it warm the flower of you into being.
- Now open your eyes and receive that it is all true, it is all here, it is all now . . .

## September 26
## Putting Down Pain

The time has come to put our stones
    down.
For hands clutching stones can't freely
    drum.
And hearts fisting the past can't freely sing.

It only took me a lifetime to learn. But the lesson is as profound as it is simple. As long as we clutch to one thing — be it a stone, or rail, or weapon — our hands cannot open or reach for anything else.

The timeless and essential drama of living

into the unknown resides in this simple sequence. We must risk putting down the stone or stick or gun we are grasping, in order to build or touch or make music of any kind.

It reminds me of a friend who wouldn't let go of his past. He clutched it like a rope and was afraid that if he let go, he would fall. But as long as he fisted his history in this way, he couldn't embrace the love that was before him, and so, he never healed.

It is unavoidably true: hands must be emptied before they can be filled anew. It is the same with our hearts. It is why courage, day by day, is necessary.

- Sit quietly and bring to mind one thing you are fisting with your heart.
- As you exhale, open your hands and try to let the feeling loosen in your heart.
- Practice using your hands to open your heart.

# SEPTEMBER 27
# LEANING IN

Few situations can be bettered
by going berserk.
— MELODY BEATTIE

It was the philosopher Michael Zimmerman

who told the story of being a boy in school when someone passed him a pair of Chinese handcuffs, a seemingly innocent thimble-like casing with an opening at each end. It was passed to him without a word, and, of course, through curiosity, he slipped his left forefinger in one end and then his right in the other.

Mysteriously, what made them handcuffs was that the more you tried to pull your fingers out, the tighter they held you. Feeling caught, he panicked and pulled harder. The small cuffs tightened. But suddenly, it occurred to him to try the opposite, and as he leaned his fingers into the problem, the small casing slackened and he could gently and slowly work his fingers free.

So many times in life our pulling in panic only handcuffs us more tightly. In this small moment, the philosopher as a boy reveals to us the paradox that underscores all courage: that leaning into what is gripping us will allow us to work our way free.

- Sit quietly, and bring to mind a situation you feel stuck in or a position you are being stubborn about.
- As you breathe, try to relax your self-protection so you can lean into the situation slightly.
- Note how this feels. Note if the energy around the situation loosens.

## ABOUT FORGIVENESS

---

The pain was necessary to know the truth
but we don't have to keep the pain alive
to keep the truth alive.

This is what has kept me from forgiveness: the feeling that all I've been through will evaporate if I don't relive it; that if those who have hurt me don't see what they've done, my suffering will have been for nothing. In this, the stone I throw in the lake knows more than I. Its ripples vanish.

What it really comes down to is the clearness of heart to stop defining who I am by those who have hurt me and to take up the risk to love myself, to validate my own existence, pain and all, from the center out.

As anyone who has been wronged can attest, in order to keep the fire for justice burning, we need to keep burning our wounds open as perpetual evidence. Living like this, it is impossible to heal. Living like this, we become our own version of Prometheus, having our innards eaten daily by some large bird of woundedness.

Forgiveness has deeper rewards than excusing someone for how they have hurt us. The deeper healing comes in the exchange of our resentments for inner freedom. At last, the wound, even if never acknowledged by the other person, can heal, and our life can continue.

It is useful to realize that the word *forgive* originally meant both to give and receive — to "give for." In keeping with the original meaning, we can see that the inner reward for forgiveness is the exchange of life, the give and take between our soul and the Universe.

It is hard to comprehend how this works, yet the mystery of true forgiveness waits in letting go of our ledgers of injustice and retribution in order to regain the feeling in our heart. We can only hope to begin this exchange today, now, by for-giving what's broken in each other and imagining through love how these holy pieces go together.

- As you breathe, let yourself feel the pain of a wound that you carry. Let yourself feel the pain of keeping the wound open as evidence of what you've suffered.
- As you breathe, let yourself put the indignity, the injustice, the woundedness down.
- As you inhale, take in the softness and the freshness of the air.
- As you breathe, forgive the wound — that is, exchange the part of you that is defined by this hurt for the part of you

504

that, without your consent, keeps healing.

# SEPTEMBER 29
## CONSIDER OR ENTER

If you try to comprehend air
before breathing it,
you will die.

We can only consider things so long. After a
while, all the information — all the options
and opinions — will begin to weigh us down.
After our deeper eyes have seen the situation,
all the well-meaning voices telling us what we
should or should not do will start to feel like
strings we can't cut through.

This was poor Hamlet's fate. He over-
thought his life away. He over-considered
which way to go until he felt stalled and op-
pressed by just being in the world. It is
natural enough to be cautious and thoughtful, especially when faced with important
decisions, but often the only way to know
what awaits us is to live it.

This brings to mind the revelation that
came upon a Hindu sage centuries ago. One
day in the middle of their morning prayers,
the sage suddenly rose and ushered his
students away from the monastery. He rushed

about them and shooed them back into life like little ducks, proclaiming, "The day is to be experienced, not understood!"

- Center yourself while holding a glass of water and an empty cup.
- Consider the choices that await you while pouring the water from one glass to the other.
- When you tire of the pouring, breathe deeply and drink the water.
- Now enter your life.

# SEPTEMBER 30
# WE ARE RARE

We are rare,
not perfect.

With our hands full of groceries, our heads full of things to do, our hearts full of memories, and our dreams full of plans, we tend to think if we could only get away or finish crossing off the things on that list, if we could only undo what has been done or do what needs to be done, we might then live more completely, more perfectly. But we are human beings, flawed colorful beings that eat plans and memories for food.

This is a deep paradox at work in us. For

though we aspire to self-mastery and peace of mind, we are only momentarily whole. As conscious beings living in bodies, we are worn down by the days until we flash open to everything. These are moments of enlightenment, when the clarity and compassion of centuries rise in us, and we are suddenly more than we are, only to trip on the garbage the very next day or to say something hurtful the very next minute to the one we love most.

I used to think of these come-downs as failures, as evidence that I wasn't trying hard enough, and they would prick me with slivers of inadequacy. I often felt discouraged, as if there were something essential I just couldn't learn. For a while, I felt deeply flawed.

But I have come to understand that this is only the earthiness of our human condition. It is not to be corrected or eliminated or transcended. Just accepted.

We are in moments pure and ageless as light, and with the very next breath, we drop things or bruise the treasures of a lifetime. We need to soothe ourselves, not blame ourselves. We are rare, not perfect, and seem destined to know all there is briefly, only to pound it into bread.

- Sit quietly and recall a lighted moment in which life appeared especially clear to you.
- Now recall a moment in which you hurt

507

yourself or a loved one and feel the result of your clumsiness.

- Without judging yourself, hold that earthly reminder of your humanness in that clearness and let the two soften each other.
- Enter your day with both clarity and compassion for your humanness.

# OCTOBER 1
# THE FLY AT THE WINDOW

Faith is the state of being ultimately concerned.
— PAUL TILLICH

It can't be helped. We return through different questions to the same central issue: How do we live fully? How do we live in such a way that the wonder of feeling outfuels the pain of breaking?

I'm not sure. I am only trying myself; each of us a tiny will striving to find and ride the Universal current without perishing. But faith seems crucial; the ability to inhabit the breadth and depth of our compassion, to know, even in the dark center of our pain, that somewhere out of view there is joy and wonder; that even when we tumble we are part of a current larger than our own design.

508

This is a hard bit of consciousness to ask for. Yet, even failing, faith — the life of concern — is possible.

In actuality, the infinite coherence of all things and events continues like a great bottomless stream, and we like fish have but once choice, to find and ride the flow. That stream is God, or the Tao, as the great Chinese sage Lao-tzu terms it, and the strength that lifts us when our tiny wills merge with that stream of being is the sacred luminosity we experience as grace.

Once in the stream, the life of preparation ends, the life of defense ends, the measuring of individual traits ends. Fear somehow gives way to Trust. Control somehow evaporates into Surrender. The fish and stream are for the moment one. The sacred moment and God are always the same. There is nothing else to live for — even the declaration changes, for it is no longer *a living for,* but *a living out.* Always the inner out, and once out and kept open, the Whole flows in.

So, faith is no more than the willingness and bravery to enter and ride the stream. The mystery is that taking the risk to be so immersed in our moment of living in itself joins us with everything larger than us. And what is compassion but entering the stream of another without losing yourself?

I remember one summer I was at the window when a fly near the latch was on its back spinning, legs furious, going nowhere. I thought to swat it, but something in its struggle was too much my own. It kept spinning and began to tire. Without moving closer, I exhaled steadily, my breath a sudden wind, and the fly found its legs, rubbed its face and flew away. I continued to stare at the latch hoping that someday, the breath of something incomprehensible would right me and enable me to fly.

- Visit a stream, if you can, and drop leaf after leaf in its flow.
- Watch each leaf be carried downstream. Note its dips and turns.
- Note how effortless it is for each leaf to be carried along.
- Note how the leaves have no sense of where they are going.
- Close your eyes, listen to the water, and meditate on how your life is such a leaf in the stream of God's time.
- Feel the days like water around you. Enjoy the ride.

# October 2
# The Red Kingdom

I've never felt a pain that didn't bear a
   blessing.
   — Gene Knudson Hoffman

I know this to be true. From broken marriages, to losing a rib to cancer, to being laid
off after eighteen years of teaching, there has
always been a gift waiting once the ache and
fear and grief have settled.

To be clear, it is not the disease or injustice
that is a blessing. Though I am grateful for
how my life has forever changed for experiencing cancer, I would not wish cancer on
anyone.

But, as cries are absorbed into silence, as
the sun always rises just when the night seems
like it will never end, as the sky holds everything flying and everything falling, there is
something indestructible at the center of each
of us; though the pain of being transformed
and rearranged while still alive often feels
unbearable.

Even as a boy, I cut my finger open with an
X-Acto knife — I still carry the scar — and
after crying and stomping around, I marveled
to see the red kingdom within for the very
first time.

- Center yourself and recall a time when you were healing from either a physical or emotional injury.
- Breathe deeply and ask yourself if, once the pain subsided, you were able to reexperience the world freshly.
- When you can, describe all this to a loved one, noting what this injury cost you and what this injury opened you to.

# OCTOBER 3
## SO UNUSED TO EMOTION

We are so unused to emotion
that we mistake any depth of feeling
for sadness, any sense of the unknown
for fear, and any sense of peace for
    boredom.

We are so schooled away from the life below that anything beneath the surface scares us. But the need to look beneath the surface doesn't go away. In part, this accounts for the barrage of violence we see in films; as the introspective need to look within, once denied, comes out anyway in big stories of people being ripped open, in chases that end with the opening of bodies against their will. Denying the need to look within only empowers it in another direction, and we find ourselves paying to sit in the dark, unable to look and unable to turn away, as people like ourselves are physically and psychologically forced open.

We each do this in a more personal way, too. In my thirties, I was unwilling to look deep within at the source of my low self-esteem, but found myself digging in the garden with an unexpected urgency, eager to uncover some root I couldn't name. I have also found myself over the years picking at myself, at cuticles and blemishes, picking at little wounds until they bleed, and I have slowly realized that this is my soul's need to look beneath the surface diverted by my refusal to do so.

My own struggle to open my heart has been a long one. I have been married twice, have survived cancer and a cold mother, have tried to hold onto friends like food for twenty-five years, and all that has fallen away. I use solitude now like a lamp to illumine corners I've never seen. And though I am scared at times that, after all this way, I will come up empty, I still believe that going inside and bringing whatever I find out makes all the difference.

When we bring up what we keep inside, it is sacred and scary, and the rest of us don't know if we want to touch or not, like reaching from a ladder into a nest of baby birds. It's too soft and sacrilegious. It seems a place where human hands do not belong. But I invite you anyway. Go on — let others reach in honestly — so we can say, "This is who I am when no one's looking." For each of us is a fledgling that eventually, if fed, will fly.

- Sit quietly before a mirror with your eyes closed, and meditate on an insecure part of yourself.
- Breathe deeply, and try to lift the source of this insecurity into your awareness.
- Now open your eyes and look into the mirror. Examine your face gently.
- See both your insecurity and your awareness holding it. . . . Accept who you are.

# OCTOBER 4
# OUR ALL-EMBRACING NATURE

No individual exists in their own nature, independent of all other factors of life. Each has the totality of the Universe at their base. All individuals have, therefore, the whole Universe as their common ground, and this universality becomes conscious in the experience of enlightenment, in which the individual awakens into their own true all-embracing nature.

— LAMA GOVINDA

Imagine this spiritual fact: the whole Universe is at the base of who we are. What the whale sees as it rushes to the surface is beneath all human seeing. What the eagle feels brushing under its wings is beneath all human question. What the uppermost tree leaf knows of light as it spreads open for the first time is beneath all attempts to love. The essence of every living thing is embedded, dormantly potent, in the energy of heart that waits beneath the skin of heart. As Lama Govinda so touchingly puts it, enlightenment is an experience in which all of that *essential relation* becomes more than knowable, it becomes palpable; and being so touched, essence to essence, a pre-existing spiritual quality of Oneness is enlivened.

Imagine that beneath all our distrust there is a stream of ongoing Oneness, and the only way to enter it is to take off our distrust and bad experience like clothes. Imagine that in entering that stream naked we reach, for the moment, with every hand that ever reached.

I confess that I have known moments that open beneath the grid of time where light is more than light and yet only light, where the soft wind through the remaining yellow leaves falling on the pond is today and a hundred years ago. I usually enter these moments alone. It is how I climb my way to God.

But quietly, when daring to love, to hold nothing back, I have gone there with others.

515

And in those moments of total embrace — of life and each other — we look both out and in, and all is aglow. And it becomes clear that all true lovers meet here, climbing through their lives to a moment no one else seems to understand, where to be together is to be alone, where to touch the skin is to touch the spot of God within that was born to be touched.

In this way, enlightenment is the experience — *the feeling* — of Oneness of All Life, more than the putting on of wisdom.

- Simply breathe and meditate with your arms and hands open.
- As you inhale, imagine that you are joined to everything at the point you can inhale no more.
- As you exhale, imagine that the totality of the Universe is drawing you back into its dailiness.
- Allow yourself to embrace and be embraced.

# OCTOBER 5
# WAKING CLOSE TO THE BONE

Seeking life everywhere,
I found it in the burn of my lungs.

I have awakened and closed for nearly half a century: have run from and stopped, run to and stopped, climbed and stopped, lifted and stopped. I ask questions that can never be answered and live like an answer to all that is never asked. Like an ant building temporary homes, I keep moving what should be left alone and dropping what can't be carried, and, in the highly charged space between the skin of the world and the skin of my soul, experience rushes.

Now, simply by waking, waves of feeling pulse close to the bone, and this continual pulse is so deep it aches. It is the ache of being alive. I used to think this ache was sadness, but now know it is deeper than not getting what I want or losing what I need. This waking close to the bone is the pulse from which both joy and sadness rise, where pain and wonder meet. Now I wake on stubborn fall days that resist the cold, I wake before the sun, the world wet with anticipation, and feel this ache, the way the Earth feels its core grind about that central fire that no one sees. It is the slight burn of being here.

- Wake early, if you can, and meditate on whatever mood is present.
- Breathe deeply, and meditate on the feeling beneath this mood.
- Breathe steadily, and meditate on the pulse beneath that feeling.

517

- Meditate, if you can, on the pulse of being that lives in your bones.

# OCTOBER 6
# TWO WAYS TO FEEL WIND

There are two ways to feel wind:
climb into the open and be still
or keep moving.

Everyone alive embodies both being and doing. The wind we create by running is the energy of becoming, and the wind that comes to us by stilling ourselves is the energy of being.

Being human, there are endless times we need to be still and as many times that we need to move. But much of our confusion as modern citizens comes from trying to have the one we are more comfortable with substitute for the other.

Those of us who struggle with being still often can't find the native wind, while those of us uncomfortable with living in the world can retreat into a stillness that is open but often void of the energy of living.

Yet these concerns are more seamless than how we tend to discuss them. My godson Eli captured the oneness of being and becoming when going for a walk the autumn he was six. He and his father were standing in an open field bordered with maples and willows when a wind lifted through. It so excited Eli that he began to twirl and spin and run with his arms wide through the brightened trees. Out of breath and stunned, he tugged at his father's sleeve, exclaiming, "Daddy! Daddy! If you run too fast, you can't tell what's real!"

Amazingly, there is great insight in children. And great innocence. They carry a wisdom they often live but seldom know. Ironically, we spend our lives trying to regain that treasured state, where being and doing are inseparably one.

- Which comes to you more easily, being or doing? Why do you think this is so?
- What would you like to change about your energy of doing?
- What would you like to change about your energy of being?
- Wholeheartedly choose to spin with your arms wide in an open field the next chance you get.
- What else feels like this for you? What sort of involvement brings being and doing together for you?
- Wholeheartedly choose to involve yourself this way at least twice in the next two weeks.

# OCTOBER 7
## UNTIL WE LIVE IT

We come with all these parts
and no instructions how they go together.

It is so tempting to want the answers before we begin the journey. We like to know our way. We like to have maps. We like to have guides. But we are more like a breathing puzzle, a living bag of pieces, and each day shows us what a piece or two is for, where it might go, how it might fit. Over time, a picture starts to emerge by which we begin to understand our place in the world.

Unfortunately, we waste a lot of time seeking someone to tell us what life will be like once we live it. We drain ourselves of vital inner fortitude by asking others to map our way. At the end of all this stalling, though, we each have to venture out and simply see what happens.

The instructions are in the living, and I confess that of all the times I thought I liked this or didn't care for that, not one was of my choosing or yours. For as the Earth was begun like a dish breaking, eternity is that scene slowly reversing, and you and I and the things we're drawn to are merely the pieces of God unbreaking back together.

520

- Center yourself, and bring to mind how fresh today is.
- With each breath, drop your preconceptions about where you are going and what you must do.
- Simply breathe, and know that everything is possible, and everything, even this day, is unknown until you live it.

# OCTOBER 8
## BREAKING THE JAR

A man raised a baby swan in a glass jar,
but
as the bird grew it became stuck in the jar.
The man was caught now, for the only way
to free the thing was to break the jar, killing
the swan.
— ZEN SAYING

This parable speaks powerfully to the clear containments we set about the ones we love, never imagining that who and what we love grows. What we set up as parameters, out of fear or arrogance or even out of the best intentions of protection, can suffocate the very thing we hold precious.

Even more devastating and subtle are the ways in which we jar ourselves. If our mind is the man raising the baby bird, then the swan

521

is our heart. Too often, in an effort to protect ourselves from being hurt, we place our soft and growing heart in a clear jar of distrust, never dreaming that the heart continues, like the baby swan, to grow. Too often, we can contain our way of being within our way of surviving.

This is how we can wall in our hearts over time. And even the most unassuming and cautious of beings can find themselves having to break their hearts — their way of feeling in the world — in order to free themselves of their hardened clear resolve.

But many of us simply live within the hardness, if we can call such a constraint living. With such suffocation of heart in mind, Rachel Naomi Remen wisely asks, "Is it possible to live so defensively that you never get to live at all?" At the heart of her question and this little Zen story is the difference between surviving and thriving, between existing and living, between resignation and joy.

As human beings, our distrust builds a hardened resolve over our innocence, the way that silver tarnishes when exposed to air. Only the quiet, daily courage to be can let the air soften our hearts again.

- Imagine the last time you felt vulnerable or hurt, but didn't show it.
- What has happened inside you for not

showing your hurt?
- Imagine that moment of vulnerability again, now in the safety of your solitude.
- Soften the moment and let the original feeling through.
- Receive yourself the way you would have wanted others to.

## OCTOBER 9
## BURNING OUR WAY OUT

The soul hovers like a sun within:
burning its way out
without ever leaving center.
We call this — the burning out — passion.

From where does our passion come? It is not taught. It is only allowed through. Or not. When resisted, it carves out the heart daily. When allowed through, it rises and swells and almost drowns us with its heat. Yet somehow the steady tending of its release — not stopping it and not drowning in it — this steady, tender humility of holding our lips open to the rush of inner light, letting the vibrancy of all feeling rush by our open mouths — this is the rhythm of grace; this is the source of all song.

Despite gravity, against gravity, in counterpoint to the weight of the world, a glowing heat that can be blocked but not contained emanates through all beings as love, thought, longing, and peace. When letting this vibrancy through, we open the common heart that lives beneath all human longing and the fire at the core begins to rise.

This rising forth is what I live for. It is what keeps me alive. If I were a dancer, I would only try to scribe this endless rising against the sky, over and over, giving it away and away. Oh the heart like a whale has no choice but to surface. Or we die. And having surfaced, we all must dive. Or we die. And more than books or flowers or thoughtful gifts that show I know you, the dearest thing I can give is to surface with the sheen of my spirit before you. And so I look for the truest friendships, watching the deep for spirits to surface all wet with soul.

- Sit quietly, and as you breathe, feel the vibrant glow at the core of who you are.
- Breathe steadily, and let this passion rise in you with no aim or intent.
- Breathe slowly, and as you begin to feel its heat, look at the simple things around you.

# OCTOBER 10
## TALENT

It is the world that is enlightened
and we who are intermittent.

Like radios, we struggle through our static to
receive wavelengths that are always there,
and, being human, we are unable to sustain
the clarity necessary to apprehend the magic
inherent in everything. So we vacillate from
the extraordinary to the ordinary, time and
time again, and most of us blame the world.

It is not surprising, then, that though we
feel intermittently gifted, our gifts are ever-
present. For if enlightenment stems from a
clarity of being, then talent is no more than a
clarity of doing, an embodied moment where
spirit and hand are one. The chief obstacle to
talent, then, is a lapse in being. It is not that
people have no talent, but that we lack the
clarity to uncover what it is and how it works.

Talent, it seems, is energy waiting to be
released through an honest involvement in
life. But so many of us check whether we have
power with the main switch off — the switch
being risk, curiosity, passion, and love.

With this in mind, happiness can simply be
described as the satisfaction we feel when we
are in ultimate accord, however briefly, in be-

ing and doing. In those unified moments, our purpose is *life* and our talent is *living* it in its most immediate detail, be it drying the dishes or raking the leaves or washing the baby's hair.

So when I can't find my purpose, I beg myself to sit in a field in the sun watching ants in hopes that I will meet my clarity. When I am convinced I have no gifts at all, I implore myself to search for the switch, to try something out of view, to gamble on what is remotely calling. When I lapse between comets, I try to watch fish swim and hear birds glide while I trudge out of synch. And in a tremor of faith, I know if I don't try at all, it will all return as surely and swiftly as light fills a hole.

- Center yourself, and bring to mind the last time you experienced your being and doing as one. It might have been while shoveling or gardening or listening to music.
- Breathe slowly, and think of this ability to experience oneness, however briefly, as one of your talents.
- Try, during your day, to apply this talent once.

# OCTOBER 11
## BEING DOWNSIZED

Our life experiences will have resonances within our innermost being, so that we will feel the rapture of being alive.
— JOSEPH CAMPBELL

Recently, a friend said to me, "Everyone I know has to work obsessively and is worried about losing their jobs, being downsized and eliminated." I confess, there are times I worry about this, too. There is no minimizing the hardships that arise beyond our control, especially when we have others to care for. Yet, despite all this, there are countless stories of people whose lives truly find their meaning after events force them to give up careers that they have been devoted to.

This is not new. Even the mythic Odysseus, after being a sailor all his life, after finding his way home after ten years of war and ten more years of wandering, even he was downsized, forced into retirement.

There he was, pining to return to his glory days at sea, when a soothsayer came to him in a dream and said, "Take your favorite oar and go inland until no one has heard of you, and then go farther until no one has heard of an oar or the sea. Plant your oar there and start a garden."

Life may downsize the things we rely on or how we see ourselves, but our spirit waits like a song in a blanket. No matter how dear the tapestry, there is something more dear in each of us that waits for the blanket to be lifted, so that our spirit can sing.

- Consider a change of vocation you are facing.
- Consider how your work has helped to define who you are.
- Close your eyes and think of your work as the glass, and who you are as the water.
- Meditate on what other kinds of work you can pour yourself into.

# OCTOBER 12
# WE TEND TO CLING

I envy the tree,
how it reaches
but never holds.

Things that matter come and go, but being touched and feeling life move on, we tend to cling and hold on, not wanting anything to change. Of course, this fails and things do change. Often, we are stubborn enough to go after what we think is leaving, trying to manipulate and control the flow of life. Of course, this fails, too.

We can't stop life from flowing. So we are left with feeling what was and what is, and we call the difference loss. But all the clinging and holding on only makes it worse. Now, new things come, and some of us anticipate the loss and just let the things of life go by without feeling them at all.

I have done all these things, but when clear enough and open enough, I try to let things in, to let things touch me. I try not to poke and pull at them as they move through. It doesn't eliminate loss, but when trusting enough to let this happen, I am tuned like a harp held up to wind.

- Sit quietly, and bring to mind a feeling you've tried to hold onto.
- Breathe evenly, and bring to mind a feeling you've cut off.
- Breathe slowly, and bring to mind something you are feeling deeply right now, and try to allow it in without interfering with its presence.

# OCTOBER 13
## WISDOM OF THE TORN HEART

A flag goes boneless as it assumes
the shape of the wind that snaps it
and so I love.

The lesson of the flag challenges our trust in the fabric of our lives. It asks us not to resist the wind of spirit that comes along. For the vital energies of life come upon us in sudden gusts of experience, and we can only unfold our true selves if we let go of our resistance and realize that our purpose, after all our suffering, is as simple and beautiful as that of a flag.

The great poet Rilke says, "I want to unfold. I don't want to stay folded anywhere, because where I am folded, there I am a lie." Once again, we are invited to live in the open. We are encouraged and challenged to unfold past our fear, so that the appearance of life larger and older than us might flap us into full living.

For sure, this is not easy, as all our bad experience and protective upbringing has us ready to resist anything sudden or powerful. Yet, even when we trip and fall, we learn soon enough that it is the arm that stiffens and resists that breaks. Often, our resistance only makes things worse. As the Chinese sage Lao-tzu said 2,500 years ago, "The hard and stiff will be broken. The soft and supple will prevail. . . . Whoever is stiff and inflexible is a disciple of death. Whoever is soft and yielding is a disciple of life."

So, to stay among the living, we are often asked to summon a courage not to resist. This is different than turning the other cheek or submitting to dominant forces in our lives. Rather, this is meeting the world in all its painful variety with feet spread and arms open, neither accepting everything nor rejecting everything, but leaning into what is nourishing and letting the rest move on through.

In this way, the heart becomes a torn flag that knows no country, and over time it is the little tears of living in the open that we must give thanks to. For it is the slight rips we suffer that let through the blasts too painful to carry.

Perhaps this is wisdom, the earned humility of our suffering that doesn't try to hold onto everything. Perhaps this is the wisdom of the torn heart that lets us keep going.

- Center yourself and let your breathing be the wind of feeling that unfurls your heart.
- Simply allow yourself to feel one recent moment of pain and one recent moment

531

of joy. Let each move through you like wind through a flag. One after the other. Again and again.

- With each breath, practice not resisting by leaning into each feeling, and, without holding onto it, let each feeling through.

# OCTOBER 14
## AT THE PACE OF CREATION

The first breath
is always life-giving.

Slowing how we think and feel and take in the world is directly related to being centered. The wisdom traditions all have some form of meditation or prayer that is aimed at slowing us into this center, where the very pace of creation breathes. In their own way, all spiritual practices help us reclaim this centeredness, because being centered in this way plunges us, again and again, into that unseeable stream in which life is continually vital and refreshed.

At the pace of creation, all things breathe the same way. So, when we slow and open and center ourselves, we breathe in unison with all of life, and breathing this way we draw strength from all of life. When we slow down and breathe, we reach like trees into everything open, and whole skies of cloud drift in unison with the dreams of an entire people. If we can slow to the pace of creation, truth will sweep like a flock of birds from the mountains we climb. At the pace of creation, the beginning enters us and we are new.

When courageous enough to relax our soul open, the pace at which our mind thinks slows to the pace at which our heart feels, and, amazingly, together, they unfold the rhythm with which our eyes can see the miracle waiting in all that is ordinary.

- Close your eyes and slow your breathing until you feel centered.
- Once centered, open your eyes, and breathe in unison with the life around you.
- As you speed up during your day, take a slow breath in unison with something small that is near you.

# OCTOBER 15
# TO AFFIRM OUR PERSON

Wisdom tells me I am nothing.
Love tells me I am everything.

And between the two
my life flows.
— NISARGADATTA MAHARAJ

Having survived the inhumanity of the Holocaust and the death of her husband, Dr.
Elkhanan Elkes, the revered elder of the
Kovno Ghetto in Lithuania, Miriam Elkes
told her son, years later, of two objects that
sustained her: "One was a piece of bread,
which she always hid about her person; the
other a broken piece of comb. She kept the
bread in case someone needed it more than
she; and no matter what, morning and night,
she would comb her hair to affirm her person."

What Miriam Elkes carried, and how she
used what she carried, is a profound example
of how the spirit can turn ordinary objects
into living symbols that can help us live.

For what she carried — the bit of bread
and her broken comb — and why she carried
them, speaks to the wisdom of love itself, and
makes me ask, What small thing do we each
carry that we can give to others more in need
than we, and what constant gesture do we
each carry by which we can affirm our person?

To carry these questions alone is life-
sustaining. For to carry the smallest crust of
bread or truth that we can offer others always
reminds us of two essential facts: that we do

not live this life alone, and that no matter the severity of our own circumstance, we have something to give to others. The fact of this does not invalidate our pain, but affirms our worth, that even in pain we can be of value.

We all live somewhere between nothing and everything, and to reenact, along the way, the smallest gesture of valuing your life is to carry out God's work. Only by affirming our person can the human stalk of spirit break ground and grow into something free.

- Center yourself, and breathe your way to the spirit's pause that waits beneath whatever hardship you may be facing.
- As you breathe slowly, let your heart bring to your awareness what small thing you have that you can offer others more in need than you.
- As you breathe freely, let your spirit give your body a gesture by which you can affirm your person.
- Breathe in and affirm your person, breathe out and offer your gifts to the world.

# OCTOBER 16
## HEART AND PATH

Look at every path closely and deliberately.
Try it as many times as you think
    necessary. Then ask yourself, and
    yourself alone. . . .
Does this path have a heart? If it does, the
path is good. If it doesn't, it is of no use.
                    — CARLOS CASTANEDA

It takes six million grains of pollen to seed one peony, and salmon need a lifetime of swimming to find their way home, so we mustn't be alarmed or discouraged when it takes us years to find love or years to understand our calling in life.

Everything in nature is given some form of resilience by which it can rehearse finding its way, so that, when it does, it is practiced and ready to seize its moment. This includes us.

When things don't work out — when loves unexpectedly end or careers stop unfolding — it can be painful and sad, but refusing this larger picture keeps us from finding our resilience. Then, sadness can turn into discouragement, and pain can spoil into despair.

As the many grains of pollen birth the one flower and the many eggs spawned birth the one fish, each person we love and each dream

536

we try to give life to brings us closer to the mystery of being alive. So, we must try as many times as necessary until our many loves become the one love, until our many dreams become the one dream, until heart and path feel the same.

- Sit quietly and bring to mind your disappointments of dream and love.
- Breathe gently, and try not to be brought too fully into your sadness.
- Instead, breathe deeply and try to see each, not as a failure, but as a shimmering bead on a necklace your life is making.
- Breathe cleanly, and let these gems lead you to the next.

# OCTOBER 17
## REFLEX OR RESPONSE

I did not survive
to be untouched.

The emotional patterns of our lives are very strong. They often come into being because we've needed them to survive. But sooner or later, we all arrive at moments where the very thing that has saved us is killing us, keeping us from truly living. Being invisible once kept us from being hurt, but now we are vanishing. Or listening once kept us in relation, but now we are drowning in our unheard cries. Or avoiding conflict once kept us out of the line of fire, but now we are thirsting for contact that is real.

Early in my life, I learned to protect myself, and this meant that I became very good at catching things. In fact, I never went anywhere without my catcher's mitt. No matter what came at me, nothing could surprise me. And while this saved me from the unpredictable assaults of my family, and even helped me in my odyssey through cancer, it eventually had a life of its own. Everything — birds, women, friends, truth — was intercepted by the quick reflex of my mitt. Eventually, nothing got through, and the very thing that helped me survive was now keeping me from being touched. The softness and wonder of the world was vanishing from my life.

But I did not survive to live at a distance from things, and so I began the long and painful process of putting my mitt down, of regaining choice about when and how to protect myself. I began to realize that letting life in was a deeper way to survive.

In doing this work, I began to experience an amazingly thin lining of breath, which I believe is in us all. Beneath it lives our impulse of heart, our true and genuine response to all that we encounter. Above it lives the reflex of our emotional survival, the quick twitch of our patterning.

It seems our ability to be authentic and free can't touch us until we breathe our way below the twitch of our patterning. Often, this requires outlasting the anxiety of needing to catch or fix what comes our way, so we can truly respond from the center of our being.

There is, after all, a difference between helping someone because if you don't you will lose their love or some sense of your own image as a caring person, and helping someone because your impulse of heart moves you to their aid.

We are, each of us, in a repeatable war between defending ourselves from hurts that happened long ago and opening in innocence, again and again, to the unexpected touch of life.

- Sit quietly until you slowly find your way to that thin lining of breath that surrounds your heart.
- Allow into your awareness one current pressure you are feeling from a loved one.
- From that thin lining of breath, in and out, try on the different ways you can respond.
- What response has helped you survive in the past?

- What response will help you live more fully now?
- Which feels more life-giving?

# OCTOBER 18
# HONEY OF MY FAILURES

Last night, as I was sleeping,
I dreamt — marvelous error! —
that I had a beehive
here inside my heart.
And the golden bees
were making white combs
and sweet honey
from my old failures.

— ANTONIO MACHADO

It seems impossible, but every humbled life has cried it is so: The sweetness of living comes to us when the very humanness we regret and try to hide, our seeming flaws and shameful secrets, are worked by time and nature into a honey all their own. Ultimately, it is where we are *not* perfect — where we are broken and cracked, where the wind whistles through — that is the stuff of transformation.

Like other people, many of the things I've wanted to be have crumbled over time into cinders that have sparked the very next dream. And the hurtful things I've never

540

meant to say have thickened my tongue over time into a kindness I didn't think possible. And each time I've failed at being what someone else needed or wanted or hoped for, each time I've failed at being what *I* needed or wanted or hoped for — each failure at love has solidified into unexpected learnings. The painful shavings of one love have become the spices of joy in the next.

They say that Cupid's shafts, when not landing in the heart, were ordinary arrows that wounded the innocent. Like Cupid, we try so hard, but missing, hurt those along the way until we land squarely in the heart. And, when we miss, we are wounded as much as those we wound.

None of this lessens the pain of our journey, but it gives me comfort that our failures — our unexpected stumblings — are the very human paste from which we are made sweet.

Just know, when everything is falling apart, that you are preparing the ground of you for something ripe that can't yet be seen, but which, in time, will be tasted.

- Sit quietly with a trusted friend and meditate on one relationship you believe you failed at.
- After a period of silence, discuss how you think you failed.
- Discuss how you carry this failure, how it effects your current relationships.

- Identify, if you can, one way you have softened and grown in your heart for having experienced this failure.
- Though the relationship didn't last, bear witness to one sweetness that lingers from it.

# OCTOBER 19
## OUR SENSE OF CALLING

Every year, around the scalp of the planet, the caribou run the same path of migration along the edge of the Arctic Circle. They are born with some innate sense that calls them to this path. And every year, along the way, packs of coyote wait to feed on the caribou. And every year, despite the danger, the caribou return and make their way.

Often nature makes difficult things very clear. What feels like confusion is frequently our human refusal to see things for what they are. What lesson do the caribou shout to us with the thunder of their hooves as they deepen the crown of the planet? They are evidence, even as we speak, of the fact that in every living thing there is an inner necessity that outweighs all consequence. For the caribou it is clear what it is.

For spirits carried in human form, it is a

blessing and a curse that we don't always know our calling. Part of our migration is the finding out. What *is* it we are called to, beneath all formal ambition? The caribou tell us that, though there are risks and dangers that wait in the world, we truly have no choice but to live out what we are born with, to find and work our path.

These elegant animals bespeak a force deeper than courage, and, though some would call the caribou stupid, the mystery of their migration reveals to us the quiet, irrepressible emergence of living over hiding, of being over thinking, of participating over observing, of thriving over surviving.

In regions near the Arctic, the caribou are not just seen as animals living out an instinct at all cost. Rather, it is believed that their endless run, no matter what stands in their way, is what keeps the Earth turning. And somewhere, beneath all hesitation and despair, it is our endless call to being, in each of us and all of us together, that keeps the fire at the center of the Earth burning.

- Sit quietly and ask yourself what you are called to. If you don't have a sense of inner calling, please read on anyway.
- Describe what arises without any conclusion. If you feel called to sing, do not conclude you need to become a singer. If you feel called to paint, do not con-

clude you need to become a painter. If you feel called to plant, do not conclude you need to become a gardener.
- Stay with the essence of what arises. Receive it as an energy that lives inside you and not as a goal you have to achieve.

# OCTOBER 20
# THE ROAD BETWEEN

To stand up and be worn
to something deeper
is a pledge that living
forces us to keep.

I drove 500 miles down the California coast with the mountains on the left and the ocean on the right. For days they spoke to me of standing up and wearing down. Of course, I was driving a road we have made down the middle. During the fourth day, the road became a ribbon. It was here it was most beautiful.

I found the world out there all in here, and now I know: The current of life requires us to stand up, again and again, and we are not defeated when we are worn down, just exposed anew at a deeper level. We are meant to live between the two.

In this way, life keeps getting more and more precious. It is a natural law like gravity or osmosis: Stand up to be worn bare. It is how everything in the way is thinned, so we can feel just how thoroughly alive we are.

- Sit quietly, and bring to mind a time when you stood up to something you had to face.
- Breathe deeply, and consider in what way the experience wore you down.
- Center yourself, and name, if you can, how this standing up and wearing down changed you.

# OCTOBER 21
# HAVING HONEST FRIENDS

If you tell me you already understand, I feel a little pessimistic. If you say you do not understand, I feel more optimistic.
— THICH NHAT HANH

This Vietnamese monk, so renowned for his insight, helps us remember that no one can live up to their image of themselves. We can only live out our questions.

I have learned from both sides — from being the one with all the answers and from being the one with all the questions — that

545

there is no real bond with others until we share the evidence of who we are and not just our conclusions. It's taken a long time, but I finally get it. I cannot have both truth and love in my life until I speak from the "I" and stop putting all my pain into "you," until I own all my stumblings and stop projecting my misfortunes on to everyone nearby.

I have a friend. His name is Alan. We have known each other for twenty-nine years, across eighteen states, and through storms we swore would never let up. We held each other when marriages failed, through accidents and cancers. We held each other up when our grandmothers died.

I have seen him in the rain where words can't reach him. I have even seen the rain that is his alone. And here, now, because we've dared to open our small windows to each other, because we've broken down in front of each other with fragments of what we thought was truth, we have the privilege of asking again, as if for the first time, "Who are you?"

I look at him, after all these years, without protection, and I say, "I want to know you. Whatever you have withheld, whatever I have not been able to hear, let us sit in the clearing and understand each other like old birds whose wings are used now more to huddle than to fly."

Having an honest friend — one before

whom you can dump all your heart's pockets and still feel that you are worth something — is a form of wealth that will buy you nothing but will give you everything. And mysteriously and rightly, to find such a friend, we must be such a friend.

- This is a meditation around risk. Center yourself and breathe freely, and bring to mind someone you would like to be closer to.
- Breathe deeply, and recall a belief you have expressed to this person.
- Now meditate on the personal experience that led you to this belief.
- Breathe freely, and safely, and make a vow to share some of this experience the next time you are together.

# OCTOBER 22
## STAYING PRESENT

I am as all mortals are,
unable to be patient.
— PABLO NERUDA

It is so difficult to wait, and yet nothing short of patience can give us access to the nature of wholeness. In part, this is because the mystery of life in its totality is incomprehensible, and what can be understood often speaks in a language so slow that we seldom stick around long enough to hear it. As the great Chilean poet Pablo Neruda confirms, patience is a gift that waits beneath our very human agitation. Yet only through the incredibly difficult effort of staying present will life's forces reveal to us their powers of Oneness.

I recently went to the ocean and listened much of the night to the surf, and the next morning I was surprised to see that the tide had receded to reveal a cliff that had been submerged. I was now able to walk on what revealed itself, out into the sea. And the water rising about me — spraying and slapping what normally can't be seen — made me realize it is the same with our pain. For only when we can outwait the dark will the sharpness of experience recede like a tide to reveal what has survived beneath it all. Often what seems tragic, if looked at long enough, reveals itself as part of a larger transformation.

I also remember coming upon a clearing in the woods so densely overgrown that it felt depressing, for nothing seemed capable of getting through. Something in my own makeup resembled this and made me return there several times. But it was finally in winter, without its leaves, that this same clearing undressed itself as a magnificent bed of light that happened to be on the crest of a beautiful hill. It humbled me to realize that winter can be freeing, too, and that I am often overgrown with memories and reasons and twigs of mind that block me from the light.

So often, in our agitation and impatience, we hurry off, annoyed and troubled, in search of love or peace, never imagining that where we first looked is now letting light through or sprouting its truth. It takes months for a crab apple to shake the crab and find the apple, and even longer for joy to split its human bark.

- Breathe deeply, and center yourself in the dense woods of your heart.
- Go to the clearing from which you understand yourself.
- Sit beneath the many memories and reasons and feelings that have grown like leaves in your heart.
- Feel how the record of what you've lived through keeps the light from getting through.
- Without analyzing or becoming nostalgic, without thinking at all, breathe deeply and let your breath release a light-blocking leaf of heart.
- Let your deep centered breathing be a soft wind that starts to strip your heart free.

# OCTOBER 23
# THE WISDOM TO SURVIVE

My mom said she learned how to swim.
Someone took her out in the lake and threw
her off the boat. That's how she learned
how to swim. I said, "Mom, they weren't trying to teach you how to swim."
— PAULA POUNDSTONE

Reframing what happens to us can be a
healthy way to survive terrible things, or it
can become a veil of denial that keeps us
from moving on. Often, we simply have to
trust that we will see the truth of things when
we are strong enough and ready.

Yet the danger in not seeing things as they
are or were is that we can start to believe that
in order to learn something we need someone
to throw us off the boat, or out of the relationship. If we can't see the difference between
the cruelty or hardship we experience and
the wisdom waiting in our reflex to survive,
we can find ourselves needing crisis and pain
in order to learn. While much learning comes
from crisis and pain, not all of it needs to.

We don't need something to go wrong in
order to change.

• Sit quietly, and bring to mind one

change you are afraid to make in your life.
- Breathe deeply, and ask yourself: are you waiting for someone to push you off the boat?
- Breathe gently, and don't worry now about what to do or how, simply exhale and feel the wisdom to survive and grow waiting inside you.

# OCTOBER 24
# THE WAY THINGS ARE

Be content with what you have;
rejoice in the way things are.
When you realize there is nothing lacking,
the whole world belongs to you.
— LAO-TZU

Beyond what we need to survive, to better ourselves has come to mean having as much as one can store, and as such has turned into an addiction in our modern world. Such a want to have things comes from a sense of scarcity, an anxiety that something is missing, which owning will somehow soothe.

But to better ourselves inwardly is another matter. The closer to heart we take this, the more we find ourselves trying to inhabit what we have carried since the beginning. This want comes from a sense of abundance, a yearning to unlock the mystery of what is already there.

This difference became stark for me while struggling with cancer. For while I prayed for things to be better, my prayers were answered when I awoke one morning content to be who I am, no matter what was happening. Though things were not as I wanted, there was truly nothing lacking, and I vowed, as the nurses started their morning rounds, that I would trade places with no one, spirits with all.

- Center yourself and feel the reality of your life this morning.
- Let your breath take you, for the moment, beneath your dreams of betterment.
- As you exhale, feel the soreness around all you want.
- As you inhale, feel the mystery at center where nothing is lacking.

# OCTOBER 25
## TO THE CORE

No one lands where they aim.
Not even God.

We are so quick to condemn this or exile that,

to ostracize the breaker of promises, when the truth is that nothing in nature arrives as imagined. In fact, because the space between what we intend and what we do is often great, we keep beginning. Because the gap between what we feel and what we say is often surprising, we keep trying. Because the field between what we experience and what we understand is so vast, we keep growing.

This is pointedly different from deliberately living contrary to what we believe and say. That is deceit and hypocrisy. But most of the time, we humble creatures simply miss the mark. We aim, mean well, and fall short, or wide, or overreach what we set out to do.

I've come to believe that this is all part of the friction of the inner life of things becoming outer. Just as we learn in grade school about refraction, about how a stick placed in water will not stay where we put it, what we feel and think and aim for shifts once entering the world, never quite where we imagine it.

It is, despite our frustration, what makes life interesting and love hard. Each of gets the chance, repeatedly, to announce, with all the certainty we can muster, our own version of "The world is flat," only to live into the humility of what has always been true.

When I think of the beliefs I have declared over my lifetime and how they were broken like trees in a storm, or the vows I swore to keep at all cost only to deny knowing God like Peter, or the pride with which I would never kneel only to be brought to my knees by pain — when I accept the fragile way that the human journey unfolds, these become less mistakes and more the way that nature works.

We grow into truth, one self at a time: questioning, declaring, aiming, missing, questioning again. As fruits are all encased until ripe, light comes full term in the dark and truth ripens in the heart. The only way to know the truth is to live through its many casings.

- Center yourself, and meditate on the spirit within you that has survived all the different selves you've been.
- Breathe deeply, and focus on one truth you swore by that you now know is no longer true.
- Breathe slowly, taking the time to shed with each breath any embarrassment, shame, or sense of failure that might arise from seeing this.
- With humility, love the fruit that is you that has ripened within these different casings.

# OCTOBER 26
## THE EFFORT TO LISTEN

> What is so important that we have time to read all the books on love and relationships but we do not have time to listen to the heart of our lover?
>
> — MOLLY VASS

We all suffer, at times, from the effort to study something instead of living it. Or from the effort to fix or advise rather than to listen and to hold. But as the theologian Paul Tillich puts it, "The first duty of love is to listen."

When I think of the times I have truly listened in my life — to the sea's endless lapping, to the sighs of my grandmother when she thought no one was near, to the pains of others that I have caused — it is receiving these simple truths that has made me a better man.

So often when we refuse to listen, we become obsessed with remaking the world in our own image, rather than opening the spirit within us to the spirit of what is.

At the deepest level, ours is not to make ourselves heard but to be still enough to hear. As the Native American Elder Sa'k'ej Henderson says, "To truly listen is to risk being changed forever."

- During your day, take five minutes and stop making, stop doing, stop thinking . . . and just listen. . . .

# OCTOBER 27
# THE WORLD BODY

Earth Mother, you who are called
by a thousand names. May all remember
we are cells in your body
and dance together.

— STARHAWK

If you've ever flown, you know that from just below the clouds, the roads are like arteries and the cars like cells. From above the traffic, it becomes clear that though we all have places to go we just keep circulating through the streets. We race and pause and stop and start, never sure if the road we are turning on to will be congested or barren and free.

For example, every other day, I flip my blinker and drive down Washington Avenue. Some days, there isn't a car and the lights are all green. Other days, I have to wait, and I get irritated. But whether I'm early or late by my time, the dilation and constriction of events is something beyond my control.

In truth, like little cells, we race up and down pathways collecting and dispersing, feeling crowded then lonely, and somehow just doing so keeps the world body healthy. Like blood through a body, we are life pumping through the streets. Even waiting at a light, we are helping life go on.

- The next time you find yourself in a crowd, slow down and feel life circulating about you.
- For the moment, let go of where you are going, and simply breathe.
- Breathe out your concerns, and feel yourself as a healthy cell whose simple movement is cleansing the world body.

# OCTOBER 28
## BUDDHA AND ANGULIMALA

I have stopped.
You have not.

— BUDDHA

There is a story of how, just before he was hung, Angulimala, the murderer, became an Arahant, or worthy one, because of his encounter with Buddha. Angulimala had seemingly been so driven from his own life that he was taking the lives of others. Perhaps it was timing, the readiness of a man about to die confronted with the unwavering presence of an authentic spirit; no one will ever know. But it is said that the two stood before each other for a very long time, and when the silence seemed to part some veil from Angulimala's eyes, Buddha said to him, "I have stopped. You have not stopped." This was followed by an equally telling silence, after which the fortress of cruelty that Angulimala had built around his heart crumbled. It is said that, though Angulimala was hung with a rope made from the finger-bones of his victims, in the moments between Buddha's words and his own last breath, Angulimala truly lived.

Of course, such a story is a penetrating riddle. What had this man *not stopped* that enabled him to murder? And what had Buddha *stopped* that enabled him to be enlightened? Though we will never know, we can suggest that the thing not stopped might be any form of running from the risk and pain of being alive, such as denial, hiding, projection. For any form of running from the truth of ourselves can lead to such a numb existence that one can become violent in order to feel. If we don't stop running, we can murder ourselves again and again by taking the lives of others, either physically through violence or sexually through conquest or emotionally through dominance and control or professionally through power.

Ultimately, however you enter this riddle,

we are both Buddha and Angulimala, and we repeatedly need to have this conversation with ourselves in order to stay compassionate and real.

- Center yourself, and with your inbreath, let the Buddha in you say, "I have stopped."
- Breathe deeply, and with your out-breath, let the Angulimala in you say, "I have not stopped."
- Inhale slowly, and even if you're not sure how, enter your day with a commitment to stop running from the truth of your life.

# OCTOBER 29
# OUR ABILITY TO TRY

If you try to teach before you learn
or leave before you stay,
you will lose your ability to try.

There are so many ways we can divorce ourselves from our own experience. I can remember, as a young man fearing the pain of being hurt by love, I became endlessly involved in advising others in their struggles with love. I can remember, when fearing the sadness and pain of conflict with dear ones,

559

leaving notes rather than facing them in person, trying to leap over the need to go through the real stuff face to face. I can remember, when facing the next horrific chemo treatment, trying to anticipate and prepare endlessly for every possible instant of pain and fear, only to discover that no amount of preparation can keep me from my experience.

Each of these separations — teaching before learning, leaving before staying, anticipating rather than entering — left me drained of my deepest resource, the energy of my life force. Removing myself, even from pain, only left me pale and unable to continue.

When needle or hand or rain or sun hits the skin, the only thing to do is meet its exact touch from the inside. For this moment of inner meeting outer releases an electricity of spirit that gifts us with a tenderness for being awake.

- Sit with a trusted loved one, and after centering yourselves, take turns:
- Let your loved one slowly place their palm on your heart.
- As their hand reaches and lands on your heart, practice meeting its touch with the energy of your inwardness.

# OCTOBER 30
# THE ART OF FACING THINGS

What people have forgotten
is what every salmon knows.
— ROBERT CLARK

Salmon have much to teach us about the art
of facing things. In swimming up waterfalls,
these remarkable creatures seem to defy gravity. It is an amazing thing to behold. A closer
look reveals a wisdom for all beings who want
to thrive.

What the salmon somehow know is how to
turn their underside — from center to tail —
into the powerful current coming at them,
which hits them squarely, and the impact
then launches them out and further up the
waterfall; to which their reaction is, again, to
turn their underside back into the powerful
current that, of course, again hits them
squarely; and this successive impact launches
them further out and up the waterfall. Their
leaning into what they face bounces them
further and further along their unlikely journey.

From a distance, it seems magical, as if
these mighty fish are flying, conquering their
element. In actuality, they are deeply at one
with their element, vibrantly and thoroughly

561

engaged in a compelling dance of turning-toward-and-being-hit-squarely that moves them through water and air to the very source of their nature.

In terms useful to the life of the spirit, the salmon are constantly faithful in exposing their underside to the current coming at them. Mysteriously, it is the physics of this courage that enables them to move through life as they know it so directly. We can learn from this very active paradox; for we, too, must be as faithful to living in the open if we are to stay real in the face of our daily experience. In order not to be swept away by what the days bring, we, too, must find a way to lean into the forces that hit us so squarely.

The salmon offer us a way to face truth without shutting down. They show us how leaning into our experience, though we don't like the hit, moves us on. Time and again, though we'd rather turn away, it is the impact of being revealed, through our willingness to be vulnerable, that enables us to experience both mystery and grace.

- Sit quietly and meditate on the last time you opened yourself to the life coming at you.
- In recalling this, try to focus on three things: the way that opening yourself caused you to unfold, the way that being hit squarely changed your life posi-

tion, and where leaping like a salmon landed you.

- Breathe steadily, and invite the lessons of opening, being changed, and landing into your heart.
- Breathe slowly, and realize that you are in this process now.
- Relax and turn the belly of your heart toward the day.

# OCTOBER 31
## ONLY WHILE LOVING

If you had a sad childhood, so what?
You can dance with only one leg
and see the snowflake falling
with only one eye.

— ROBERT BLY

I flew all the way to South Africa, carrying all my troubles with me, like oversize bags that no one would check, and there in the sun that lit up Capetown, I saw a boy on Green Street dancing on crutches.

I put my bags of trouble down to watch. When he was dancing, the crutches were light as drumsticks bouncing off the street. When he stopped, they became crutches again. Only while dancing, or while watching the dancer, did this make sense.

563

Now that I'm back, I approach things differently. For only while telling the truth does the truth lighten us. When we stop, it turns massive. I left some of my bags on that corner of Green Street somewhere below the equator. Now I carry less and try to dance on my crutches. For only while loving do the pains of feeling lighten.

- Bring to mind a scar that you carry.
- Feel the legitimacy of its weight.
- Now try to see if you carry a crutch to support the weight of your scar. If you do, loosen your grip.
- Breathe deeply, and play with your crutch.
- Breathe fully, and for the moment, put it down.

# NOVEMBER 1
# THE NEXT MOMENT OF LOVE

To allow oneself to be carried away by a multitude of conflicting concerns, to surrender to too many demands, to commit oneself to too many projects, to want to help everyone in everything is to succumb to violence. The frenzy of the activist neutralizes his or her work for peace.

— THOMAS MERTON

Merton wisely challenges us not just to slow down, but, at the heart of it, to accept our limitations. We are at best filled with the divine, but we have only two hands and one heart. In a deep and subtle way, the want to do it all is a want to be it all, and though it comes from a desire to do good, it often becomes frenzied because our egos seize our goodness as a way to be revered.

I have done this many times: not wanting to say no, not wanting to miss an opportunity, not wanting to be seen as less than totally compassionate. But wherever I cannot bring my entire being, I am not there. It is like offering to bring too many cups of coffee through a crowd. I always spill something hot on some innocent along the way.

Helen Luke speaks to all this when she talks of the trap of good works. She refers to "those who take refuge from themselves in an unreflective pursuit of good, pouring all their energy into the redemption of society and other people, while blind to their own personal darkness."

It seems the old adage is a place to start: Do one thing and do it well. Though I would offer it as: Do one thing at a time and do it entirely, and it will lead you to the next moment of love.

- Center yourself and think of the many kindnesses that you feel called to do.

565

- As you breathe, let your heart glow around one.
- Without thinking, pray for the others, but devote yourself today to the one.

# NOVEMBER 2
# THE HUNT FOR TRUTH

I take a wolf's rib and whittle
it sharp at both ends
and freeze it in blubber and place it out
on the fairway of the bears.
And when it has vanished
I move out on the bear tracks,
roaming in circles
for days.

— GALWAY KINNELL

The way that Eskimo hunt bear for food is powerfully captured in Galway Kinnell's poem "The Bear." Yet just as Eskimo hunt food for survival, we often find ourselves searching for an inner food known as truth. For the authenticity of living is not just an interesting idea or an eloquent feeling. Authenticity, the experience of truth, is our richest food. Without it we will freeze to death.

Two lessons happen to Kinnell's Eskimo that are difficult to take in. On the third day out, the hunter is starving as much as the hunted, and at nightfall he stoops as he knew he would to gnash down a bear turd sopped in blood.

What this tells us is that no matter what we say we will or will not do, no matter the imperious standards by which we judge ourselves and the world, we humbly can't know what we will do when starving for truth. And rightly so, for life on Earth often brings us to our knees so that something can take root. When dying of cancer, I, a proud Jew who vowed never to kneel, found myself on my knees before a Catholic healer who laid hands on the tumor on my brain. While feeding on truth can disrupt the ways we like to see ourselves, it can also deeply affirm that we as human beings are resilient beyond anything we can imagine.

A second imperative occurs when the Eskimo, seven days out, is half-frozen as the bear finally dies, and he is forced to enter the gutted cavity of the bear to survive the cold. For those of us who search for truth in cold modern streets, we are told here that arriving at the truth is not enough. We need to put it on, to inhabit it, to actually enter and wear the truth.

So where do we begin? Well, the Eskimo also teach us how to hunt for truth in the way they fashion their bait. Not by intellectual debate or esoteric study, but by risking something of ourselves, by placing something troublesome and sweet in the open. By offering something essential from our hunger and coating it with our vulnerability, we call the greater truth into the open with the smaller. Humbly and unavoidably, the need for truth will lead us into the unexpected living of our lives beyond all images of perfection.

- Is there something you have done that you vowed you would never do?
- Do you consider this to be a triumph or a failure?
- What prompted you to act this way? Was it courage, necessity, or was it a mistake?
- How has your life changed for this unexpected experience?

# NOVEMBER 3
# IN THE CARE OF SOMETHING UNSEEN

Genius is a crisis that joins the buried self, for certain moments, to our daily mind.
— WILLIAM BUTLER YEATS

We have been trained to think of genius as an unusual brilliance of mind, an ability to retain or calculate or conceptualize uncanny amounts of information. But the original sense of *genius* means attendant spirit — being in the care of something unseen but near. It is really another definition of wholeness or God, another way of acknowledging the Tao, the unseeable stream we all swim in.

What Yeats offers us is an insight into life on Earth. The great Irish poet suggests that crisis is an unexpected jarring of our ways that brings us into contact with our attendant spirit.

I'm reminded that the Chinese ideogram for danger also means opportunity. This is not to suggest that we seek out danger, but that we look for the openings, when broken by experience, by which we can find our connection to the unseeable stream we often forget we are a part of.

Perhaps the purpose in crisis, if there is one, is not to break us as much as to break us open.

- Sit quietly and feel the unseeable stream you are a part of.
- Breathe slowly and meditate on your genius, your attendant spirit.
- Breathe softly, and expose whatever crisis you are in to your attendant spirit.
- If you can, move through your day feeling both your crisis and the depth of your genius. Let them join.

# NOVEMBER 4
## BEHOLDING OTHERS

Once for each thing. Just once; no more.
And we too, just once. And never again.
But to have been this once, completely,
even if only once: to have been
at one with the earth,
seems beyond undoing.
— RAINER MARIA RILKE

I was visiting a friend who asked me, "How do you prepare for meeting people you respect? How do you know what to ask or say?"

I'd never thought about it, but realized with his asking that ever since my cancer experience, I enter every meeting with another being saying to myself, "If I only have this time on Earth with this person, if I may never see them again, what is it I want or need to ask, to know? What is it I want or need to say?"

I find I come upon others now as if I have just crossed a desert and each of them is an oasis. The truth is that each living spirit we encounter is a depth to gently swim in, a miracle that can quench our thirst. Honoring others in this way has opened me to wisdoms that would otherwise run silent beneath my time on Earth.

- Sit with a trusted loved one or friend, and with your eyes closed, meditate on just how rare it is to be alive at the same time.
- When you are fully feeling this awareness, open your eyes and behold each other.
- Breathe slowly, and if you have only this time together, let the one question you would ask rise within you.
- Behold each other and ask.

# NOVEMBER 5
## PLANS AND PLANNING

Plans are useless, but planning is invaluable.
— WINSTON CHURCHILL

We easily confuse plans with planning, dreams with dreaming, and love with loving. The wisdom waiting within what Churchill says is that we live like hungry fishermen: sewing and casting our nets, though we never really know what they will catch, never really know what will feed us until it is brought aboard. So, as Buddhists say, to be a good fisherman you must detach yourself from the dream of the fish. This makes whatever is caught or found a treasure.

When I look at all the books I've written, I must confess that every one has been discovered along the way to other plans. What I envision when I begin is never what is actually written. The same can be said for my career path. For me, the most meaningful job experiences have been completely unforeseen, the result of seizing heartfelt opportunities that appeared along the way to other dreams. I must also confess that though I've imagined love and lovers often, each person I've been blessed to love has come to life beyond all imagining.

Certainly, there are times we need to anticipate what is coming and times we need to be spontaneous. But too much is made of choosing either way. Plans are kindling to every fire, and no two fires are the same. We just need their heat and light.

- Center yourself and think of your current plans for happiness.
- As you breathe, lay your plans before your heart like sticks of kindling.
- Not knowing what fire they will light in you, enter your day looking for the spark.

# NOVEMBER 6
## WHEN WE SQUINT

And when we squint, we think we see like a tiger, while the truth like the sun spills everywhere but through our slits.

We have all heard the gritty advice that when things get tough, we need to dig in. This often translates to an aggressive, alert stance. We hone our focus and thinking, readying ourselves for anything. Unfortunately, when we steel ourselves for battle, our focus narrows and we can cut out as much of what we need as what we fear.

I am not suggesting that we stumble through life without thought or focus. Rather, I'm offering a deeper sense of what it means to be alert. There is a telling difference between the sharp line of a laser ray and the wash of sunlight over a field, between the sharpness of a mind in crisis and the wash and warmth of an open heart. When we need it most, it is nearly impossible to see ourselves with compassion from the slit of a narrowed mind all tensed for battle.

A few months after the tumor vanished from my head, I bumped into a very bright friend in a restaurant who was tenacious in pursuing what I had done to defeat the tumor. I kept telling her of the enormous surrender that had overcome my life and that I didn't really know how to account for the miracle. She squinted terribly, as if blocking out the glare of the mystery, and insisted that I was evidence of what mind could do over matter. As she squinted, I could feel her heart close. It was very sad. We've had little to say to each other since.

I have also found myself from time to time unable to stay in the feeling of a moment because my alertness in crisis, like a periscope shooting up, pulls me out of my heart, and the next thing I know, I am lost in the analysis of problem solving, of calibrating advantages and liabilities. Like my friend, when I squint, insisting solely on my own will to power me in the world, I close myself to the mystery, and I notice I become sad, having little to say to myself.

This has taught me that attention to detail can be mistaken for the act of caring. The truth is that being alert often requires us to widen our focus and to see with what the Sufis call "the heart's eye." For though surprise and crisis can make us squint like a tiger and show our claws, it is the effort to enlarge and stay open that helps us the most.

- Before a mirror, with your eyes closed, meditate on a confusion or problem that

is troubling you.
- Allow yourself to think about its circumstances and possible solutions.
- Now look at yourself in the mirror and note the tension in your face and how it affects your eyes.
- Staying before the mirror, again meditate with your eyes closed and try to relax your analysis. Try to look at the confusion or problem with your heart's eye, without trying to solve it.
- Now look at yourself in the mirror, and note if and how your face and eyes have changed.
- Discuss the difference with a trusted loved one.

# NOVEMBER 7
# THE WATERS WITHIN US

Spirit like water
is a source of life.
We cannot live dry.

The more we are worn by experience, the more of an inlet we become and the more the waters of life wash out of us. This is why tears come more easily the longer we are here.

Perhaps wisdom is nothing more than the unsayable waters rising within us to swell

575

around the eye, the way that oceans soften land, evidence of that inevitable tide that takes a lifetime to rise.

We are so afraid of the waters within us that we often tense as soon as we see tears, asking what's wrong, when perhaps we need to ask those at sea, what do you see?

- Sit quietly and recall the last time you cried.
- Breathe slowly and revisit the feeling of release.
- Breathe into that release, and look beneath what caused you to cry.
- Breathe deeply, and feel for the unsayable wisdom rising to cover you.

# NOVEMBER 8
# WE ARE ALL MADE DELICATE

We are all made delicate or we perish.
Isn't this the cloth our griefs sew?

The hard things break. The soft things bend. The stubborn ones batter themselves against all that is immovable. The flexible adapt to what is before them. Of course, we are all hard and soft, stubborn and flexible, and so we all break until we learn to bend and are battered until we accept what is before us.

This brings to mind the Sumerian tale of Gilgamesh, the stubborn, hard king who sought to ask the Immortal One the secret of life. He was told that there would be stones on his path to guide him. But in his urgency and pride, Gilgamesh was annoyed to find his path blocked, and so smashed the very stones that would help him. In his blindness of heart, he broke everything he needed to discover his way.

With the same confusion, we too break what we need, push away those we love, and isolate ourselves when we need to be held most. There have been many times in my life when I have been too proud to ask for help or too afraid to ask to be held, and in the frenzy of my own isolation, like Gilgamesh, I have smashed the window I was trying to open, have split the bench I was trying to hammer, and have made matters worse by bruising the one I meant to be tender with.

The live bough bends. The dead twig snaps. We are humbled to soften from our griefs, or else, in brittle time, become the next thing grieved.

- Meditate on a situation you are now facing in which you are being hard, stubborn, and resistant.
- Look at your stubbornness. What are you preserving by being hard? What

577

might break if you continue being resistant?

- Now look beneath your stubbornness. What do you fear will happen if you bend to the situation? What might be gained by softening?

# NOVEMBER 9
# DIVING HALF-BLIND

We carry within us
the wonders we seek
without us.

— THOMAS BROWN

The cormorant and common mure are sea birds that dive half-blind looking for food. As they go from surface to bottom, air bubbles get caught in their feathers, and this makes them shine. Thus, as they dive, they turn silver.

So too, we; for don't our bubbles of pain get trapped in our feathers, turning to jewels the closer we get to the current under everything? This is a baptism of true feeling: the deeper we go, the slower the world; the slower the world, the softer our way. So we must keep calling each other into the depths of what we know. For below the surface, we all shine. Diving in, we all turn silver.

Given to air alone, the cuts of this world burn. But when we dare to enter what is deep, the bruises we carry soften and glow. In truth, the more we accept our limitations and surrender to the depths below our woundedness, the more the vastness holds us up. There is no way to know this but to dive.

- Center yourself and hold a pain or ache that you carry; hold it gently before you.
- As you breathe slowly, surround your pain or ache with a loving kindness meditation that keeps broadening your prayer for all living things.
- Allow this silent prayer to subside.
- Now, if you can, feel your pain or ache slightly softened by your love for the world.

# NOVEMBER 10
## LIFE ON THE EDGE

You are that which you are seeking.
— SAINT FRANCIS

When I feel lonely, my first thought is that you hold the key to my loneliness. When I feel confused, my first thought is that you (or someone neither of us knows) is more clear, if I can only find them and get them to speak.

When wanting respect, my first thought is that it is waiting on the other side of some mammoth achievement I must devote myself to. I try so hard to find what I need or want outside of myself, certain it is waiting for me somewhere just over there.

In the end, seeking only brings us to the edge of knowing ourselves. If we never look inward, we tend to become experts at life on the edge, while seldom unlocking what all our seeking means. We can become masters at climbing the mountains of the world instead of breaking trail to the center of our woundedness. We can become masters at driving fast cars through the night instead of moving through the dark corners of our mind. We can become masters at seducing strangers in the name of love instead of embracing the softer, less perfect aspects of who we are.

Seeking in the world has always been a way to mirror to us where we need to work inwardly, but seeking danger outside has always been a way to divert the soul's cry for us to take a genuine risk inside.

- Meditate on something you are seeking. It may be love, power, wealth, or the thrill of jumping out of a plane, or the recognition of being famous.
- Now imagine that what you seek already lives within you, and as you breathe,

hold what you seek before your mind's eye like a door you must enter if you are ever to be whole.
- Inhale deeply, and feel what you seek as a part of your spirit that needs attention.
- Exhale deeply, and though you may not know how, give yourself this attention.

# NOVEMBER 11
## SUSTAINING WONDER

In one atom are found all the elements of the earth; in one motion of the mind are found all the motions of existence; in one drop of water are found all the secrets of the endless oceans; in one aspect of you are found all the aspects of life.

— KAHLIL GIBRAN

As humans we are relentlessly in cycle. The mind builds a shell to protect its turtle-spirit, but the shell muffles the spirit, till outgrowing the shell we devise ways to break it. We build the shell, then tear it down. We build it thinner. We tear it down. Yet only between constructions are we thoroughly touched. Only between encasements are we punctured by love.

But we are not to be blamed. All of nature

581

is conscripted to such a cycle. Trees grow moss, silver tarnishes, the mind is dulled by the growth of its conceptions; and likewise, a storm removes the moss, a scratch breaks through the tarnish, and crisis reveals the raw surface of the mind.

Time builds and erodes and we are transformed, yet the same. Wind gathers sand to a dune and tide undermines the dune. It's how the early years pack us and the later ones softly flood us without a sound. We have no choice but to withstand the film that constantly builds and to endure the erosion that inevitably follows.

Of course, for humans this dance of film and erosion is not merely physical. It affects our thinking, feeling, seeing, and being. How easily and repeatedly we dull and brighten. How easily we become chronic amnesiacs of spirit, drifting into observation and analysis when we stop participating and experiencing. Then we wake one day forgetting the feel of life, while incredibly attuned to its silhouette. We can see it so clearly, each perplexity and nuance, yet why can't we feel it. In this way, the mind grows thoughts and words the way the planet grows trees, so much that we no longer see the heavens, and so we need to chop down what we think and say, and yes, silence is an ax.

In truth, our aliveness depends on our ability to sustain wonder: to lengthen the moments we are truly uncovered, to be still and quiet till all the elements of the earth and all the secrets of the oceans stir the aspects of life waiting within us.

- The next time you walk outside, let the cold air wash over your closed eyes.
- Take a deep breath, and let the air wash off the film of memory or thought you are struggling with.
- Feel your blood flush your face, and open your eyes freshly.

# NOVEMBER 12
## BURNING THE WRAPPER

From the beginning,
the key to renewal has been shedding,
the casting off of old skin.

The Polynesians say the world began when Taaora — their name for the Creator — woke to find himself growing inside a shell. He stretched and broke the shell, and the Earth was created. Taaora kept growing, though, and after a time found himself inside another shell. Again, he stretched and broke the shell, and this time the moon was created. Again, Taaora kept growing, and again, he found himself contained by yet another shell. This time the breaking forth created the stars.

In this ancient story, the Polynesians have carried for us the wisdom that we each grow in this life by breaking successive shells, that the piece of God within each of us stretches until there's no room to be, and then the world as we know it must be broken so that we can be born anew.

In this way, life becomes a living of who we are until that form of self can no longer hold us, and, like Taaora in his shell, we must break the forms that contain us in order to birth our way into the next self. This is how we shed our many ways of seeing the world, not that any are false, but that each serves its purpose for a time until we grow and they no longer serve us.

I have lived through many selves. The first of me, so eager to be great, to set things ablaze, shunned everything that was ordinary. I hunted the burn of a champion's hip and wanted to be a great musician too — to be famous and extraordinary. But as I grew, the notion of fame left me lonely in the night. Thrones, no matter how pretty, have only room for one.

The second of me wanted to be covered by waves, inhale the stars, and move like a song. Now I wanted to be the great music itself. But to be the great thing was still as lonely as it was magnificent.

The third of me gave up on greatness. It

was how I let others draw close. I asked more questions, not really interested in answers, but more, the face below the face about to speak.

And then during cancer, there came yet another self — there, bent and distorted in the hospital chrome as the late sun flooded my pillow. I was dead in the chrome, alive on the pillow, a quiet breath between — dead, alive — at once. And oddly, it did not scare, for I felt the pulse of life in the quiet breath, and the place to which I transcended is here.

Almost dying was another shell I had to break. It has led me to realize that each self unfolds, just one concentric womb en route to another, each encompassing the last. I would believe in arrival but for all the arrivals I've broken on the way.

- Breathe slowly with your eyes closed, and feel one aspect of your current world that seems confining.
- Rather than focusing on the people or circumstance involved, try to feel this confinement as the threshold of your next growth.
- Meditate on how the piece of God within you might stretch and stand more fully, so that being who you are more completely will break the shell of this confinement.
- Pray to understand that none of this is

bad, but simply necessary for the growth of your soul.

# NOVEMBER 13
# TO MARRY ONE'S SOUL

Being true to who we are
means carrying our spirit like a candle
in the center of our darkness.

If we are to live without silencing or numbing essential parts of who we are, a vow must be invoked and upheld within oneself. The same commitments we pronounce when embarking on a marriage can be understood internally as a devotion to the care of one's soul: to have and to hold . . . for better or for worse . . . in sickness and in health . . . to love and to cherish, till death do us part.

This means staying committed to your inner path. This means not separating from yourself when things get tough or confusing. This means accepting and embracing your faults and limitations. It means loving yourself no matter how others see you. It means cherishing the unchangeable radiance that lives within you, no matter the cuts and bruises along the way. It means binding your life with a solemn pledge to the truth of your soul.

It is interesting that the nautical definition of *marry* is "to join two ropes end to end by interweaving their strands." To marry one's soul suggests that we interweave the life of our spirit with the life of our psychology; the life of our heart with the life of our mind; the life of our faith and truth with the life of our doubt and anxiety. And just as two ropes that are married create a tie that is twice as strong, when we marry our humanness to our spirit, we create a life that is doubly strong in the world.

- Sit quietly and center yourself.
- Meditate on the fact that being centered includes your confusions and worries, the way a lake is a home for many birds and fish.
- Breathe gently, and let your breath be the water.

# NOVEMBER 14
# THE COST OF SPLITTING

To birth the baby and to dwell on the baby at the same time engenders madness.
— CHÖGYAM TRUNGPA

Try as we will, we cannot be both participant and observer at the same time without split-

587

ting ourselves. Madness it seems is the cost of splitting ourselves in the midst of our experience. To dwell on our next gesture or reply while a truth is being shared splits the heart's capacity to feel. To dwell on our bodies while making love splits the capacity of two hearts to bond. To dwell on our reward while performing a kindness splits our authenticity.

It is at times the hardest thing a human being must do: When looking in the eye of a dear one, we must look in the very eye of that dear one. When stepping on a dried leaf, we must be there stepping on the very dryness of that hardened leaf. When feeling the face of a stranger's dog, we must without distraction feel the dog's panting in the cavern of our heart.

- Center yourself, and as you meditate, see yourself in the room meditating.
- With each successive breath, practice shedding first the room and then the room of your mind.
- As you breathe, try not to think or watch anything; just feel for the air coming and going.

# NOVEMBER 15
## DYING INTO NOW

In the end, everyone is aware of this:
nobody keeps any of what he has,
and life is only a borrowing of bones.
— PABLO NERUDA

Three years from my surgeries, I am taking a shower, and there, on my head, along the scar, is the beginning of a pimple. In thirty seconds, I am tripping into a cascade of "what ifs." What if this is another tumor? What if it is spreading? As the water pelts me, my fear runs wild. I can see myself in the doctor's office, undressing for surgery, walking the halls in recovery, lying down for chemo, getting weaker, dying. There and back. In thirty seconds.

My heart is pounding, naked in the shower. I so want to live. I am so awake, finally at peace, but what if this is true? What shall I do? Where shall I go? But in this moment, the shower rinses me over and over, and I come home. If this is true, if I am to die soon, I know what I will do. . . . I sigh more deeply than I ever thought possible. . . . I will finish my shower. . . .

In that moment I learned that everything is right where we are. No matter our pain or distress, all of life is in whatever moment we wake to. I could clearly see and feel how our fear of death makes us run, though there is nowhere to go. Yet mysteriously, I learned that there's a ring of peace at the center of every fear, if we can only get to it.

Every time I shower now, I try to remember that we cannot live fully until we can first accept our eventual death. Otherwise, we will always be running to or running from. Only when we can accept that we are fragile guests on this Earth, only then will we be at home wherever we are.

- In the shower, let the water rinse your mind of both indifference and fear.
- Breathe fully and feel the clear drops hit your skin.
- Breathe deeply and give thanks for being alive.

# NOVEMBER 16
# THE MOMENT OF DAWN

There's a sun in every person — the you we call companion.

— RUMI

It is essential to realize and embrace the paradox that while no one can go through your journey for you, you are not alone. Everyone is on the same journey. Everyone shares the same pains, the same confusions, the same fears, which if put out between us, lose their edges and so cut us less.

A very touching story from the Talmud captures this soft paradox of how we all journey alone together. A Rabbi asks his students, "How do you know the first moment of dawn has arrived?" After a great silence, one pipes up, "When you can tell the difference between a sheep and a dog." The Rabbi shakes his head no. Another offers, "When you can tell the difference between a fig tree and an olive tree." Again, the Rabbi shakes his head no. There are no other answers. The Rabbi circles their silence and walks between them, "You know the first moment of dawn has arrived when you look into the eyes of another human being and see yourself."

- Sit quietly and try to breathe your way to center.
- Simply breathe your heart open, and try to feel both your aloneness and what you share with every other human being.
- Breathe deeply and slowly, and try not to comprehend this, but just to feel it.

# NOVEMBER 17
## DO YOU WANT TO LEAVE?

Walls are worn away a grain at a time,
and hearts are opened a feeling at a time.

Susan and I were sitting in an ice cream parlor when the two couples next to us began to get loud. They were just having a good time, but I was feeling a bit inward and intruded on. I felt the need to go. I leaned over to Susan and asked if she wanted to leave. She, in her contentment, said, "No. I'm happy here." Then seeing consternation on my face, she asked, "Do you want to go?"

In that simple moment in a booth in an ice cream parlor, I realized that for much of my forty-nine years, I have tried to take care of my needs by indirectly projecting them on those around me and then acting as if I am taking care of the other person. As the ice cream was melting, I understood myself. I laughed, shook my head, felt embarrassed, then sighed deeply, and importantly voiced the obvious, "Yes, I'd like to leave."

This indirect way of trying to get what I need by planting my feelings as needs to be attended to in those around me has been a way to hide my vulnerability, while still managing to appear as a kind and other-centered person. I realize I am not alone in this malady. It is often so subtle and so close to our healthy way of relating to others that we seldom realize the manipulation and deceit involved.

Of course, this indirectness lives in us because somewhere along the way, we become convinced, often with good harsh reason, that to voice directly what we need is asking to be hurt. Yet I know of no other way to reverse this hiding of who we are than to catch ourselves humbly in each instance and to rise out of our private cave, admitting the indirectness and saying what we feel and what we need as soon as possible.

Still, the energy wasted in trying to quietly get others to behave in ways that will satisfy our needs remains a major source of anxiety and alienation. Rather than prevent us from being hurt, indirectness and dishonesty only heighten our isolation from what it means to be alive.

Underneath it all is the fundamental truth that as trees have leaves that are nicked and eaten, human beings have feelings that are just as worn by the act of living. We have a right to these. They are evidence of our human seasons.

- Recall the last time you asked someone to do something rather than express what you needed directly.

- What prevented you from expressing your needs directly? What were you afraid of?
- Imagine what you would have said if you had lived that situation more directly.
- Now practice expressing yourself directly by replaying that situation aloud, even though you are by yourself.
- Enter the day feeling the ease of living directly.

# NOVEMBER 18
## THE PUPPY IN THE POUND

Everybody can love in the place where they are. We can all add our share of love without leaving the room.
— HELEN NEARING

At dinner, a friend who was interviewing for a job shared how she sometimes felt too eager for their acceptance. She said she found herself inwardly yelping, like a puppy in the pound, "Pick me! Pick me!"

We all laughed, because we all do this. At some point of inner confusion, we assume that we are orphaned of all gifts and possibilities. During these painful times, we imagine that we are so small in what we have to offer that we become desperate to belong anywhere at any cost.

To make matters worse, we then hide parts of who we are, certain that if the potential boss or partner or new friend were to know all about us, they couldn't possibly accept us.

Once inside this thinking, it is hard to repair, and the challenge, repeatedly, is to stop giving ourselves away. For what good is it if only a sliver of you remains? What good if only your ear is accepted and the rest of your body must be kept out of view? What good if only your obedience and good manners are accepted and the rest of your passion and personality must be kept in hiding?

In truth, no one can live with a sliver; for slivers, even of gold, are near-impossible to hold.

- Center yourself and bring to mind a time you felt the need to be accepted.
- Let that feeling come and go, and as you breathe, bring to the surface if you can that part of you that so wants to be loved.
- Breathe thoroughly, and let each inhalation be an embrace of your very human longing by your very ancient spirit.

# November 19
## That Feminine Thread

In how you have come
is the secret
to how you must go.

In Greek mythology, there is a story of a man, Theseus, who in order to find his way home, had to find his way through a labyrinth that led him to a dark center, where he had to kill a powerful beast, a Minotaur. The only way he could return to the light of daily life was to trace back the thread he had unraveled on his way in, which was given him by a kind woman, Ariadne.

Stories like this carry wisdom we must encounter if we are to become whole. Each of us has a beast at center which we must confront if we are to live peacefully in our days. But like Theseus, making our way back into the light is only possible if we retrace with kindness and love our dark way in.

This is how after years of feeling mistreated, I can find myself mistreating others and, suddenly, I feel humbled. This is how in giving myself away to be loved, I finally, after years, arrive at the dark loveless center of that way, and the only way out is to follow the small thread of accepting who I am until it leads me back to where I began, except this time I weep to know my place in the world.

- Sit quietly with your palms open.
- Breathe thoroughly, and in your right palm, meditate on the nature of your labyrinth, your way to your beast.
- Now breathe just as thoroughly, and in your left palm, meditate on the nature of your feminine thread, your way out to the light.
- During your day, open your palms and become familiar with both your labyrinth — your way in — and your feminine thread — your way out. Both are friends.

# November 20
## Commitment and Risk

The moment one definitely commits oneself, then Providence moves too. All sorts of things occur to help one that would never otherwise have occurred. A whole stream of events issues from the decision which no one could have dreamed would have come their way.

— W. H. Murray

We'd all like a guarantee before making a

decision or taking a risk, but the irony is that taking the risk is what opens us to our fate. It's like wanting to know what things will taste like before putting them in your mouth. It just can't be figured out that way.

I always seem to be relearning that real commitment comes before I know where anything is going. That's what listening to your heart is all about. Without jumping off its perch, the bird would never fly. Without jumping out of your heart's silence, love is never possible. Without asking to be whole, the divine essence waits inside everything the way bread hardens if never bitten into.

For me, as I look back, being a poet came after committing to speak though I had no idea what I needed to say, and the grace of being loved has come into my life after admitting freely that I wanted to love though I wasn't sure how.

If we devote ourselves to the effort to be real, the Universe in all its forms will find us, the way that wind finds leaves and waves find shore.

- Center yourself, and with each breath, commit your being to where you are.
- After a while, walk slowly about the room, and with each step, feel commitment in the landing and risk in the lifting.

# NOVEMBER 21
## AS FAR AS WE CAN MANAGE

Wherever we stop
is the summit.

I was climbing Trail Ridge Road through the Rocky Mountains, determined to make the Continental Divide, when two sharp feelings pierced me almost at once. I, who have never had any trouble with heights, felt rushes of fear as I drove on narrow stretches 12,000 feet up. I was also filled with the irrevocable truth that everything-there-is is wherever we are.

This all made me stop and walk the tundra above the treeline. There, I was overcome with the sudden truth that I could go no farther, and that I had no need to go any farther. Can it be that this journey through the mountains mirrors the journey through our lives? Is our suffering like the dizzying, gut-wrenching narrow passes through these ancient rocks? Do we simply move on until we can't, and in accepting our humanity, does the peak come to us?

What an unlikely truth. I traveled as far as I could manage, and there on the bare scalp of the Earth, I realized that where I can go no further is my destination. This is the wearing of heart that no one can escape. Despite all our noble efforts to reach some treasured peak — be it a dream of wealth or love — we carry the summit within. And it is always the effort and exhaustion — the very journey itself — that opens the view which is everywhere. For the summit is not so much arrived at as we are worn open to it.

I felt the truth of arriving at wherever my human limitations had left me, knew somehow it was enough, and I let out a cry like a vapor. We are as bare as these crags being worn by endless wind, and, regardless of the maps we carefully draw and pass down, we arrive at what we've always had when we use up everything we've saved. In this way we are brought to humility.

Once accepting our frail humanity, we can see how stubbornly fragile living things are. We can see how it takes just a thin lick of water down a mountain crack to strengthen a root and a bare lick of love through our stony hearts to blossom a soul.

- Earlier we asked these questions, which seem worthwhile to explore again. So breathe deeply, and see what they touch in you now.
- What is it about being human that you are most grateful for?
- What is it about being human that continues to surprise you?

# NOVEMBER 22
## GRIEF

If pulled, grief is a thread
that will leave us naked in song.

A friend took me to the redwoods, where the trees talk with God, and it was a thick-barked tree five or six hundred years old that made me think Grandma was near. It's been twelve years since she died, and though no one understands, I carry her behind my left eye where the spirit sees. I leaned into that ancient tree, making small noises. The laurel leaves rustled. The younger trees creaked along with me. I miss her terribly. And though I resist feeling the loss and emptiness of not having her around, when I lean into that grief, it always in aftermath makes everything more vibrant, more real.

I've learned that grief can be a slow ache that never seems to stop rising, yet as we grieve, those we love mysteriously become more and more a part of who we are. In this way, grief is yet another song the heart must sing to open the gate of all there is.

In truth there is a small one who suffers in each of us, an angel trying to grow wings in the dark, and as this angel learns how to sing, we lose the urge to hide. Indeed, when one heart speaks, all hearts fly. This is what it means to be great — to speak what feels unspeakable and have it release what waits in us all.

- Sit quietly, and if there is some loss you are grieving, allow its feeling to move through.
- Breathe evenly, and with each breath, imagine the angel in your heart trying to sprout its wings.
- Breathe deeply, and know that each feeling felt is another feather.

# NOVEMBER 23
# RISK AND TRUTH

Empower me
to exercise the authority of honesty,
and be a participant
in the difficult ordinariness of now.
— TED LODER

Once there were two friends, and one was very daring in the way she met experience, always trying new things, always breaking new paths. The other was more timid in the world, but had the strength to look directly at the truth of any situation. They helped each other grow.

In time, they fell in love and became partners: the one leading them into new experience, the other showing them the truth of where they'd been. This worked for many years, but eventually, the one who was daring wanted to go farther and farther into the world and the one who could see the truth of things wanted to go further and further into his sense of truth.

Eventually, they had to go their own ways, which was very sad. But the one who was daring had to discover her own ability to see the truth, and the one who could look directly at any situation had to discover his own ability to break new paths.

It took another lifetime, but they met again, these friends who had become lovers who had found their own way, and while each needed the other less, they wanted each other more.

- Center yourself, and as you exhale, open your heart to the place in you that risks.
- Breathe deeply, and as you inhale, open your mind's eye to the place in you that sees truth.
- Breathe steadily until your heart and mind's eye start to merge.
- Breathe evenly, until the place in you that risks touches the place in you that sees truth.

# NOVEMBER 24
## THE NEED TO CONTINUE

Older now, you find holiness
in anything that continues.
— NAOMI SHIHAB NYE

The longer I wake on this Earth, the louder the quiet things speak to me. The more I experience and survive, the more I find truth in the commonalties we all share. The more pain softens me, the deeper my joy and the greater the lessons of those things that live in great stillness.

Before I had cancer, I used to complain so much, annoyed that every chore would need to be done again, that the grass would grow back as soon as I'd cut it. Now I am in awe how it will grow no matter what you do to it. How I need that knowledge.

Now, twelve years from that bed, I am standing in a gentle rain, each drop a whisper of simple things I will never understand. Now, there is only air in the sky of heart waiting to rain. Now, I am thinner, grayer, brighter, less able to say, and my heart has learned more on this side than it will ever let me know. Now, I want to learn how to kiss an orange, unpeeled, and taste the juice.

Twelve years ago the unasked-for growth

disappeared, and — praise this life — I have been shedding ever since. Now, all that remains is my armless heart wanting to live.

- Sit quietly and consider your thoughts as leaves and your heart as the tree.
- Breathe slowly, and try to listen to the soil you share with everything.
- Breathe deeply, and meditate on what is oldest in you.

# NOVEMBER 25
## COMPASSION

I have just three things to teach:
simplicity, patience, compassion.
These are your greatest treasures.

Compassionate toward yourself,
you reconcile all beings in the world.
— LAO-TZU

At first, we might ask, How can being compassionate to yourself reconcile all beings in the world?

To understand the gift of this, we need to recall the analogy of the Spoked Wheel, in which each life is a separate and unique spoke, and yet all lives, like those spokes, meet in a common hub or center. That's why when we tend our deepest center, we care for all souls.

Another powerful way to realize our interconnectedness is to imagine the human family as a stand of aspens growing by a river. Though each tree appears to be growing independently, not attached to the others, beneath the soil, out of view, the roots of all the trees exist as one enormous root. And so, like these trees, our soul's growth, while appearing to be independent, is intimately connected to the health of those around us. For our spirits are entwined at center, out of view.

Once realizing this, it becomes clear that we have no choice but to embrace the health of our neighbors as part of our own health. I felt this deeply in the many cancer rooms I sat in. I know these things to be true: in cutting off strangers, we cut off ourselves; in choking roots, we choke our own growth; in loving strangers, we love ourselves.

Having come this far, I believe that Laotzu's third instruction tells us that if we are aware of our own suffering with the wish to relieve it, we will overcome distrust and reestablish a close relationship with all other living things. In deep and lasting ways, when we heal ourselves, we heal the world. For as the body is only as healthy as its individual cells, the world is only as healthy as its individual souls.

Across the centuries, we have this timeless

medicine: Live directly, wait, and care for your soul as if it were the whole world.

- Breathe slowly, and feel your heart constrict and dilate as your eyes do.
- Breathe slowly, and care for your soul with each breath. Feel your heart expand. Feel your sense of self open.
- Breathe slowly, and feel your sense of the world open as you care for your soul.

# NOVEMBER 26
## THE KINSHIP OF GRATITUDE

When you make the two one,
when you make the inner as outer
and the outer as inner — then
shall you enter the kingdom.
— JESUS

The goal of all experience is to remove whatever might keep us from being whole. The things we learn through love and pain reduce our walls and bring our inner and outer life together, and all the while the friction of being alive erodes whatever impediments remain.

But the simplest and deepest way to make who we are at one with the world is through the kinship of gratitude. Nothing brings the

607

worlds of spirit and earth together more quickly.

To be grateful means giving thanks for more than just the things we want, but also for the things that surmount our pride and stubbornness. Sometimes the things I've wanted and worked for, if I actually received them, would have crushed me.

Sometimes just giving thanks for the mystery of it all brings everything and everyone closer, the way suction pulls streams of water together. So take a chance and openly give thanks, even if you're not sure what for, and feel the plenitude of all that is living brush up against your heart.

- Sit quietly and meditate on what keeps you from knowing yourself.
- Breathe deeply, and lower your walls with an offering of gratitude that is not attached to any one thing.
- Now inhale with gratitude and exhale what remains in the way.
- Repeat this several times throughout your day.

# NOVEMBER 27
# THE TRUTH ABOUT MORNING

There is a vastness that quiets the soul. But
sometimes we are so squarely in the midst
of life's forces that we can't see what we're
a part of.

The truth about morning is that it is the
small light of the beginning breaking through,
again and again. It is a wisdom so large and
clear, one which carries us through our lives
so quietly and completely that we seldom see
it.

Day after day, we are covered with the dust
and grit of what we go through. It tends to
weigh us down, and then we think and
scheme and problem solve. Then we worry if
it will all really work, and if it is the right
thing to do. It all makes us dark and clut-
tered.

But despite our stubbornness of concern,
we tire and must turn what has happened
over to the hammock of night. This is a good
thing. For no matter how unfinished we
seem, the letting go into sleep is nothing
short of a quiet miracle.

This letting go into sleep is an innate,
reflexive form of meditation, no different than
a fly rubbing its face or a doe licking its fawn.

Sooner or later, without discipline or devotion, despite our resolutions and mistakes, we each must sleep. We must surrender to the quieting of all intent and regret, so that the small light of the beginning can rise in us, again and again.

There is no escaping this profound simplicity: what happens covers us like dirt. It covers our hearts and minds, till, at the shore we call exhaustion, we slip into the waters of sleep in a daily sort of baptism, so we can begin again.

So whenever you feel urgent or overwhelmed, whenever you feel pressed to figure things out or to rethink the unthinkable . . . rest . . . so that the endless beginning — which some call the voice of God — might break through what has happened. And you will wake feeling like dawn.

- This is a bedtime meditation. Breathe slowly, and bring to mind one intention you had today as well as one regret.
- Breathe evenly, and let your breath blow the intention and regret far enough away that you can see them clearly.
- Center yourself, and realize that though these thoughts and feelings come through you, they are not who you are.
- Leave these thoughts and feelings out-

side of you, and use each breath to bring you closer and closer to the letting go of sleep.

# NOVEMBER 28
## DEVOTION

Sincerity is that which flows out of your genuine innermost self. Without this, honesty
is mistaken and insufficient. It is like trying to move in a boat without an oar.
— MOCHIMASA HIKITA

It is one thing to see accurately. It is another to allow yourself to feel what you see with sincerity. And still another to allow your actions in the world to be formed by both honest seeing and sincere feeling.

All this reminds me of the stained glass master in Europe who would teach three ways of seeing as necessary to create a sacred window. First, she would say, there is the need to see what image of life shapes the window. Next, there is the need to fill the window with color. And finally, there is the act — the pledge — to let it all come alive by placing it in the light.

How like stained glass we are. Honesty enables us to discover the images of life that

611

shape us, the images that scratch and stain us with experience. But these are nothing without the sincerity of heart that will fill them and us with color. And then, if we are to come alive at all, we must place ourselves in the light.

We all know how sudden and brilliant a stained glass window can be: dirty and opaque one moment and breathtaking as soon as the sun floods it and we can see it from the inside. We are the same: sacred windows in the making. So to place ourselves in the light and to see each other from the inside are the most important skills we can learn.

When we do these things we are practicing devotion. This may sound difficult but it is no different than how we coordinate the eye, hand, and mouth to eat every day. It is basic and necessary, and, after we learn, we do it every day without thinking.

- This is an eating meditation. Place a bowl of cereal or fruit before you.
- Breathe deeply and eat slowly.
- As you see your food, think honesty.
- As you lift your food, think sincerity.
- As you take your food in, think devotion.

# NOVEMBER 29
## THE ANGEL OF RELATIONSHIP

The angel seeing us is watching
through each other's eyes.
— RICKIE LEE JONES

When we can look into each other, however
briefly, without any agenda or scheme of
desire or need, something indescribable and
essential makes us more than we are by
ourselves. This is the difference between looking in a mirror and looking into the eyes of
someone you love.

It seems the angel of relationship can only
appear when our hearts pump our eyes open.
It is such a powerful feeling that many things
can go wrong. I can feel an aliveness that I
think is only in you because it has been
awakened between us. So I might only want
to be with you and thus abandon myself. Or
you, feeling stirred way down in your depth,
might be frightened by such a feeling, and
thinking it is I who poked you there, you
might run from the most beautiful thing to
come your way.

But like the summer sun I chase to feel it
set on my face, I am not it, nor is it me. Yet
between us rises an unrelenting beauty that

no one can have, though we can't live without it.

- Sit with a loved one or trusted friend, and breathe in silence while looking gently and steadily in each other's eyes.
- As you breathe, notice the feelings that rise between you and know that the angel of relationship is appearing and setting like the summer sun.

# NOVEMBER 30
# WHAT WE HOLD DEAR

What we hold dear
can heal the world.

There is an ancient story of a group of pilgrims searching for the holy land. They wandered for days to the bank of a very wide river. It was too deep to cross, and there was nothing to build with. One of the pilgrims prayed for guidance, and a voice appeared urging each to give up something they held dear. From this they could build a raft. For only that which they held dear would be strong enough to hold them up as they crossed into the holy land.

There was immediate conflict and suspicion. The one who heard the voice was accused of trying to steal what mattered most to everyone. Finally, four of the stranded pilgrims agreed. Each offered what seemed useless to the others: a stone, a feather, a piece of driftwood, a page from a book no one understood. Mysteriously, as they slept, the dearness they had placed in these things flowed together and they woke to find a magnificent raft.

Once on the other side, the one who gave up the feather heard another voice. It said that the holy land was right where they had landed. The four pilgrims settled on the far bank within view of the others who would not cross. That night, they burned the raft to cook their food and the voices told them that the holy land is wherever what you hold dear holds you up and then turns to food.

The wisdom carried in this ancient myth is that what we fear is most private mysteriously belongs to everyone; that is, once shared, the things we hold dear release a power that is healing. This is not to say that we should give up what is healing us in the midst of its becoming dear to us. Rather, the story urges us to relinquish personal icons so that they may continue to heal others.

It reminds me of a relic of a saint someone gave me when I was ill, a chip of bone from someone centuries ago who began a religion I was not a part of. But as I held this relic and prayed and worried and sweat through my terror, it became precious to me.

Once well, it became a sacred charm for me, until one day the person who gave it to me fell terribly ill and needed it back. I was afraid to give it up and felt naked without it, but giving it up made everything holy.

I have since, when the time proved right, given away other precious things I have lived with — crystals and books and personal treasures I have long enshrined. For only in use do they again become healing. It is the giving of what is dear that helps us cross the river.

- Center yourself and meditate on something that has personal power for you, something you hold dear. It might be a shell or stone that you have prayed with. Or a special candle you burn when troubled.
- Breathe deeply, and give gratitude for its dearness to you.
- Breathe deeply, and pray for the clarity of heart to know if and when it might be right to give this dear thing to another.
- Do not act on this today. Do not give this up if you still need it. Do not hold on to it tighter if you fear letting it go.
- Simply breathe now with a willingness to know if and when such a moment might come.

# DECEMBER 1
## CANDLES AND COCOONS

Dreams are candles
to help us through the dark.
Once used, they have to melt.

Very often, we define ourselves by what we want or dream of. I want to be an actor or a musician or president or a grandmother. I dream of being famous, of going down in history, of being a hero or a heroine. Yet when our lives shape us differently, we often think we have failed, that we are settling for less, because we weren't good enough to become or have what we wanted.

Certainly, as we experience our limitations, this sometimes feels true. Yet even through our limitations, we *evolve* rather than fail, the way a caterpillar becomes a chrysalis becomes a butterfly, and the succession of life's trials is precisely the unfolding we need to find our bliss and rightful place in the order of things.

The truth is that what we want or dream of doesn't always last. It tends to serve its purpose in our development and then fades away, losing its relevance. And we can do enormous damage to ourselves by insisting on carrying that which has died.

As a teenager, I wanted very badly to be a

professional basketball player. My gifts were enough to hide my limitations for a while and I played in high school and in college. But when I stopped playing my sophomore year in college, I discovered my calling as a poet. This carried me for almost eighteen years until cancer opened me to the uncovered life of spirit.

I did not fail at being a basketball player nor did poetry fail me. More accurately, my inwardness evolved with enough life experience, so that moving bodily in the air evolved into the poet's dance of feeling which then evolved into the spirit's grace of being. I no more failed in my desire to be a basketball player than the cocoon fails the butterfly, though the form of the dream was painful to lose.

Living up to a dream is rarely as important as entering it for all it has to teach.

- Try to recall the first dream that really took hold of you.
- What did you want from this dream?
- What has the dream taught you and where has it led you?
- Is the essence of that dream still with you?
- Do you have a dream now?
- What is it teaching you?

# DECEMBER 2
## AN INVITATION

Yours is to live it, not to reveal it.
— HELEN LUKE

Helen Luke was a very wise woman, deeply grounded in the life of the spirit. I knew Helen during the last two years of her life. During that time she was a mentor to me. These words are from our last conversation. They troubled me, for I have spent my life becoming a writer, thinking that my job has been just that — to reveal what is essential and hidden.

In the time since Helen died, I've come to understand her last instruction as an invitation to shed any grand purpose, no matter how devoted we may be to what we are doing. She wasn't telling me to stop writing, but to stop striving to be important. She was inviting me to stop recording the poetry of life and to enter the poetry of life.

This lesson applies to us all. If we devote ourselves to the life at hand, the rest will follow. For life, it seems, reveals itself through those willing to live. Anything else, no matter how beautiful, is just advertising.

This took me many years to learn and accept. Having begun innocently enough, there arose separations, and now I know that health resides in restoring direct experience. Thus, having struggled to do what has never been done, I discovered that living is the original art.

- Center yourself and think of your life as a story not yet written.
- Breathe slowly, and relieve yourself of the responsibility to record your own story.
- Breathe deeply, and imagine your path as the patch of sky a bird flies through.
- Now just breathe and fly. Enter your day, and breathe and live.

# December 3
# Hospitality

At heart, hospitality is a helping across a threshold.

— Ivan Illich

In Dante's *Divine Comedy,* Virgil lovingly guides Dante through the hell of denial and the purgatory of illusion, up to a passage of fire that Dante must cross alone, beyond which he becomes authentic. Earlier in history, Aaron guides his brother Moses off

Mount Sinai back into the world, where the prophet must live what God has shown him. Even in Eden, if we can get past the punitive tellings we have heard so often, God ushers Adam and Eve to the threshold of the world, offering them the bruised and wondrous life of genuine experience that only those who are human can know.

These are deep examples of spiritual hospitality, of helping kindred spirits further into their living. Truly, the most we can ask of others is for their guidance and comfort on the way — without imposition, design, or thought of reward. This is the hospitality of relationship: for family to help us manifest who we are in the world, for friends to bring us to thresholds of realness, for loved ones to encourage us to cross barriers of our own making into moments of full aliveness.

This is the honest welcoming to table, without judgment of what we eat. Often the purpose of love is for others to guide us, without expectation or interference, as far as they can go, so that we might begin.

It reminds me of a dream I had when ill, in which I came to the edge of a forest where the narrow, lighted spaces called to me. I stood there through many opportunities till an ageless woman of great resolve appeared, saying, "You can't start, I know, and if I were kind, I'd see you halfway in, but I am more than kind. You must enter alone. I will meet you on the other side."

I'm not sure if that feminine presence was God or an angel or the peace of my own spirit, but its strong and gentle guidance was enough for me to make it through, and I never saw her again. But now, when I love by clearing paths that I and others may or may not take, I feel her in my hands.

This speaks to one of our deepest callings of love — that special hospitality for the injured, the strong action of compassion that makes it possible for those in pain to heal themselves. It calls mysteriously and arduously for the clearing of confusion and the comfort of what is real. It is the way that we who have suffered can take our turn, lifting the head of whoever has fallen, bracing their exhausted neck to drink, knowing we can never drink for them.

- Breathe deeply, and meditate on one act of guidance and comfort you have received that asked for nothing in return.
- As you exhale, offer gratitude for that gesture of hospitality.
- As you inhale, feel your own capacity for guiding without interfering. Feel your own capacity for giving comfort without needing anything in return.
- As you enter your day, practice anonymous guidance by leaving a gesture of kindness or truth in the path of others.

Leave half a sandwich where the home-less gather, or leave a book open to a passage of wisdom, or leave a flower on a bus seat.
- Help the world by leaving a trail of who you are.

# DECEMBER 4
# WORK AND PASSION

Don't ask what the world needs. Ask what makes you come alive, and go do it. Because what the world needs is people who have come alive.
— HOWARD THURMAN

I remember when in college, many of us were herded into teaching because there seemed a need in the job force. But by the time we graduated, teaching jobs were scarce. The same thing happened fifteen years later when I was teaching college. Many of my students were herded into the study of business. But a few years after graduating, there were very few jobs.

This is another way that scarcity can direct our lives. Often when we shape our interests around what others need, we wind up selling our chance at happiness for what we think will be secure. But while supply and demand may work on paper, it can build a loveless life in the world.

This is why finding what we love, though it may take years, is building a life of passion. For what makes you come alive can keep you alive, whether you are paid well for it or not. And beyond the fashion of the job market, a life of passion makes us a healthy cell in the body of the world.

- Center yourself and allow the things that stir you to come into your heart. It may be as simple as watching a candle flicker or running in the wind.
- Breathe freely, and just feel how these things affect your whole body and being.
- When you can, discuss with a loved one what makes you come alive.

# December 5
## Pursue the Obstacle

Pursue the obstacle.
It will set you free.

When I came upon the mountain, I was in a hurry. I thought it would take too long to make my way around, so I set out to break a path through. Each rock and branch felt like

624

a waste of time. If only the mountain weren't in the way. I cut my legs and arms as I rushed along. It grew harder to breathe, and I lost all sense of direction. Now I had to climb high enough to see.

Once I broke the treeline, something in me had to see the top. Then I hurried my way up, and strangely, as I worked the climb — step after step — I kept rising, but felt as though I were going nowhere. Finally, I broke the clouds. I had never seen sun on top of clouds. I sat in a clearing on a cliff, the light on top of my head, like a cloud. Suddenly, reaching the top or getting beyond the mountain no longer seemed important. I liked it up here and felt that I could live on the mountain. But I had to return. I had to eat. I needed love. But now when someone asks about breaking through what's in the way or being in a hurry, I look both ways and say, "Pursue the obstacle. It will set you free."

This story invites us to honor each obstacle as something flowing in its own right in the Universal stream, to see ourselves and the obstacle as two limbs of the same tree drifting in the same river, bumping into each other, and even blocking one another for a moment.

Looking at obstacles this way, we are asked not to oppose what blocks us as something mounting its will against our own. For the obstacle will simply give our resistance back to us. We are being asked not to empower or perpetuate the life of the obstacle, but to step aside if we can with openness to the energy of the obstacle — much like the ancient art of Aikido, where instead of blocking a punch, you help the punch move past you.

All the while we are invited to question that in us which insists that what is before us is an obstacle in the first place. It may not be so. It may be so. It may be something small that our history of struggle has enlarged into tragedy or bad luck.

So if we can, we must focus on our relationship to the stream and not to the things being carried alongside us. If something appears to be blocking our way, we must try to understand what is moving it and what is moving us. If our movement in the world is still blocked, perhaps we are meant to be still. We must try not to damage ourselves unnecessarily by trying to force a movement to happen before its time.

- Identify the biggest obstacle in your life at present. What is it keeping you from?
- Describe the obstacle as a piece of nature that has its own history. Is it like a shell being broken by the surf, or a stone tumbling in a landslide, or like a small deer frightened in the middle of a busy road?

- How is what you want or need colliding with what it wants or needs?

# DECEMBER 6
# THE COLOR OF TRUTH

The best and most beautiful things in the world cannot be seen or touched . . . but are felt in the heart.
— HELEN KELLER

There is an ancient Chinese art of painting on porcelain. It requires, more than skill and precision, a deep trust and patience in the process. It involves painting thin layers of pigment, one at a time, on the porcelain, letting each dry and soak into the porcelain itself. But even when dry, the pigment doesn't yet reveal its color. You never know what the color will be until the porcelain is fired in the kiln — that is, until the pigment is burned into the porcelain itself.

This is remarkably like the life of questions that come from living. We use the brush of our feelings to paint our questions into our heart. But only after the fire of experience, only after our felt questions are burned by experience into our heart, only then do we see the color of truth emerge.

So there are no answers to the deeper questions of living, only the emerging colors of truth which we must find the trust and patience to live into.

- Sit quietly and bring to mind the color of a truth you have personally lived into.
- Using your breath, unravel this truth back to the questions you had before living it.
- Note the difference and share the story of this truth with a friend.

# DECEMBER 7
## WE HAVE THIS CHOICE

The heart is a strong shore
and the ocean has many moods.

With each day, we have this choice: we can build walls, block ourselves from the light, and suffer a dampness in the soul. Or we can live barely, shine on through, and suffer the nicks of erosion for living in the open.

Most of us, myself included, live behind walls that were started by others and finished by ourselves. Very often, we fear each other without reason — the wall builders and those who shine on through. But it really comes down to how to make it through life — safely or fully. I confess this comes from one who struggles to shine on through, because in the end, not being touched by life is not that safe after all. What I've learned is that the more I risk being who I am — like a sun daring to shine — the thinner the walls need to be outside me.

My first experience of this was a painful moment as a boy in which my mother had ordered me to do something. We were alone in my room, and I said no. I don't remember what it was she asked of me, only that her demand was demeaning and unnecessary. I wasn't belligerent, just quietly firm. I remember fearfully building a wall as fast as I could in anticipation of her anger. I had barely prepared myself when she drew her arm behind her head and slapped me with a vengeance. The wall hadn't worked. My very soul had been struck.

She went to strike me again, but by this time my soul had somehow reflexed into a strength of selfness that she couldn't penetrate. I glowed. She stalled in midswing and called my father to enforce her demand. He felt my brightness, but held the line and struck me too. By the time he landed, I was shining through. It hurt, for sure, but I was protected.

There are times walls are necessary, but more often we can protect ourselves by being who we are. Neither hiding nor revealing ourselves will prevent our share of pain, but in being who we are, we get to be a part of the Universal stream, not just a nut in a shell waiting to fall.

- Center yourself and meditate, by turns, on your sense of the wall you look out from and on your sense of who you are that does the looking.
- Breathe steadily. As you inhale, close your fist and feel your wall.
- Breathe slowly. As you exhale, open your hand and feel who you are.
- After a time, practice bringing who you are out beyond your wall by inhaling and exhaling with your hand open.
- After a time, stand and move about the room outside of your wall. Note how this feels.

# December 8
# In the Source-Place

Take a pitcher full of water and set it down in the water — now it has water inside and water outside. We mustn't give it a name, lest silly people start talking again about the body and the soul.

— Kabir

We can't help it. We make too much of where

we end and where others begin. Yet only after declaring healthy boundaries can we discover and experience the true common water of spirit that Kabir talks about. It can be confusing. But, though we are not always eloquent or clear in what comes out, everyone is clear as water in the source-place where mind and heart start as one.

As Teilhard de Chardin said, "We are not human beings having a spiritual experience. We are spiritual beings having a human experience." Entering our days with this perspective can make a difference. It provides the ocean for our small pitcher of a life.

It helps to remember that despite all our struggles for identity, despite the weight of living, there is an irrepressible ounce of spirit in each of us, a wellspring we carry within, that can be blocked but not contained. It emanates through all beings as the longing for love and peace.

When opening our longing, our honest want for love, we open the fountainhead of spirit, and then, like Kabir's pitcher, we are water living in water, love living in love, a small thing alive in a big thing alive, a breath inside a wind.

- Sit quietly, and as you breathe, think of yourself as Kabir's small pitcher of water.
- Breathe deeply and freely, and think of

the unseeable world of spirit around you as an ocean that carries you.

• Breathe slowly and cleanly, and try to feel how you and the life around you are made of the same thing.

# DECEMBER 9
## THE WORK OF LOVE

Love courses through everything.
— FAKHRUDDIN IRAQI

I recently learned that the first form of pencil was a ball of lead. Having discovered that lead, if scratched, would leave markings, people then wrestled with chunks of the stuff in an attempt to write. Through the work of many, the chunks were eventually shaped into a useable form that could fit the hand. The discovery became a tool.

I am humbled to confess after a lifetime of relationship that love is no different. Be it a lover or a friend or a family member, the discovery of closeness appears in our life like a ball of lead — something that if wrestled with, will leave markings by which we can understand each other.

But this is only the beginning. The work of love is to shape the stuff of relationship into a tool that fits our hands. With each hardship

632

faced, with each illusion confronted, with each trespass looked at and owned, another piece of the chunk is whittled and love begins to become a sacred tool.

When truth is held in compassionate hands, the sharpness of love becomes clear and not hurtful.

- Bring to mind a significant relationship that you are struggling with.
- As you center yourself, pray that the love you share continues to finds its form.
- As you enter your day, stay pliable and open to becoming a tool.

# DECEMBER 10
## QUESTIONS PUT
## TO THE SICK – IV

When was the last time you listened to the stories of others?
— QUESTION PUT TO THE SICK BY A
NATIVE AMERICAN MEDICINE MAN

I found myself in a psychodrama group that met every other week for two years. I didn't have any idea what psychodrama was and would never have tried it, except that the man who led the group was a sage to me. I knew he had more to teach me, and I had vowed to myself to participate in whatever he was doing.

It turned out that psychodrama was a process by which we each took turns bringing to life a part of our inner story in the hope that by acting out dreams or current conflicts or unresolved pieces of our past, we might with each other's help unfold some wisdom that would help us live our lives.

I didn't want to go first, and it was several weeks before I found the courage to take my turn. At first, I thought I'd just wait on the perimeter and watch how this would all unfold. But unexpectedly and with great gravity, I began to see that each person's story, no matter how different from my own, would suddenly be about a part of me that I'd never given voice to.

I discovered that taking part in another's dream or conflict or unresolved past was just a deeper way of listening, a deeper way of being present. The reward for such deep listening was the incredible honor of first witnessing a living model of human courage, and then finding comfort and healing in the surprise that our stories are really all the same.

It seems the ancient Medicine Men understood that listening to another's story somehow gives us the strength of example to carry on, as well as showing us aspects of ourselves we can't easily see. For listening to the stories of others — not to their precautions or personal commandments — is a kind of water that breaks the fever of our isolation. If we listen closely enough, we are soothed into remembering our common name.

- Breathe slowly, and mediate on being open and receptive today.
- As you move through your day, give over your energy to listening.
- As you hear the stories of others, be aware of when one touches a part of your own story.
- If you can, offer a thread of your own story as a gift in return.

# DECEMBER 11
## INSIDE GRAVITY

Inside gravity,
the same things happen,
just slower.

When a plate breaks, we call it an accident. When a heart breaks, we call it sad. If it is ours, we say tragic. When a dream breaks, we sometimes call it unfair. Yet ants drop dirt and manage more and birds drop food and peck again. But as humans, when we drop what we need, philosophies and complaints abound.

It's not that we moan, but that we stop living to hear ourselves moan. Still, stars collide and histories begin. In our world, something is always letting go and something is always hitting the Earth. Often that which lets go survives by releasing, by not holding on until what needs to go is ripped from it. Often that which is hit survives by staying soft, by allowing what hits it to temporarily shape it the way stones shape mud.

As humans, we take turns letting go and being hit. Love softens this process, and peace slows it down, until in moments that are blessed, we seem to play catch with what we need.

- As you inhale, bring to mind what is currently hitting you and how you might soften to lessen its impact.
- As you exhale, bring to mind what is currently needing to move away from you and how you might open yourself to more easily release it.

# DECEMBER 12
## THE TREASURE AT OUR FEET

It is not easy to find happiness in
 ourselves,
and it is not possible to find it elsewhere.
— AGNES REPPLIER

If forced to name them, the biggest obstacles
to peace are ourselves and the world. Often
en route to the truth of my soul, I get stuck
in my self or lost in the world. Or the reverse.

Still we carry the treasured essence within.
It is always with us, very near though it may
seem far, and there is no place else to find
the treasure but underneath our agitation. It
waits there like gold on the bottom of a shallow lake, and though we stand in the water,
the treasure at our feet, this stirring of our
reflection keeps us from seeing. More often
than not, I need to stop moving and thinking
and fixing, and simply reach within myself.

So run, if you like, for it will all come with
you. Or think and reason as many times you
must, for your heart will outlast the ripples of
your thought. Or blame the things of this
world if you need to, for the things you blame
will eventually disappear.

Then you and I will still be left with ourselves and the world and the treasure at our feet.

- Center yourself, and if there is something you are running from, inhale and let it catch up with you.
- Sit quietly, and if there is something you are trying to reason away, exhale and let it touch you.
- Be still, and as you breathe, let the forces of the world touch you and move on by.
- Now reach if you can with your breath for the treasure waiting within.

# DECEMBER 13
# WHEN WE SPEAK

I have only now realized that something endless has broken ground in me, and I have no choice but to live and love until it grows me like a tree.

I met an old man at a gathering, and when everyone went on their way, he leaned into the hushed space between us and talked to me as if we were trees. Scratching his chin, he said, "We start out thin and green, and each time the sky grows dark, we think we will break, but the downpour makes us grow, though never straight, always twisting for the light, and, strangely, the more we reach above the earth, the deeper something in us fingers its way down, and it is this — our unseen fingers reaching for the core — that keeps us from blowing away. Now there is no more running and very little swaying, and up till now, there have been many languages, though none that could be heard, just a creak at dawn and a moan at night, and sooner or later, we are brought down. It doesn't matter how. We are undone. But stacked we burn, and here the poetry rises from us, leaving wisdom in the ash."

Then, he left. I wasn't sure what had happened, but I think his story had to do with humility and with how all that we experience is really kindling for when we truly speak. Somehow we grow through all the things that seem so dark, and with each season, our roots thicken and deepen and spread to bear our weight of living in the world.

But what is the "being brought down," the "being undone"? Perhaps it is anything — disappointment, loss, unexpected change — that brings us, humbly, closer to the earth. Perhaps any upending of our very personal designs allows us to feel our bond more fully with other living things.

Yet what does it mean for us to be stacked so we can burn? Perhaps this is about being simplified to the point that what has grown within us can rise out of us with a passion for being alive. Perhaps after two marriages and the coming and going of the dearest of friends, I can, when stripped of my bark, utter something hot and clear about what it means to love. Perhaps after losing a rib and gaining my life, I can, when set aflame by the moment at hand, cough up some cinder of what it means to live off truth.

Experience, it seems, wants to burn out of us, and whether what comes out is intelligent or pretty, the purpose of all fire is to light and warm. Perhaps as the farmer on the edge of winter must gather wood to make it to spring, we each must gather our experience and set it ablaze to keep our lifeblood healthy and warm.

- Sit quietly, before a fire if you can, and meditate on one key experience that has unexpectedly shaped who you are.
- Breathe long and softly, and let this life-changing experience that lives in you rise like a small flame.
- Breathe evenly, and give a simple word or two to this small flame.
- With your eyes closed, repeat the words that have surfaced several times and let your own experience warm you.

# DECEMBER 14
## FREEING OURSELVES

It's hard to tell the truth, but once told, it's hard to keep it back.
— SHARON GREEN

Whatever truth we feel compelled to withhold, no matter how unthinkable it is to imagine ourselves telling it, not to is a way of spiritually holding our breath. You can only do it for so long. Of course, the longer we keep our truth hidden, the more difficult it is to give it voice, or so it seems, because while the pressure is building, we are running out of air. But we are never more than a heartbeat from freeing ourselves of that awful isolation, never more than a gulp and a cough from falling back into the open.

All the while, the power of being hidden keeps us from the vitality of living, and so the healing value of telling the truth is in how it returns us to the pulse of what is sacred. Just as important as the respect and trust gained for telling the truth is the release of that terrible pressure that keeps us hidden and isolated. This is the embodied gift of truth which like breathing keeps us alive.

• Center yourself, and as you breathe,

imagine it is your truth that you are inhaling and exhaling.
- During your day, take time to inhale your truth and release it back into the world.

# DECEMBER 15
## GOYA AND MELVILLE

The sun doesn't stop shining
because people are blind.

It is a hard challenge to stay true to ourselves in the face of indifference. Rejection and opposition are painful, but being treated as if you don't exist is quietly devastating. This soft puncture is particularly human. Eagles soar and glide for hours in canyon air, and the fact that no one knows does not lessen their ability to fly. But for us there is a constant elusive heroism in being who we are, especially when we are misunderstood, judged, or ignored. Somehow our need for love gives tremendous power to the opinions of others, and so, we are required to guard against turning our lives over to the expectations of others.

A great example of hearing one's deeper self is the Spanish painter Goya. Writing about Goya, Andre Malraux tells us that after going deaf in 1792, the painter understood that "to allow his genius to become apparent to himself it was necessary that he should dare to give up aiming to please." It is both touching and instructive that Goya couldn't fully realize his God-given gifts until he went deaf to the demands of those around him.

One of the saddest examples of being ignored is the novelist Herman Melville. Having survived many years at sea against his will, Melville had authored several best-selling sea adventures. But when he opened his soul and wrote *Moby Dick,* two things happened: one of the greatest novels ever written by an American was birthed, and the American public laughed at the great white whale and its maker. He was ridiculed and dismissed.

This deep and sensitive man was so wounded by this that he painfully withdrew, and at the age of thirty-two, at the height of his powers, he virtually stopped writing for nearly forty years. Tragically, he extinguished his inner voice because those around him couldn't hear.

I carry both Goya and Melville around with me as reminders of how precious and unique each of our gifts is. No one can really know what you are called to or what you are capable of but you. Even if no one sees or understands, you are irreplaceable.

- Sit with a trusted loved one, and take turns describing a time that you felt inwardly bound to a person or situation that no one else seemed to understand.
- What made you stay true to what you were feeling?
- How well do you know that part of yourself?

# DECEMBER 16
# FULLY KNOWING THE ROAD

If you come to a fork in the road,
take it.

— YOGI BERRA

Like the koans of Zen monks and the wit of Shakespeare's jesters, we may never know if the sayings of this baseball legend are utter nonsense or utter wisdom. But the longer we stay with them, the more they reveal.

What this one says to me is not to stall too long at the crossroads of life, not to hesitate our way out of living. We can't experience everything, and taking one road will always preclude another, but agonizing over which to take can eventually prevent us from knowing any road.

Even when taking one road, keeping the other alive in our mind for too long is the beginning of regret. In fact, giving over to regret is a way to resist our limitations, a way to still take the other road with us. It's the heart's way to be stubborn. Ultimately, keeping the other road so actively with us only keeps us from fully knowing the road we have chosen.

We are beautifully limited creatures, capable of great moments of full living, but we can't have it all or experience it all. We can only, paradoxically, experience all there is by giving ourselves completely and humbly to the small path we are drawn to.

- Center yourself and consider a decision you are facing.
- Breathe slowly, and try each path on once, no more.
- Return to your day and try not to replay your choices. Simply let your deeper self tend to these things for you.

# DECEMBER 17
## HEALING OURSELVES

---

In this world,
hate never yet dispelled hate.
Only love dispels hate.
This is the law,
ancient and inexhaustible.

— BUDDHA

One of the most difficult things about healing from being hurt by others is how to put wounds to rest when those who have hurt us will not give air to the wound, will not admit to their part in causing the pain. I have struggled with this deeply. Time and again, I find myself confusing the want for justice with the need for a witness of the wound.

Physical wounds are hard to miss, but emotional wounds are seldom visible. This is why they must be looked at and acknowledged if we are ever to heal. Yet so often, our pain is compounded by the very human fact that we may never agree on the nature of what happened. If we do, we may never admit it to each other. Or the amends we feel we so deserve may go with the hurtful one to the grave.

As with so many other crucial negotiations of life, what's required is to honor what lives within us. We must bear witness to ourselves, for there is no power as embracing or forgiving as the authority of that portion of God that lives in each of us.

- Sit quietly until you begin to feel safe, and bring into view a wound that hasn't healed.
- Breathe steadily and look directly at the wound, bearing witness to yourself and all you've been through.
- Breathe fully, and let your compassion

for yourself be the air to cleanse the wound.

# DECEMBER 18
# LIGHTING OUR WAY

One does not become enlightened by imagining figures of light, but by making the darkness conscious.

— CARL JUNG

If Jung is right, then perhaps Paradise is no more than seeing the light forming in the dark. Perhaps being awake is paying attention to the ongoing moment of life that we so often take for granted, that moment — like conception, like seed cracking open — that is happening even as you read this.

Yet, as a headlight grows filmed by driving through all kinds of weather, the gift by which we perceive gets covered by experience, and our ability to see is diminished until we clean the gift. This is a lifelong process, one that never ends, but always begins.

So the care of one's being is imperative and continuous, as simple and hard as wiping the residue of experience from your mind and heart, letting your original face again light the way. Though, like scratching the middle of your back, we often need each other to regain our sense of Oneness.

It helps here to tell an old Sufi story about a thirsty man who follows a muddy stream into a cave. He carries a lantern, holds it before him, and finds the clear source which he can drink from. When feeling muddied and troubled, we must not drink from the mud, but trace its source carefully. Carrying the lantern of our spirit before us, we must enter the darkness of our troubles if we are to drink clearly again from the source. This is making the darkness conscious, and compassion is swaying your small light near others too troubled or muddied to see their way.

- Sit quietly with your eyes closed, and feel the light of spirit in every cell of your body.
- As you inhale, feel each cell brighten.
- As you exhale, feel a slight increase of light around you.
- During your day, when feeling troubled, stop and breathe slowly and light your way.

# DECEMBER 19
## SUGAR IN THE TREE

As someone sitting beneath a tree
can imagine the earth from above the
    trees,
a heart encumbered by reality
can know eternity.

As a boy, I spent many hours at sea on a thirty-foot ketch my father had built. When the sea would get rough, I'd go below where the noise and motion of the deep would pound the hull, and every toss and lurch would feel sudden and pointed.

Finding me there, my father told me how sailors, when feeling seasick, have always made their way on deck to look at the horizon. While that doesn't prevent the pitch and drop of waves in a storm, it is somehow less upsetting if the larger context is kept in view.

I have kept this wisdom close to me when pitched in storm. In truth, whether facing cancer or riding the insecurity of repeated rejection or trying to surmount the most profound moments of loneliness, my greatest pains and fears have been lessened when I've managed to keep the largest sense of life before me like a horizon.

This is the difference between despair and

faith, between the narrow point of doubt and a view long enough to sustain all life-giving possibility. It seems we suffer more when huddled below, and though the eternal perspective, the horizon of all time and all life, doesn't remove us from our storms, it does make things bearable.

During the hardest times, keeping my eyes on the horizon has helped me endure such things as the loss of a rib, and a marriage, and a job I loved. For staying where we can keep God in view allows the ups and downs to be somewhat predictable. It even shows that suffering has its rhythm. Keeping the larger view can be the difference between thinking life is cruel and knowing that experience is a powerful ocean. In ways that truly matter, God is always in the horizon, and faith is making our way on deck, despite our pain.

- Wherever you are — in your bedroom, at your desk, or on a bus — sit quietly and see yourself sitting there from above your bed or desk or the bus you are riding.
- Breathe slowly, and be both where you are and above where you are.
- Now feel the stress or pain of what you are carrying this instant.
- Breathe slowly, and try to see yourself in your life and from above your life,

and feel both your pain and the Universe surrounding your pain.

- When you find yourself huddled in your pain, try to breathe your way to the horizon.

# DECEMBER 20
## BELIEVING

Believing is all a child does for a living.
— KURTIS LAMKIN

Picasso once said that artists are those of us who still see with the eyes of children. Somehow, as we journey into the world, more and more gets in the way, and we stop questioning things in order to move deeper into them and start questioning as a way to challenge things that we fear are false.

As a child I used to talk to things — birds that flew overhead, trees that swayed slowly in the night, even stones drying in the sun. For years, though, I stopped doing this freely because of what others might think, and then I stopped altogether. Now I learn that Native Americans do this all the time, that many original peoples believe with their childlike eyes right into the center of things.

Now, almost fifty, I am humbled to recover the wisdom that believing is not a conclusion, but a way into the vitality that waits in everything.

- When you can, talk with a child about how they see the world.

# DECEMBER 21
## NOWHERE TO GO

There is nothing to do
and nowhere to go.
Accepting this,
we can do everything
and go anywhere.

One of the basic notions of Taoism is that the world in all its mystery and difficulty cannot be improved upon, only experienced. We are asked to believe that life in all its complexity and wonder is complete as is — everchanging and vital, but never perfectible.

I've come to understand that this doesn't prevent our being involved. On the contrary, accepting that the world can do quite fine without us allows us to put down the burden of being corrective heroes and simply concentrate on absorbing the journey of being alive.

Thus, our work is not to eliminate or re-create anything. Rather, like human fish, we are asked to experience meaning in the life that moves through the gill that is our heart. Ultimately, we are small living things awakened in the stream, not gods who carve out rivers. We cannot eliminate hunger, but we can feed each other. We cannot eliminate loneliness, but we can hold each other. We cannot eliminate pain, but we can live a life of compassion.

I only came upon these notions after experiencing them. Faced with dying, the opportunity to change the world was taken away. It was all I could do to survive being changed by the world. This sent me into a sudden depression, but soon I found what remained to be liberating. Stripped of causes and plans and things to strive for, I discovered that everything I could need or ask for is right here — in flawed abundance.

Since then, my efforts have turned from trying to outrun suffering to trying to express it, from trying to achieve joy to trying to discover it, and from trying to shape or better the lives around me to accepting love wherever I can find it.

- Sit quietly and simply let your heart breathe without focus.
- Try not to think and also try not to not think.
- Exhale your pressures and arrive where you are.

- Breathe deeply, and accept the jewel and grit of this moment.

# DECEMBER 22
# THE LESSON

---

God breaks the heart again and again and again until it stays open.

— HAZRAT INAYAT KHAN

When young, it was my first fall from love. It broke me open the way lightning splits a tree. Then, years later, cancer broke me further. This time it broke me wider, the way a flood carves the banks of a narrow stream. Then, having to leave a twenty-year marriage. This broke me the way wind shatters glass. Then, in Africa, it was the anonymous face of a schoolboy beginning his life. This broke me yet again. But this was like hot water melting soap.

Each time I tried to close up what had been opened. It was a reflex, natural enough. But the lesson was, of course, the other way. The lesson was in never closing again.

- Center yourself, and concentrate on the part of your heart that is breaking open right now.
- Ease the pain by breathing deeply

through the break.
- Try if you can, just for a moment, to leave your heart open and look inside the break.

# DECEMBER 23
# A SURETY OF ROOTS

You didn't come into this house
so I might tear off a piece of your life.
Perhaps when you leave,
you'll take something of mine:
chestnuts, roses, or a surety of roots.
— PABLO NERUDA

Perhaps the most stubborn thing that keeps us from knowing love is distrust. Certainly, we have more than enough reason in our world to be cautious, alert, and guarded against being hurt or taken advantage of.

But the fact remains that in spite of all the news and terrible stories that we pass on at parties, there is no other doorway into kindness and all its gifts but through the gentle risk to open ourselves, however slightly, and try. The question we must ask, that I ask myself every day, is which is more debilitating: to be cut off from love or to be scarred by the pain of being hurt?

What makes Neruda such a great poet is

the largeness of his heart, and through his large kindness, he suggests that giving heals and that until we step into that space between each other and try, nothing can happen. But once we do, giving and receiving become the same, and we all grow stronger for going there together.

- Center yourself, and bring to mind three small gifts you are willing to give away. They may be tangible or symbolic or gestures of kindness.
- Wrap each gently in your breathing.
- Bring these gifts with you into your day.
- Before you come home, give them away.

# DECEMBER 24
## IN A BURST OF ONENESS

When wax and wick work best,
light and heat are all that's left.

Like a candle, our wick of spirit is encased in our humanity, and when our spirit is touched, we light up until all we know melts and changes shape for the burn of our experience. Repeatedly, our sweat and struggle burns our sense of self and world away, so that our Divine spark can be released, again and again. These moments of Spirit-Lighting-Up not only rearrange our lives, but they light and warm those who stay near.

In such moments, we become one with what we see, and this sudden Oneness is what the faithful of all paths have called Love. And in the illumination of Oneness called Love, all that's left is a willingness toward birth, an urge to be touched by something timeless and fresh. All that's left is the want of deep parts in strangers. To relish the waking over being awake, the burning over being burned, the loving over being loved.

When we can be — no matter how briefly — at one with what we have in common with all life, we are rewarded beyond attachment and ownership. This is the difference between becoming a singer and becoming the song. This is the best of ambition: that the dancer melts into the dance, and the lover melts into the act of love, and the builder melts into the thing being built, until in a burst of Oneness, dancer and lover and builder are one.

Perhaps momentarily, when swimming with the stream, we are the stream; when moving with the music, we are the music; when rocking the wounded, we are the suffering. Perhaps momentarily, when thinking without masks, we are pure thought; when believing without doubt, we are God. Perhaps love is an instrument we play for all we're worth in an orchestra yet to be convened. Perhaps this is why, in the fullest moments of loving or knowing or being, we go nameless and time-less and breathless — everything about us used up, like a candle, burned over and over, just to light entire rooms with our flicker.

- Watch someone doing something they love. It could be as simple as gardening, cleaning a treasure, grooming a pet, stacking wood, or washing a child.
- Observe in detail how they attend their task.
- What lets you know that they love what they are doing?
- Is there a moment where they seem to be one with what they love?
- What can their act of loving teach you?

# DECEMBER 25
# BEGINNING AGAIN

The glory around you
is born again each day.
— THE MUPPETS' VERSION OF
*A CHRISTMAS CAROL*

Creation is ongoing. The world begins anew each day. This is the miracle that makes not a sound, but which changes everything, if we can be quiet enough to feel it happen. When we can participate in this, we begin anew each day.

Consider how the sun washes the Earth with its heat and then clouds dissipate, and grasses grow, and stones crumble when no one is looking to reveal a smoother, deeper face. It is the same with us. In a moment of realness, the clouds in our mind clear and our passion is restored, and our walls crumble when no one is looking. It all continues and refreshes, if we let it. It all renews so subtly.

We think it is night that covers the world, but everything living is re-created in that mysterious moment of rest that blankets us all. And each time you blink, if you pause to let your heart flutter with nothing but air to flutter about, each time you open your eyes, you can begin again. It's true. This is the moment of resurrection, the opening of our eyes.

- Sit quietly and look at the things about you, common as they may seem.
- Breathe deeply, and close your eyes and pray to see everything again for the first time.
- Breathe slowly, and open your eyes and enter your life again as a pilgrim.

# DECEMBER 26
## INSIDE THE WIND

---

Sometimes I go about with pity for myself
and all the while Great Winds are carrying
me across the sky.

— OJIBWAY SAYING

Our crucial task when in pain or despair is
not to let the sour feelings spill into everything, so that we stain our sense of the world.
Yet we must also take care not to so contain
our feelings that they fester and infect our
sense of ourselves. Somewhere between these
two extremes waits the life of healthy expression, not personalizing everything and not
painting the world with our troubles.

Our inner work is often most demanding
when we are sad and afraid, for we can so
easily be overwhelmed by the power of these
emotions that we can start to believe the
world less possible or ourselves diminished.
Once feeling less than, we stop feeling the
truth of what is genuine and start losing
touch with the Great Winds of life.

Yet, somehow life has a way of carrying us
along whether we are aware of it or not. Just
as the stream carries both the hungry fish
and the sleeping one downstream, the Great
Winds carry both the agitated heart and the

peaceful one into tomorrow.

Thus the work of prayer, when we feel least like praying, is neither to inflate or deflate the world or ourselves, but to restore our connection to the powerful currents of life.

- Sit quietly, and after a time open yourself without words to the mood of prayer.
- Breathe slowly, and pray to feel the Great Winds surrounding you.
- Breathe steadily, and feel your breath mix with the currents of life.

# DECEMBER 27
# THE BEAUTY OF IT

If all I have is Now,
where will I look for Joy?

Without hope for the future, without hope that things will change, with no hope of finding what's been lost, and no hope of restoring the past, with only the risk to crack open all that has hardened about me, what will I do with what I have?

At first, this might seem scary or sad, but as a tired swimmer comes ashore surprised to find pearls washing through his legs, I lift my tired head again and again to find all I need is right where I am.

But being human, I stray and dream of lives other than my own, and soon I am busy wanting something else, somewhere else, someone else; busy imagining something just out of reach to strive for.

It leads me to say if you are unhappy or in pain, nothing will remove these surfaces. But acceptance and a strong heart will crack them like a shell, exposing a softness that has always been, exposing a soft thing waiting to take form. It glows. I think it is the one spirit we all share.

- Center yourself, and with your eyes closed, imagine what you want.
- Breathe slowly, and with your eyes open, realize what you have.
- Reverse the process. Close your eyes and realize what you have. Now breathe slowly, and with your eyes open, imagine what you want.
- Keep doing this until what you want and what you have start to become the same thing.

# DECEMBER 28
## INTEGRITY

---

Integrity is the ability to listen to a place inside oneself that doesn't change, even though the life that carries it may change.
— RABBI JONATHAN OMER-MAN

Much of our journey throughout this book has been about discovering that place inside and cultivating the ability to listen to it, while having compassion for the life that carries it.

It moves me to share the story of a troubled man who, exhausted from his suffering and confusion, asked a sage for help. The sage looked deeply into the troubled man and with compassion offered him a choice: "You may have either a map or a boat."

After looking at the many pilgrims about him, all of whom seemed equally troubled, the confused man said, "I'll take the boat."

The sage kissed him on the forehead and said, "Go then. You are the boat. Life is the sea."

As we have discovered so many times, we have everything we need within us. This ability to listen inside is our oldest oar. You are the boat.

• Sit quietly and put down all your maps

663

for the moment.
- Let your breath take you safely out to sea.
- Breathe gently and bob there . . . and simply listen. . . .

# DECEMBER 29
## SING THEN

---

As long as we sing,
the pain of the world
cannot claim our lives.

Through cancer, through growing up in America, through learning about the innumerable struggles for freedom around the world, all different but the same, through being with the people of South Africa, it has become very clear that giving voice to what is inner is essential to surviving what is outer. No matter where we live or whom we love, no matter what we want or what we can't have, this is the lesson I can't repeat or learn enough.

When everything in life presses from outside of us, we have no choice but to sing like scared children relying on their song to stop the pain, the way that fire stalls the cold. This is the secret of all spirit, why it cannot stay inside, but must be brought from within us into the world. For it is the song from within that keeps the pain of living from snuffing our lives. It is the song from within ignited, again and again, that keeps the world going. When we do this for ourselves, we do it for every child not yet born.

As night and day take turns on this massive Earth spinning nowhere, the song we share within takes turns with the catastrophes of living. When we go silent, the age goes dark.

Sing, then, in whatever tongue your pain has taught you. Sing, though you have no training and never went to school. Sing, because the cry from all the places you have kept quiet will stall the cold, will soften the danger, will keep the world possible for one more turn. . . .

- Deeply and simply, close your eyes and let whatever is inside you begin to rise.
- Exhale everything that seems in the way, and give voice to the piece of the infinite that dwells within you.
- Release a cry or gasp or sigh, and feel the world continue.

# WE BECOME THE EARTH

In seeking what is essential,
we become essential.

I have always been amazed how the deepest things are intangible: love, doubt, faith, confusion, peace, wisdom, passion. Where are they? They can't be held in the hand like fruit or turned in the lap like pages of a sacred text. Yet they shape our lives. This has always been the driving mystery of all sacred wisdom: The only things worth saying are those things that are unsayable.

It is quite humbling to realize that we spend a lifetime gaining grain after grain of this wisdom, working to understand it and struggling to express it and share it, only to become more and more a part of it, unspeakable ourselves. Over time, we age into a stillness that breathes like stone, exposed beyond resistance.

Perhaps this is the most poignant of paradoxes, nature's safeguard against letting too much of the mystery out. We take years of living to squeeze a few precious words from all that will not speak, and steadily, being shaped by our suffering and polished by our joy, we become the Earth, knowing more and

666

saying less. Ironically, after a lifetime, we may finally have important things to say, just as we lose our ability to say them. Yet this doesn't diminish all we try to say. For the fact that sound always ends in silence doesn't make music any less precious to our souls.

It seems the more we live through, the less we can surface. I recall visiting Grandma Minnie when she was ninety-four. I had found the steamship ticket with which she had come to this country in 1912 as a girl. There was a strange and beautiful name on it, Maiyessca. This was her birth name, never spoken in this country. I put the yellowed ticket in her hand. Her eyes widened and I could feel the big old fish of her heart swim up near the surface, stirring waters that had been still for eighty years. Lifetimes passed between us in silence. She trembled and coughed up a chuckle, saying only, "I forgot I ever came."

There is nothing sad about this. Rather, it feels inevitable and holy that we should become what we seek. We start out wanting to know love and living long enough, we become love. We start out wanting to know God, and suffering long enough, we become God. Over time, the heart expands from within and all our skins thin until we become something elemental, rounding to the next grain of wisdom to be found.

- Sit quietly with a trusted friend.
- Breathe deeply and meditate, each of you, on your own history of love, letting the wordless feelings stream through you.
- After a time, try to honor this wordless stream by letting a single word or phrase rise within you.
- Write down this word or phrase and hold it in silence near your heart.
- Without looking, trade pieces of paper and meditate in silence with your friend's written phrase near your heart.
- After a time, simply read each other's word or phrase aloud.

# DECEMBER 31
## I SEE YOU

I See You!
I Am Here!

For centuries, African Bushmen have greeted each other in this way. When the one becomes aware of his brother or sister coming out of the brush, he exclaims, "I See You!" and then the one approaching rejoices, "I Am Here!"

This timeless bearing witness is both simple and profound, and it is telling that much of our modern therapeutic journey is suffered to this end: to have who we are and where we've been be seen. For with this simple and direct affirmation, it is possible to claim our own presence, to say, "I Am Here."

Those people in our lives who have validated our personhood by seeing us and exclaiming so are the foundations of our self-worth. Think of who they are. For me, the first to rejoice at my scrambling into the open was my grandmother. If not for her unequivocal love, I might never have had the courage to express myself at all. And, after all, isn't art in all its forms the beautiful trail of our all-too-human attempts to say, again and again, I Am Here.

It is important to note that being seen enables us to claim our lives, and then it becomes possible to pass the gift on to others. But just as important as bearing witness is the joy with which these Bushmen proclaim what they see. It is the joy of first seeing and first knowing. This is a gift of love.

In a culture that erases its humanity, that keeps the act of innocence and beginning invisible, we are sorely in need of being seen with joy, so we can proclaim with equal astonishment and innocence that of all the amazing things that could have been or not, We Are Here.

As far back as we can remember, people of the oldest tribes, unencumbered by civilization, have been rejoicing in being on earth

669

together. Not only can we do this for each other, it is essential. For as stars need open space to be seen, as waves need shore to crest, as dew needs grass to soak into, our vitality depends on how we exclaim and rejoice, "I See You!" "I Am Here!"

- Sit with a trusted loved one, and with your eyes closed, meditate on their essence as you know them.
- When filled with their presence, open your eyes and declare with joy and sincerity, "I See You!"
- Allow your loved one the space to proclaim in return, "I Am Here!"
- Switch roles, and repeat this process of first seeing and first knowing. If moved, live your life this way.

# GRATITUDES

I want to honor and give thanks for the deep presence of others who helped shape me into an open container that could receive and birth this book. Gratitude to the Fetzer Institute, a soil of spirit and love in which I have taken root and grown. To the Fetzer Board of Trustees for their belief in people. To the Fetzer Program Roundtable, who listened to and discussed many of these entries. To the Fetzer staff for their perpetual welcome. To Rob Lehman for his endless vision and spiritual friendship. To Molly Vass for her courage of love. To Carol Hegedus for her delicate ability to listen from the center. To Joel Elkes for the sweet wisdom he gives everyone with his eyes. To Parker Palmer for the rootedness of his very large heart. To Wayne Muller for the joy of his company and the gift of his compassion. To Maggi Alexander for the integrity of her care. To Megan Scribner for her willingness to journey further. To Mary Williams for always being there.

671

Gratitude to David Blustein and Pearl Mindell for guiding me deeper into the truth. To Robert Mason for more than words can say, my brother. To Susan McHenry for the tender, affirming home you give my heart.

Gratitude to Tom Callanan for believing enough to show my work around. To my research assistants, Elizabeth Roche and Samantha Berman, for their patience, care, and friendship. To my editor, Mary Jane Ryan, who encouraged me to write this book when I had only five entries written. Your belief and precision helped birth this book. To the 260 inquiring souls around the world who took the time to read and respond to these reflections via e-mail each week. And to Melody Beattie, the pioneer of this daybook form, for opening a way to bring spirit more fully into our ordinary days. And to the voices of all those teachers quoted herein for carrying their pain and awe across the ages to the altar of today.

# COPYRIGHT ACKNOWLEDGMENTS

674

675

# ABOUT THE AUTHOR

**Mark Nepo** is a poet and philosopher who has taught in the fields of poetry and spirituality for over twenty-five years. Nominated for the Lenore Marshall Poetry Prize, he has written three books, *Acre of Light, Fire Without Witness,* and *God, the Maker of the Bed, and the Painter,* and has contributed to numerous anthologies. As a cancer survivor, he remains committed to the importance of inner life. Through both his writing and teaching, Mark devotes himself to the life of inner transformation and relationship, exploring the expressive journey of healing where the paths of art and spirit meet. For eighteen years, Mark taught at the State University of New York at Albany. Currently, he serves as Scholar-in-Residence and Senior Advisor for the Fetzer Institute in Kalamazoo, Michigan, a nonprofit foundation devoted to the wholeness of mind, body, and spirit as it informs our individual and communal health. He lives in Albany,

New York, and continues to give readings, lectures, and retreats.